A confused person's guide to therapy, counselling and self-help

talk yourself better

Ariane Sherine

ROBINSON

ROBINSON

First published in Great Britain in 2018 by Robinson

Copyright © Ariane Sherine, 2018

3 5 7 9 10 8 6 4 2

A CIP catalogue record for this book is available from the British Library

ISBN: 978-1-47214-133-0

Typeset in Adobe Garamond Pro by Hewer Text UK Ltd, Edinburgh
Printed and bound in Garamomd pro by CPI Group (UK) Ltd, Croydon CR0 4YY

Papers used by Robinson are from well-managed
forests and other responsible sources

Robinson
An imprint of
Little, Brown Book Group
Carmelite House
50 Victoria Embankment
London EC4Y 0DZ

An Hachette UK Company
www.hachette.co.uk

www.littlebrown.co.uk

NOTE: The information in this book is for guidance purposes only and is not intended
to replace any advice given to you by your GP or other health professional. All matters
regarding your health should be discussed with your GP. The author and publisher disclaim
any liability directly or indirectly from the use of the material in this book by any person.

BMA

Ariane Sherine is a comedy writer and journalist. Her work has appeared in, among others, the *Guardian*, the *Sunday Times*, the *Observer* and the *Independent*, and she has worked as a scriptwriter for the BBC, Channel 4 and ITV. She loves writing, photography, illustration, video editing and jewellery designing, and is happiest when sitting in her garden on a sunlit day with her daughter, Lily. She is @arianesherine on Twitter and Instagram, and you can support her on Patreon here: www.patreon.com/arianesherine

Praise for *Talk Yourself Better*

'Brilliant – makes a baffling world comprehensible'
Jeremy Vine

'What an excellent, long-overdue idea! A super-accessible guide through the bewildering marketplace of modern therapy to ease our noble search for help'
Derren Brown

'How do we cope with this brutal world? In this witty, revealing book, Ariane Sherine runs through the ways. An excellent, funny and thought-provoking read for all who seek answers'
Arthur Smith

'What makes Ariane Sherine's *Talk Yourself Better* stand out from the crowd is its accessibility and humour; to be able to discuss difficult things with a lightness of touch and a comedy that does not trivialise is a rare skill indeed. This combined with the honest – and often deeply moving – stories of clients and practitioners alike make this the ideal introduction for anyone considering therapy for the first time'
Brian Bilston

*For everyone struggling with mental illness.
I know how tough it can be. I hope this book helps.*

*And for my darling Lily, whose life I hope
will be easier than mine.*

Contents

Contents

Introduction

Welcome to *Talk Yourself Better*. You're probably reading this because you're wondering whether to have therapy. Maybe you have depression or anxiety like me – I would happily kick mental illness in the balls for all the years of my life it's destroyed. Or perhaps you have a different issue or problem, and are considering seeing a counsellor about it.

We've all watched films and telly programmes featuring therapists, such as *The Sopranos* – but what's the best way to access therapy in real life if you're not a Mafia boss? What's the difference between therapy and counselling, or CBT and psychoanalysis? And why pay a stranger to listen to you in the first place? Can't a good friend provide a shoulder to cry on?

All these questions and more are answered in this book. There's a short guide to therapy, which will cover all the big questions. The rest of the chapters each feature a light-hearted Q&A about a different therapeutic approach; a serious interview with a therapist from that 'modality' (fancy word for 'type of therapy') so you can decide whether it's for you; and an interview (or first-person piece) with a client who has experienced that type of therapy.

I've also interviewed some people you might have heard of, such as Stephen Fry, Charlie Brooker, David Baddiel, Dolly Alderton, Musa Okwonga, Cosmo Landesman, John Crace and James Brown (the magazine editor, not the Godfather of Soul) about their experiences with mental health and therapy – because celebrities can experience mental illness and addiction too.

If you'd like to email me to ask about anything, I'm at ariane.sherine@gmail.com.

Wishing you much happiness and peace of mind, Ariane x

Therapy: A Short Guide

What the hell is therapy, then?

At a basic level, therapy is airing your problems in the presence of another human being, who is effectively a stranger. You've usually never met them before you step into the therapy room, and after you finish therapy you generally never see them again (unless you bump into them in the supermarket, and then it might be a bit awkward, especially if you accidentally smash their eggs).

What kind of person are they? I'm guessing they eat eggs.

You probably won't be able to find out much about them, because therapy works best when you aren't aware of their history or views. For example, if you knew that they were infertile and that it caused them sadness, you might feel that you couldn't talk about how much you loved or disliked your kids, because bringing up the subject of children might upset them.

On a different level, if you knew that they were, for example, a Conservative, or went to church every Sunday, you might feel that you couldn't yell 'Fuck God and fuck the Tories!'

To be honest, I don't really want to fuck either. I can't imagine they'd be that good in bed.

Never know till you try . . . But whatever your beliefs, the idea is that you're able to talk to your therapist about anything that's troubling you, whether that's a bad relationship or the state of the world today, without worrying about what they're thinking and feeling.

But what if they hate me?

Therapy training is all about being non-judgemental, and therapy is about talking freely. Your therapist gets paid to listen to you rant

2

about anything that's on your mind, whether that's your profuse embarrassment about getting erections on the bus, or your secret fear that the FBI are tapping your phone.

And then what? Do they laugh at you?

No, they try to help you. Depending on the type of therapy, they either ask questions to enable you to find your own answers to your problems, or they help you to think your way out of irrationality.

If you're really crazy, will they report you?

No. My therapist hasn't reported me to my doctor for being paranoid and believing our sessions are being monitored by spies, which is pretty much as crazy as it gets. Therapists only report you if they think you're seriously intending to harm yourself or others.

What's to stop any old chancer from setting up as a therapist? Seems like a racket: you just sit, pretend to listen, then take the person's money.

Nothing really, though I'm not sure fake therapy happens often. But that's why you should always go through the registered therapy bodies such as the BACP (British Association for Counselling and Psychotherapy) and UKCP (UK Council for Psychotherapy) to find a therapist (see page 309 for details).

Does therapy actually work, even if it isn't fake?

It genuinely can do. When it works, it's brilliant and makes you feel as though anything is possible. It can help you overcome phobias and addictions, let go of the things that are bothering you, and gain clarity on troubling issues. When it doesn't work, it can leave you feeling despondent.

Knowing my luck, it'll be the latter. What happens then?

Then you try either a different type of therapy, or a different therapist. Because (and I can't stress this enough) if either the approach or the person isn't right for you, therapy is unlikely to work.

For example, if you dislike your therapist more than you dislike mouldy Brussels sprouts, you're unlikely to want to trust them with your innermost thoughts and fears. Maybe they're cold and unfriendly, or maybe their manner just turns you off. Whatever the reason, if you don't feel able to talk to them freely then it doesn't matter what kind of therapy they're practising; it won't be helpful.

Conversely, if your therapist is warm and kind and approachable, but you don't believe, for example, that having your dreams analysed is a reasonable way of resolving your problems, then a part of your brain will be hanging back thinking, 'This isn't going to work' – and therapy probably won't.

Why do I have to pay a therapist? Can't I just talk to my friends instead?

You can, but the problem here is that friends aren't blank canvases onto which you can project all your thoughts and fears. Your friends might be lovely – I'm sure they are. But you know them, and they know you (or at least, the version of you you're prepared to show them), which means that there are often subjects you both tiptoe around.

And therapy isn't about tiptoeing. It's about treading confidently, thudding like an elephant if you want or have to, without fear of causing offence or damaging your relationship.

There's also the chance that you'll be less likely to take umbrage at a therapist's comment, because we often allow strangers (especially professional strangers we're paying) more leeway to challenge us than friends.

Do therapists tell you what to do then? It sounds a bit like school.

Generally they aren't meant to, but I've found that some therapists do and some don't, regardless of the type of therapy they practise.

Therapists are human, and if they're watching a client mess up their life week after week, it's only natural to want to step in and stop them.

But talking broadly here: you're more likely to get questions than advice from a therapist. They're meant to help you find your own solutions to your problems.

I'm useless at finding solutions. I can't even do crosswords. Will my therapist give up on me?

In twenty-three years of therapy, I've never had a therapist tell me they can't help me. I've had a therapist leave the practice they were at, effectively ending our sessions, but I haven't been given up on. That's not to say it never happens, but it's probably not something you need to worry about.

Oh, I worry about everything. I even worry that I don't worry enough.

Then therapy could definitely be worth a try.

How do I access it, then?

You can go via the NHS, which means that therapy is free. The catch is that you have to wait a while to see a therapist, you only get a certain number of sessions, and you don't have any choice about which therapist you see.

Alternatively, you can go private and pay for therapy. There is also a third way: you may be able to access free therapy via a charity or training college.

Say I want to go via the NHS. What do I do?

You visit your GP and explain the problem you've been having, whether this is anxiety, depression, an eating disorder, addiction or another problem. Unfortunately, the NHS is very over-stretched, so unless your GP decides your problem is serious, they're unlikely to refer you for individual therapy. They may refer you for group therapy instead, or refuse to refer you.

If your problem is serious anxiety or depression, they should refer you for individual therapy, and may also suggest medication, which I cover in a later chapter (see page 279).

How do I convince them that my problem is serious?

It's best not to self-diagnose, but instead to describe your symptoms and situation. For instance, when I asked for my antidepressants to be upped two years ago, I explained that my father had just died very suddenly after we had been estranged for over two years, so I hadn't been able to say goodbye; that a former boyfriend and I had had a nasty argument five days later; and that I was feeling very low, crying a lot and finding it hard to muster any enthusiasm to do anything.

Crikey, that's a bit heavy. What did your doctor say?

Not much. They generally don't. He just handed me a prescription, which was what I wanted.

I don't like my doctor. She said I should stop having sex.

Why, did you have some kind of medical problem?

No, I got arrested for doing it in KFC. Anyhow, how do I find a private therapist?

It's best to use the search engines on the sites of the two regulatory bodies for therapy in the UK: the BACP and UKCP. You can find details of these and other useful organisations on page 309. Choosing a therapist through this method will ensure that they have the training necessary to help you.

How much will private therapy cost? I had to pay the court costs for the KFC thing, so I'm skint.

6

The average therapy session costs around £50 for fifty minutes. However, many therapists have a sliding scale for fees, so if you don't earn much you could pay far less. I've also been quoted up to £160 for a session, but that was with a leading therapist in his field.

What was he doing in a field? Doesn't therapy take place in a room?

It does, though the décor of the room very much depends on the therapist. I've had therapy in grand rooms with dusty books from floor to ceiling, and also very modern, sterile little rooms with strip lights. The only given is that there will be at least two chairs, generally facing one another.

Won't there be a couch? I've been promised a couch in the films I've seen.

It's very unlikely that there will be a couch. Sorry.

I feel cheated. It also means I can't drift off to sleep if the therapy's boring.

Therapy generally isn't boring. After all, you're talking about yourself, which is most people's favourite subject. I personally think that learning to understand yourself is one of the most fascinating and rewarding activities possible.

What's the difference between therapy and counselling? I hear both words bandied around.

Hmm, it's tricky. Many people say they mean the same thing. However, other people say that counselling is shorter-term and less intense, while therapy is longer-term and also examines the issues in question on a deeper level.

How will I know when therapy's working? Will all my anxiety and depression fade away?

Realistically, good therapy doesn't mean you'll be floating around on clouds of bliss without a care in the world forever, as happy as when you're in love and have just got a new puppy. That's not how human beings work. However good your therapist is, there will always be ups and downs.

When therapy is successful, however, a lot of people describe feeling 'lighter'. If you're having CBT for a phobia, you may be able to overcome it. And if you've come to therapy to solve a particular issue, such as guilt you've been carrying around for years, it's often possible to get closure on it.

'Closure'? That's a bit American, isn't it?

Therapy is often associated with Americans, but it actually started in Austria. As you probably know, Sigmund Freud is widely considered to be the 'father' of psychotherapy, though I'm not entirely sure who the mother is. Anyhow, the original 'talking cure' dates back to the 1880s, though I'll cover the history of each therapeutic approach in that chapter.

What else are you going to cover?

Each chapter will focus on a particular modality (e.g. CBT) and I'll interview a person who has experienced that type of therapy, along with a therapist from that approach. There will also be accounts of undergoing therapy from clients.

How did you get the clients to talk to you? Did you blackmail them?

No. Having therapy doesn't carry the same stigma it used to. For instance, several people at my workplace are open about having therapy now, or having had it in the past, including myself, and our contracts still got renewed.

So everyone spoke to you on the record?

No – some people in the book are anonymous.

Aha, so there is a stigma!

No. There's a difference between being open about having therapy – which everyone in the book was fine with – and having the private, traumatic details of your life made public. And if an account references a court case, child sex abuse or malpractice by medical professionals, there are often legal reasons why the details have to be anonymised.

Do you think it's appropriate to write a book on such serious subjects and make jokes in it?

Definitely, as I'm not joking about those things. I think this would be a very dull and depressing book without some levity to balance out the bleak subject matter.

What gives you the right to write this book, though? You're not a therapist.

True, but I've undergone twenty-three years of therapy, on and off. So here's my personal story.

Ariane's Story

I grew up with a physically violent and emotionally abusive father whom I was terrified of, and a very repressed mother.

From the age of three-and-a-half onwards, I was hit by my father for the slightest misdemeanour: spilling my orange juice, refusing to eat my dinner, wearing my clothes 'sloppily', losing a pencil eraser. I would have my trousers and knickers pulled down and would be hit hard between fifty and a hundred times, while my father told me I was disgusting, revolting and that I made him sick.

If I cried, I would be hit again, and he would ask, 'Why are you crying? I should be crying, having a daughter like you.' I learned to cry with bed sheets in my mouth, so my sobs didn't make a sound.

My mother was perpetually disappointed in me. I wasn't the child she hoped she'd have: she wanted me to be tidy, clean, obedient, organised, quiet and studious – a child like my brother. Instead, I was messy, sloppy, rebellious, chaotic, loud and, though naturally bright and creative, I didn't much care about doing well at school, and would play up in class.

This was unacceptable in the eyes of my parents, as they were academics. My mother tried to criticise me into being the daughter she wanted; I just resented her in response, and dug my heels in harder.

Throughout my childhood, I was very much alone emotionally; the only attention I received was negative, and in response to negative behaviour. Because I wasn't properly socialised, I didn't know how to behave at school, and would 'act out' and do and say shocking things in order to get attention, which meant I was ostracised and severely bullied.

I would take out my hurt, anger and frustration on my little brother at home, hitting, kicking and pinching him. On one occasion, when I did this, I remember my father holding me down and telling my brother to hit me.

When my brother was twelve and I was sixteen, he punched me in the face and gave me a black eye. We have now been estranged for over two decades; he stopped talking to me at around this point and never properly restarted.

At the age of twelve, I told my father that if he ever hit me again, I'd report him and he would be arrested. After this, when he was angry, instead of hitting me he would respond by going completely silent. The first silent period lasted for half a year, from thirteen-and-a-half to my fourteenth birthday.

He wouldn't respond to apologies, or my begging him to talk. At first, I was relieved that I wasn't being hit any more, but soon it became distressing. It wasn't just me he would do it to, either: at any one time, he would be ignoring me, my mother or my brother, for up to a year at a time.

Throughout my childhood, I was forced to eat all of the food I was given (usually soggy broccoli, hard brown rice and gloopy dhal), or one of three things would happen: I would be hit; I would be force-fed by my father, who would hold my nose, forcing my mouth to open so he could feed me; or I would find the same food on my plate for every meal – breakfast, lunch and dinner – until I finally ate it.

My lunchbox at school featured gritty bread with houmous, a dirty unpeeled carrot, grapes and unsweetened juice. I craved the white bread sandwiches, crisps and chocolate the other kids at school ate. I began throwing my lunch in the bin at school, because it tasted horrible and I was embarrassed by it.

I became sexually active at the age of fourteen, and lost my virginity a couple of months after turning fifteen, to a twenty-year-old. Throughout my teens, I was desperate to be loved, and would sleep with anyone I thought might be willing to love me. I had been an unattractive and geeky child, and the kids at school had told me repeatedly that I was ugly and that 'no man will ever fuck you'.

When I blossomed at last at the age of fifteen, I was suddenly popular with men, and was terrified of losing this appeal and being thought of as unattractive. I became insanely jealous of anyone, even celebrities, whom my boyfriends considered more attractive than me, and developed a negative obsession with a female celebrity whom I felt extremely threatened by.

Also at the age of fifteen, I stopped eating properly, was diagnosed with anorexia, and was referred both to a nutritionist at the local hospital, and for family therapy. It is perhaps a sign of my family's dysfunction that my father refused to come to therapy, and my mother didn't want my brother to attend. So it was just my mother and me in therapy, along with a therapist and social worker.

The sessions consisted of me explaining that my father was violent and abusive, and my mother contradicting me or downplaying everything I said, because she didn't want my father to go to jail or my brother to be taken into care. Understandably, it wasn't a great reflection of what therapy can or should be.

Aged sixteen, I slashed up my left arm, the start of a year of self-harming. My mother took me to our GP, who referred me to the Tavistock Clinic, a psychoanalytic therapy centre where I had individual therapy for the first time.

I loved my therapist and thought she was wonderful; she was the first adult who had ever truly taken the time to listen to me properly. She was unusually straight-talking, and would comment on the problems and material I brought to therapy (such as my resentment towards the aforementioned female celebrity) with questions such as 'But you know that's crazy, right?'

Unfortunately, she left after a short time, and was replaced by a different therapist.

I hated the new therapist, partly because she wasn't my original therapist, but also because she would say things that didn't make sense to me. She would ask, 'Do you see me as your mother?' and 'Do you think about our relationship when you're not in therapy?'

Now, two decades on, I understand why she was asking these questions, though I don't think this approach was the most helpful. I now think she was very new to therapy. Back then, I thought she was clingy and self-obsessed, and kept making the process all about her.

Because I had never been loved in a functional way, I didn't know how to accept or give love. I had never had any stability in my life – it had all been very traumatic due to my father's rages, and I had felt constant fear. When I entered my first real relationship aged fifteen, I didn't believe that my boyfriend loved me – even though I can see now that he did.

If at any point I thought he didn't love me, I would go off and sleep with someone else. Usually I would leave him first; on a couple of occasions, I was unfaithful. I would then return to him and beg for his forgiveness. He would forgive me, we would get back together, and then I would do it again. I would also tell him repeat-edly that I was bad and wrong and that he shouldn't want to be with me.

Aged sixteen, while I was crying a school bully taunted me and spat in my lunch, and I saw red and threw a Coke can hard in her face, giving her a black eye. In response, she got her stepsister's gang to wait for me after school to mete out punishment. The deputy head had to escort me past the gang after school, and it was made clear to me that the school thought I should leave.

I felt I had no choice but to leave – being beaten up badly wasn't an option. I felt let down by the school and by my parents, who didn't care enough about the situation to collect me from school.

Reading through my medical records from this period, I see that I was assessed by a number of doctors and psychiatrists, who all made the same diagnosis: borderline personality disorder (BPD). BPD is a disorder characterised by emotional instability, impulsive and reckless behaviour including self-harming, and unstable relationships.

However, I was never informed of this diagnosis. A boyfriend told me he thought I had BPD; when I asked my therapist about it, she said, 'It's not helpful to think of yourself as a collection of symptoms'. But I genuinely think that, had my GP confirmed that I had a personality disorder, it would have helped me understand myself.

It makes perfect sense, now, that I had BPD. The NHS website says: 'A number of environmental factors seem to be common and widespread among people with BPD. These include: being a victim of emotional and/or physical abuse . . . being exposed to chronic fear or distress as a child . . . being neglected by one or both parents.'

The BPD suicide rate is four hundred times the national average. A typical BPD sufferer will attempt suicide three times in their life – it is thought that 74 per cent try to end their own life – and 10 per cent of all those with BPD die through suicide.

Sure enough, aged seventeen and eighteen, I made two suicide attempts, trying to slash my wrists and throw myself in front of a train. I hated myself for my inability to complete suicide, and never confided my specific failed suicide attempts to anyone, though I did tell the doctor that I was trying to take my own life.

At seventeen, I started doing a form of fully dressed Indian dancing in men-only Asian clubs – a job that lasted until I was twenty-three. During this period, I was sexually assaulted hundreds of times, taking the men's hands off my breasts and vagina, only to have them assault me again. Outside this job, during my teens and twenties, I was sexually assaulted twelve times. When a strange man exposed himself to me on a train, I went to the police and was told, 'You'll have to get used to this, pretty girl like you.'

Aged nineteen, I went to the doctor with depression, and was prescribed five different antidepressants one after the other – mostly SSRIs. None of them helped much; they made me sick, delusional, thin, fat, but not happy. My faith in drugs and therapy was waning. I saw several more therapists intermittently during this period, and also returned to see my first therapist again, who was working at the American Psychological Association and cost £50 a session. I couldn't afford to have more than one session with her.

My unstable relationships continued, but I started to become successful as a writer. Aged twenty-one, I came runner-up in a BBC scriptwriting competition, and started to write for television. This success took my mind off my past and my failure to maintain a steady relationship. By the age of twenty-four, I was writing for primetime sitcoms and shows.

However, at that point, I also entered the worst relationship of my life. My boyfriend was more than ten years older than me. He pressured me to do things I didn't want to do sexually, and also pressured me to drink and take drugs. Every time I tried to leave him, my lack of self-worth told me that he was right and I was wrong.

Finally, I got pregnant with his baby, and we went abroad on holiday. During an argument on our final night he turned violent, hitting me in the face and making my ear bleed. He then held his hand over my mouth, suffocating me. He told me repeatedly that he would kill me.

I reported the crime to the police when I returned to Britain. Because it was committed in a different country, I had no way to press charges against my boyfriend. In addition, I was still in love with him, and was scared that he would commit suicide in response to charges being pressed, as he threatened, and that it would be my fault. I contacted my parents for help, but they refused to see me again until I had a termination.

After agonising, I eventually decided to have an abortion, which I felt tremendous guilt about. It felt like the worst thing I had ever done, and I told everyone I had had a miscarriage. My mother refused to take the day off work to accompany me for the abortion, so my father took me instead. The abortion was a miscarriage induced by pills, and was agony because my father wouldn't let me take the painkillers the clinic provided.

In the aftermath of the violent incident, as well as depression, I developed generalised anxiety disorder, extreme claustrophobia and obsessive-compulsive disorder (OCD). The generalised anxiety disorder meant I was scared of literally everything; the claustrophobia meant I couldn't even be in a room with the windows and door shut, let alone an enclosed space like a lift or the Tube; and the OCD meant I was terrified of saying or doing something that would harm either myself or others.

I cried for a year about (what I saw as) ending my baby's life, feeling like a terrible person. When I had searched for abortion information online, I had found lots of Catholic sites featuring pictures of foetuses sucking their thumbs, and warnings that I would get breast cancer or go to hell as a result of having a termination. I was so scared of going to hell, I didn't even want to go to sleep at night in case I died in my sleep.

Knowing I needed therapy, I went back to the Tavistock again, where I had the single worst experience I have ever had in therapy. The therapist was young and female with dark hair. When I told her what had happened to me – my boyfriend, the pregnancy, the violence and the abortion – her face hardened and she said in a cutting voice, 'So you thought you'd come here for some sympathy, did you?'

She was completely devoid of empathy. Had I not been so vulnerable at the time, and had I found the strength, I would have reported her; as it was, I just sobbed and sobbed as she stared at me with total contempt.

I'm not sure why that experience didn't put me off therapy altogether. Perhaps it was because I had already experienced good therapy and knew that it could work for me, or maybe I recognised that this young therapist was an anomaly. Either way, a few weeks later I found myself at Camden Psychotherapy Unit for an assessment.

The lady was middle-aged, kind and thoughtful, though I only had three sessions with her before I received a letter referring me to another therapist – with a name I recognised. She was a household name and was iconic in my industry. I thought, 'It can't be her', but when I looked at her Wikipedia entry, it said that she was now a practising psychotherapist in London. I was amazed: my parents had watched her on television when I was a kid.

When I turned up at her grand, imposing house in north London, she looked just the same as I remembered, though she was twenty-five years older. She was formidable and slightly austere. At the end of the first session, she said I would ideally have three sessions a week; I couldn't afford this, even though the sessions were only £20, so we compromised and settled on two sessions.

This therapist was too Freudian for me, with the kind of 'opaque wall' that many psychoanalytic therapists have up, like a barrier between you and their emotions. While making notes, she asked if I'd been breastfed, and told me to write down my dreams, which seemed odd. I didn't believe that dreams had any significance – to my mind, they simply indicated what had been preying on your mind before bed – and being breastfed clearly hadn't improved my relationship with my mother, as we weren't remotely close.

However, this therapist did say something I found helpful. When I told her about my abortion, she asked, 'Did it never occur to you that this wasn't a terrible thing to do?' It seems obvious, but it felt revelatory to me. To my knowledge, I didn't have any friends who had had abortions, and the only other person I knew of who had had a termination had also viewed it as a sin. Confused, I remember replying 'No'. But I think this question was instrumental in eventually allowing me to forgive myself.

I left this therapist after a few months, as I didn't feel I responded well to Freudian psychoanalysis. However, I was still having severe mental problems. My claustrophobia, brought on by being suffocated by my boyfriend, was extreme enough that I had panic attacks in any space that was even slightly enclosed, such as a bus stuck in traffic with the windows and door shut. I went to my GP, who referred me for a little-known therapy called cognitive analytic therapy (CAT).

Before this therapy started, I had cognitive behavioural therapy (CBT) with a computer at a local library, to fill my time on the waiting list. It was slightly surreal, though they allowed me the room to myself for privacy. The computer asked me a series of questions to tailor my experience, but I remember thinking how much I preferred seeing a human therapist as opposed to interacting with a machine. Luckily, I was soon given an appointment for cognitive analytic therapy.

I loved my CAT therapist. She was the first therapist I'd clicked with since my initial therapist in my teens. She was young but mature, calm and measured and reassuring. I felt that she truly cared about me and wanted to help me. CAT is directive, like CBT, but with more of a focus on your past and how it has contributed to your present.

I had been referred for CAT for my claustrophobia, but decided that I wanted to focus on my relationship problems instead, rather than face my fears.

I remember that my therapist drew me a 'vicious cycle' diagram explaining how my problems were being perpetuated by my beliefs. I was truly sad when our ten sessions were up. The CAT process meant we had to write each other goodbye letters. She said she was moved when she read mine, as it explained how much she had helped me.

By this stage, I was very pro-choice when it came to abortion – and, given the religious propaganda I'd viewed when trying to make an informed decision, very anti-religious. I had also moved into journalism and had started writing regularly for the *Guardian*. I remember telling my CAT therapist that I was planning to launch a campaign to put atheist adverts on buses that would say 'There's probably no God – now stop worrying and enjoy your life'. She laughed and laughed.

I called the campaign the Atheist Bus Campaign. When I launched it, I didn't realise how huge it would be. It generated more national and international press than any other advertising campaign that year, and went global, running in thirteen countries around the world.

The UK campaign raised over £150,000 in six months, instead of the goal of £5,500, smashing our fundraising target by nearly 3000 per cent. Instead of the projected thirty buses in London, we were able to afford eight hundred buses around the UK, as well as Tube adverts and a poster campaign.

Unfortunately, all the press and interviews meant that I received an enormous amount of hate mail from Christians. Having my inbox filled with messages such as 'I hope you die', 'I pray Jesus kills you' and 'If you come to America I will shoot you in the head' made my anxiety and claustrophobia worsen. I remember being trapped in a studio at the BBC, about to record a segment for a Radio 4 programme. I had a panic attack and called my friend Charlie Brooker, who managed to stop me hyperventilating by telling me to slow my breathing down.

Knowing I needed to take action to curb my anxiety, I tried a therapy called hypnoanalysis. The therapist was a very kind and calm lady, and the treatment cost £80 per session and consisted of me being put into a 'trance' (basically a very relaxed state) where I relived traumas of the past. I wouldn't have minded the cost had it worked, but it didn't.

Though I was becoming extremely successful, recording a *Guardian* video series, writing travel features for the *Sunday Times* and regularly appearing on national television and radio, I was also descending into mental illness. It had taken over a year from the start of the campaign, but I eventually entered a psychological downward spiral from which I didn't seem to be able to break free.

When I fell deeply in love, my brain wasn't able to cope and I started to have terrifying paranoid delusions. It felt as though the whole world was against me because I had run the atheist campaign, which my brain decided was a terrible thing to have done. I felt as though I was screaming inside, and my body couldn't stop shaking. I subsequently had a major nervous breakdown, and didn't feel able to continue with journalism for over three years.

During my breakdown, I was convinced that I was going to be killed by the government, MI5 or a religious organisation, and that all kinds of people were spying on me. I was put on a high dose of an antipsychotic called olanzapine, which knocked me out for sixteen hours a day. I got pregnant but couldn't feel any happiness through all the fear, paranoia and depression. I quickly became suicidal. When I was six months pregnant, I decided to try to find someone who would help me kill myself, and spent a lot of time on suicide forums. I began writing to a user who was planning their own suicide; thankfully, we never met up.

Because I was terrified of being monitored, I didn't want to have therapy. In my paranoid delusional state, I didn't see how it would help – how could a therapist talk me out of the fact that I was going to be assassinated? My best friend Graham persuaded me to go and see one of my previous therapists and tell her everything. I did, but her response filled me with horror. She said, 'I'm not surprised you're scared. What you did [with the Atheist Bus Campaign] was so inflammatory!' After that session, I felt worse than ever.

After my daughter was born, I was assigned a psychiatrist. He inadvertently put me on an effective drug combination, combining pregabalin with the olanzapine, and the paranoid thoughts went away. Sadly, my OCD reared its head at this point, and I became terrified of sleepwalking. Again, I felt too scared to go to therapy – a shame, as it might have helped. (Two years later, I was finally put on a drug for OCD, clomipramine, which all but cured it.)

I split with my daughter's father in 2012, as he had fallen out of love with me because of my mental illness, and our relationship had become untenable.

I soon entered a new relationship. My new boyfriend had problems with commitment, and after eight months he suggested we go for couples therapy.

This was a painful and slightly ridiculous experience: my boyfriend would repeatedly tell the therapist – a middle-aged female psychodynamic counsellor – that he wasn't in love with me, and I would respond by saying, 'What do you expect her to be able to do? If you're not in love with me, just leave me!' The therapy was unhelpful, but more because of the material than the modality.

At the start of 2015, and single again, I decided that I wanted to change career and become a psychotherapist. I wanted to help people with OCD, and carry out a form of CBT called Exposure and Response Prevention (ERP). To start with, I did an introductory counselling course at City Lit (the City Literary Institute), led by an experienced male tutor, Jonathan Izard.

He was wonderful – charming and funny and entertaining. Every session was fascinating, and I began to think that I loved counselling, that it was definitely the career for me. I got on brilliantly with nearly every member of the group, attended every session and tried really hard to do well.

I then enrolled on a degree. There was only one UK undergraduate degree I could find that featured CBT; this was based at the University of London. It was a degree in Psychodynamic Counselling and CBT (since discontinued).

I found it a hellish experience which reminded me of being bullied at school. All the trainee therapists were miserable – and the lecturers seemed miserable too. The 'experiential groups', where we had to analyse ourselves and each other, were brutal and left me in tears in front of the group twice.

I told them I had been abused as a child, and divulged my personal history; they didn't care. I couldn't believe that any of the self-obsessed trainee therapists wanted to make life better for people, and I couldn't believe the callous lecturers could teach us how to do this. I left after the first term.

However, one positive thing came out of the degree. It had been mandatory for me to start long-term psychodynamic therapy, and I found my caring, patient therapist as a result. I have now been seeing her weekly for over two years, and for much of this, she kept me on the student rate of £30 a week despite my no longer being a student. She is thoughtful and insightful, and I feel lucky to have her.

Though psychodynamic in orientation, she has a friendly manner without the 'opaque wall' of so many psychodynamic therapists. She is very astute, calm and relaxed, and I am often amazed at her powers of perception. A session with her is like having a conversation with a very wise and comforting friend. I feel as though she truly cares about me, and I look forward to our sessions.

I wouldn't say that therapy has 'cured' me, but it has made it much easier for me to deal with my past, as well as whatever life throws at me. I know that we are all works in progress, and I doubt that there will ever be a point at which I will say that I am 100 per cent well-adjusted and free of problems.

That said, wonderful things happened after starting therapy with my current therapist, things that revolutionised my whole life. I think these are due to the confidence, encouragement and support she has given me.

I restarted my career in journalism, lost a lot of weight, fell in love with my best friend of twenty years, travelled to America for the first time to get married and go on honeymoon, was offered the book deal for this book, signed with my fantastic literary agent, and secured a great full-time writing job. Although my marriage later broke down, I felt able to see the positives: I got to see America, and not everyone can say they got married in Vegas!

I would currently rate myself a nine out of ten for happiness. I feel that I am in the best place I have ever been, and that this is due in no small part to working on myself every week. I love being a mum to my amazing little girl, and feel that we are closer than ever thanks to my being happier and more balanced.

After over two decades of therapy, on and off, I know first-hand that the difference to your wellbeing between seeing a great therapist and a not-so-great one can be huge. Therapists are human and fallible, and every therapist is unique. Empathy and compassion make all the difference, and can be healing in themselves. With some therapists, I made breakthroughs in understanding myself and my behaviour; with others, I went backwards and was put off therapy for years.

As my fabulous City Lit lecturer used to say, 'Therapists aren't the first taxi on the rank – you don't have to have therapy with the first one you meet. You should take time to find the therapist who is right for you.'

Cognitive Behavioural Therapy (CBT)

I'm glad you spelled it out. I once googled CBT and was a bit shocked to be honest.

I'm not sure what you found, but it really does stand for cognitive behavioural therapy.

Oh! Nothing to do with cock and ball torture then?

No, of course not!

Sorry, my mistake.

That's OK. I'll tell you a bit about it: it was developed from behaviour therapy in the 1960s by Dr Aaron T. Beck, while he was working as a psychiatrist at the University of Pennsylvania.

Ah, this rings a bell now. This is the therapy the NHS loves, right?

Sort of. It's a short-term, goal-oriented process. It can produce quick and quantifiable results and is evidence based – that's why it's often favoured by the NHS. CBT focuses on your current problems, rather than trying to find insight from your past.

How does it work, then?

The central idea of CBT is that how we feel and behave is linked to the way we think and act. Trying to keep ourselves safe from perceived rejection or harm can have a big impact on other areas of our lives. CBT seeks to alter negative thought cycles and provide more helpful ways of viewing a situation or being compassionate towards ourselves.

Altering negative thoughts? Like mind control? Sounds a bit sci-fi, and not in a good way.

Beck referred to 'automatic thoughts' – the kind that come to us straight away, before we've really considered something. He saw that these thoughts fell into three broad categories: the client's view of themselves, of the world in general and of the future.

Instead of just accepting these thoughts, which people tend to do, CBT encourages the individual to look at a different perspective and not engage in ruminations. This would then have a knock-on effect of breaking negative cycles and improving wellbeing.

What's a negative cycle? A Boris Bike?

Let's say, for example, that you see an old friend in town and they don't acknowledge you. The automatic thought that pops into your head might be that they don't like you any more. This can lead to further thoughts that you must have done something to upset them, leading to ruminations about how you are a useless failure who no one wants to know. This is a negative cycle.

If you were then invited to a party that they were attending, you might stay at home instead because you didn't want to see them. You'd then be missing out on life, and others might be negative about you because of the way you had treated them.

I wouldn't avoid the party. I'd just slag them off on Facebook.

That's one way of coping, but could have unintended and unfortunate consequences. A CBT therapist would ask you to consider the pros and cons of your ruminating and avoidance, and whether you're truly acting within your values and best interests. You'd then be encouraged to find an alternative interpretation of the issue. It would be helpful to test this interpretation by sending your friend a message asking them how they are. You'd probably find there wasn't a problem at all.

Oh. I hadn't thought of that.

With practice and effort, you can learn to replace automatic negative thoughts with more helpful responses.

So would the positive thoughts end up being the automatic ones?

That's the aim, yes. It requires plenty of effort on the part of the client though – CBT won't work if you just turn up hoping that the therapist will fix everything for you. You might be asked to keep a journal, or make notes of your responses to situations as they come up. Crucially, it's important to test out your predictions.

I hate homework. Couldn't I skip that bit?

So you skip it, and then the therapy doesn't work, and you tell yourself that you knew it was never going to work and that you're stuck with your problems – and you keep your problem. Do you see how that's another negative cycle?

Hmmph. I suppose so. How long does the therapy last?

You would typically have between twelve and sixteen weekly sessions. When it comes to therapy, this is considered fairly short-term. The exact number of sessions required would be decided in your first appointment, where your therapist would assess your needs and identify the things you require the most help with.

So will they ask you loads of stuff about your childhood? Are they going to stroke their beard and say in a creepy Austrian accent: 'Tell me about your mother'?

No, especially if they're from the UK. Unlike some therapies, CBT is about overcoming your current problems rather than providing insight. There are different variations within the CBT world that focus more on helping to alter enduring patterns of thinking and behaving related to your personality. These include dialectical behaviour therapy and compassion-focused therapy, both of which we'll come to later (pages 59 and 72).

So is CBT mainly for depression and anxiety?

The structured approach of CBT can be applied to a number of conditions including OCD, panic disorder, post-traumatic stress disorder (PTSD), phobias and eating disorders. It can even be used for physical problems – not to cure them, but to help sufferers deal with the symptoms.

No wonder the NHS is so keen.

CBT isn't just limited to treating negative thinking, either. It can help to redefine our relationship to something, such as food in the case of eating disorders. If we change the way we think about the thing that's giving us problems, it might become less scary or intrusive. It can be easy to fall into patterns of behaviour and repeat the same mistakes.

That's what my other half says each time she takes me back. So CBT sounds like the perfect therapy – can we skip all the others and go home?

Sadly, there's no such thing as a universal solution. CBT isn't going to suit everyone, especially if they're not willing to follow the exercises suggested by the therapist. And it might not be ideal for people who need more than a limited number of sessions.

Also, as we've seen, it doesn't focus on providing insight and has drawn criticism for that. It is adaptable, though, and can be used on its own or as part of a wider treatment in both individual and group settings.

If that's all, I'd better go. I've got a lot of people to make up with on Facebook.

The therapist: David Veale

'Everyone needs to become their own therapist'

Why did you choose to become a CBT therapist over all the other therapeutic modalities?

I was attracted to CBT in the late 1980s because of the accumulating evidence of the benefits. The principles of therapy were often easy but it was difficult to do well.

Because the principles of CBT are often easy, some clients think that CBT is 'formulaic', 'one-size-fits-all' or 'for stupid people' – all opinions I've heard. But do you think that the fact that a client can easily challenge their own thoughts at home with minimal guidance is one of CBT's strengths?

Yes, absolutely. However, there is CBT that is badly done and CBT that is done well – like any other therapy. Sometimes, especially where there is an inexperienced practitioner, it may not be optimally delivered.

Equally, some of the most experienced practitioners get lazy and may not stick to protocol or be very focused. In general, if you have a particular problem like OCD, it's best to find someone who treats OCD regularly, is passionate about treating it and regularly attends continuing professional development on OCD.

Everyone needs to become their own therapist/coach and become able to talk to their 'self' in a compassionate and encouraging way to approach difficult problems – which might involve trying to see a different perspective or testing out their fears.

If you have a milder problem and are quite flexible in your thinking then you are more likely to have success on your own.

What happens in a typical CBT session? And how do you know when the session has been successful?

The first few sessions involve defining the problems, the goals the client wants to achieve and the values that they want to follow.

The therapist and client then develop a roadmap of how the problem developed and especially what is keeping the problem going – for example, the way a person catastrophises about an event, the way they ruminate about the past or are highly self-critical, or the way they avoid particular situations.

Although these processes may have short-term benefits (for example, ruminating avoids difficult thoughts and feelings), they have unintended consequences, maintain the problem and make the symptoms worse. There is a phrase that sums it up: 'the solutions have become the problem'.

Subsequent therapy sessions involve following an agenda that is negotiated at the beginning of the session.

For example, an agenda might include:

- reviewing progress towards the client's goals and symptom scores from a questionnaire
- reviewing any behavioural experiments and practice since the last session
- trying to focus on solving one or two particular problems that relate to a person's goals (e.g. being able to travel on the underground in rush hour)
- seeing how the problems fit with the existing roadmap or whether it needs to be modified
- setting up new experiments and practice from the problems identified, and finally getting any feedback from the session.

The session is done collaboratively, with the emphasis on testing out predictions and expectations to see if they are true or helpful.

Was the session a success? It depends on the feedback, whether the client continues to make progress towards their goals and whether you have set yourselves a realistic agenda to be achieved that session.

What can a client do to help themselves get the most out of therapy?

Engage in the therapy, be proactive and curious, complete the questionnaires, come up with realistic goals and complete the exercises to the best of their ability.

They can also challenge themselves, have courage, be compassionate towards themselves, tolerate discomfort and uncertainty, and not identify their self with a particular value (e.g. being perfect).

Is there anyone that CBT can't help or wouldn't be suitable for?

Sure, but this is complicated! The bottom line is when someone is not ready to change. They might need to return when things are different in their life.

The client: Anonymous

'CBT saved my life'

One morning in September 2009, I appeared as a witness in a child abuse case. I was there because for several years I worked as a community childminder, meaning I was employed by social services to provide respite care to families needing support with childcare for various reasons. There could be substance abuse issues, alcohol abuse or low-level neglect.

I'd worked with many families and knew my job made a difference to vulnerable children.

One day, I dropped Luke* back home as usual, and arranged to pick him up two days later. I'd been caring for him for six months, and in that time he'd thrived, starting to toddle, babble, gain weight and smile. He'd changed from a silent, passive, underweight one-year-old into a healthier eighteen-month-old. I loved him to bits.

The next day I got a call from the social worker in charge of the case, who told me Luke had been found dead in his cot that afternoon. The police visited me and took a statement, and his death was deemed to be non-suspicious.

I was shocked and desperately sad that Luke had lost his life. I wasn't informed of any details regarding his death. I was invited to his funeral and saw his tiny white coffin cremated. I cried.

I continued to work with other families until I moved out of the area.

Three years later, I was informed that Luke's mother and her boyfriend were being taken to court to have all children in the family permanently removed from their care following unexplained injuries to a new baby they'd had. They were fighting the order and an enquiry had been opened into Luke's death. I was required to attend.

I went, and for the first time saw photographs of Luke's dead body. There were horrific bruises on his face. His beautiful blue eyes were wide open. His death had obviously not been accidental and had been covered up.

My mind tore. I sobbed. The judge halted proceedings and I was given tissues and water. I gave my evidence and left in shock.

Luke's mum and her boyfriend were eventually proven to be the only adults in the flat when Luke was injured and died. They had tried to blame his death on their eight-year-old daughter, or me. They were proven to be liars and murderers. They did not go to prison for complex reasons, but their other children were adopted and they are not allowed to keep any further children they may have.

The day after I'd given my evidence, my GP diagnosed me with PTSD. I was unable to sleep, eat or function. I was having constant flashbacks to the photographs of Luke's body, the black bruises on his face, his blue eyes pleading for help. I wished I could have saved him. I wasn't sure I could live in a world where such evil existed.

I was lucky to be with BUPA so was seen within days by a psychiatrist who confirmed the diagnosis. He talked to me for two hours, helping me to untangle the thoughts about what had happened. He was furious that I'd been shown the photographs of Luke's body.

Those photographs had triggered the PTSD, along with the aggressive questioning of the defence lawyer who had been reprimanded by the judge for the way he was treating me. The judge later sent me a message of thanks and support.

I started CBT a few days after seeing the psychiatrist. It saved my life.

I had six months of therapy, CBT once a week plus some hypno-therapy. I was also prescribed sleeping tablets as I was having awful nightmares. I turned down antidepressants as I didn't want to get hooked, and because I had seen the numbing effect they'd had on Luke's mum.

My first CBT session was in a consulting room at a hospital. I was sick with nerves in addition to being sick with PTSD. I desperately wanted to calm the chaos in my mind but had no idea of how that was going to be possible.

The sleeping tablets my GP had prescribed were helping me to get a few hours' rest, but I was having awful nightmares and frequent flashbacks. I was barely eating, and felt constantly nauseous and anxious, jumpy and tearful. Loud noises scared me; crowds scared me; life scared me.

My therapist came to the waiting room to lead me to the consulting room. He was calm, and that helped me to calm down a bit. He asked me to tell him what had happened, and during my explanation I had several flashbacks.

I cried and he calmly handed me tissues and water. He didn't offer sympathy other than to confirm that what had happened to me was wrong. He was more focused on reassuring me that he could help me.

He explained the process of CBT, how talking about trauma enabled the brain to move on from being stuck in 'flight or fight' mode. He gave me facts to think about. This was the first time I'd ever heard of the amygdala and the mechanisms of the mind.

Despite the chaos in my head, I was fascinated by what he said. He alternated between engaging my intellectual interest in CBT and engaging my emotional responses to the trauma. I felt involved in my treatment, not passive but engaged in an active collaboration between him and me to heal myself.

I was very highly motivated to recover quickly. I have four kids who needed their mum to be back and fully functioning. My therapist quickly identified that leading me to talk about them was the route to keeping me from thinking about acting on my suicidal thoughts.

Although the CBT sessions were painful, exhausting and very difficult, I felt they were the only way I was ever going to recover from my PTSD. I knew my therapist had an excellent reputation and track record. I trusted him.

Through CBT, I learned to understand myself and my thoughts and actions. The CBT also uncovered some childhood trauma relating to my dad. That was talked through and processed.

I had hypnotherapy towards the end of my CBT. I'd expressed concern that the sleeping tablets weren't as effective as they had been, and I wasn't getting more than two hours' sleep without waking up in a panic.

I'd soon worked out that washing them down with a glass of wine bought me more hours of sleep, but I knew that was a stupid thing to do, so told my therapist. He asked if I'd be willing to try hypnotherapy to help with the sleep problems.

He talked me into a relaxed state by suggesting I let my limbs go heavy and close my eyes. There was soft music playing, wave sounds and gentle chiming of bells. I'm finding it really hard to remember what he said – a sign it worked! There was visualisation.

He asked me where I like to go on holiday and I told him about walking on a sandy beach in the warm sun. He used that image to guide me into relaxing. I know it worked with my anxiety attacks. Not so much with the sleep problems. They receded with time, although I still have occasional nightmares if I'm stressed.

I can honestly say that I was badly broken and became a much stronger, mentally healthier person as a result of the CBT.

*Names and details of the case have been changed for legal reasons.

The client: Polly Allen

'He had the personality of a wet biscuit'

Why did you first seek therapy?

I sought therapy because it was becoming difficult to pinpoint where my depression came from.

I found that counsellors wanted to downplay it as either stress or a general issue with keeping on top of student life, rather than an illness where medication alone hadn't relieved the symptoms.

For example, my initial assessment with a counsellor at university didn't go well: the counsellor's style involved trying to provoke me. He said, 'Have you ever considered that you don't want to get better?'

I was pretty insulted, as I'd actively sought counselling and was dutifully trying different antidepressants, desperate for some relief from depressive symptoms, self-harm, suicidal ideation and low self-esteem.

A counsellor I saw through my GP was equally unhelpful, but in a different way; I later learned his style is 'Freudian'. He would sit in silence for most of the hour, trying to get me to open up, with little or no prompting or questions. I felt he was essentially getting paid by the GP to do no work!

Also, he had the personality of a wet biscuit, which didn't exactly help. In contrast, I'd read a bit about CBT and knew it was about a dialogue and unpicking thought patterns, which seemed more helpful.

I think I came across online CBT via a website or forum back in 2009, and the team behind this programme wanted people with mental health issues to test it out and give feedback. It was styled as 'mood management' and was aimed at adults, but I found it quite patronising – think overly simplistic cartoon characters leading you through the exercises, that kind of thing.

Some parts were useful in theory, but it was essentially me on my computer, feeling isolated, and I don't think that aspect helped. I think it played into my self-stigma, of wanting to tell people what I was experiencing, but not feeling like I'd be accepted or understood, so just glossing over it in front of other people and plastering on a smile.

How did you go from that to group therapy?

I wasn't put forward for group therapy until a year later; I was still trying different antidepressants and getting nowhere. I got referred to my local talking therapy service, and group CBT was an option.

32

Though I had lots of friends, depression wasn't a topic of conversation with most of them – it either made them actively uncomfortable or they had their own serious issues to deal with and I felt mine didn't count, because my depression wasn't caused by a traumatic event. Group therapy appealed to me because it would involve like-minded people.

What was it like in practice?

It was sometimes patronising, but generally useful. Lots of people dropped out of the group over time, which is normal, but about eight of us stuck with it for the full ten weeks.

We were a half-and-half mixture of depression and anxiety to begin with, but most of the other depressives dropped out, except me and a woman whose depression was triggered by her husband walking out on the family.

The CBT exercises were straightforward – things like the thought tree, the thought diamond, and the standard worksheets for breaking down your thoughts and measuring in percentages how likely they were to be true.

The best bits were labelling thoughts, which I could then spot in other people: catastrophising, and so on.

We all found it difficult to put the CBT into practice, as you can't crack on with a thought worksheet if you have negative thoughts in the middle of your work shift. However, the group leaders did take us seriously.

I did feel inclined to self-censor because of the group, as it felt like some of them had more of a 'reason' to feel the way they did. I also deliberately didn't tell the group leaders about a recent overdose (which I wouldn't describe as a suicide attempt – I just wanted to end up in hospital and finally get proper treatment).

This was because they emphasised that anyone with strong suicidal thoughts or suicidal actions would have to leave the group because it wouldn't be effective for them or helpful to others. I wanted to complete the ten weeks, rather than talk about my overdose, which I was embarrassed about, and leave the group CBT.

CBT is sometimes criticised for being 'formulaic'. What are your thoughts on this?

It definitely depends on how good the practitioner is, but I'd say 75 per cent of the time, CBT is too formulaic and there is far too much of a one-size-fits-all approach.

The best therapists I've had for individual CBT haven't structured our sessions around exercises or worksheets. Their sessions have been more like a conversation, where they pull out threads and we unpick them together, rather than a childlike series of exercises, which have always had mixed results for me.

I generally find that the more realistic and down-to-earth a practitioner is, and the more emotional intelligence they have, the greater their delivery of CBT is. They make it their own and tailor it to the client. Yes, some exercises or strategies should be tried, but the session doesn't need to be clunky or awkward.

Unfortunately, some of the best CBT practitioners are being forced out of the NHS or sidelined by it, due to budget cuts, paperwork or impossibly high targets.

I ended up seeing a private therapist for CBT, starting in 2014, as nobody could treat me in the NHS – the waiting time was ridiculous. I was on a waiting list for over a year. My therapist is brilliant, but her office is a forty-five-minute drive from my house (and it used to be further than that – more like seventy minutes – until she moved offices).

My mum has to drive, because I don't drive very often. This is either because I'm having suicidal ideation about driving the car into a wall, my concentration is particularly bad, or I'm having therapy on a busy day and can't face parking. If I was getting formulaic therapy from my therapist, it wouldn't be worth the journey time.

She is sweary and funny, and she laughs at some of the overly serious people in her profession. I think you need someone who doesn't take themselves too seriously. However, she's so good that she's often called to appear in court to give testimony about a victim or perpetrator's mental health, so my appointments often change at the last minute.

As I'm not working properly, due to the ongoing effects of the depression following a major breakdown in 2014, my mum actually pays for my therapy, which I'm quite embarrassed about.

Do you think there's an issue here, in that often the only people who get great therapy are those who can afford it?

Money and affordability is definitely an issue. I spend a lot of time working on the communications and administrative side of a peer support group, Mental Health Mates, and we have a lot of people asking for advice on affordable therapy (though we are just a talking group, not therapeutic ourselves).

I often direct people to online therapist directories where you can factor in your budget in the search criteria. There are also lots of therapists who offer reduced rates for people in financial hardship, but I know people can be too proud to ask for discounts like this.

As I said before, I do feel ashamed that my mum pays for my therapy, but I don't really have an income and I'm having to live at home, so I don't have a choice. If I paid for my own therapy, I'd be well into my overdraft and would be charged overdraft fees I couldn't afford. At my worst, I was seeing my therapist once a week. She charges a fair price, no question, but it's a lot of money.

There's also a self-care issue that always gets me – if I had to pay for my own care, it would be an issue because I don't value myself enough to book appointments when I need them. I'd look at the cost and tell myself I wasn't worth it.

I bet there are people across the UK who aren't getting NHS help but, even if they have the money to spend privately, don't consider themselves 'worthy' enough for therapy. You just sit there blaming yourself instead, and seeing it as a punishment, believing you should be able to fix yourself somehow.

There's definitely a 'beggars can't be choosers' attitude from the NHS when it comes to CBT: you get what you're given, and you don't want to move to the bottom of a waiting list if you've spent months getting to the top of it. The fact that you're given a set number of sessions doesn't help.

I understand you have to have a certain number, or people would just go on and on, but I think it should be more flexible – if the therapist thinks you need five more sessions because of complex issues, you should be able to get an extension. This kind of thing might be possible with a fairer system.

In the meantime, you feel very conscious of this evaporating time, and that you should be 'better' by the end. If you're not feeling 'better', it feels like you're ungrateful or lazy. That's not to say the therapist spells it out, but you get that impression subconsciously; I felt like this, and I've met others who felt the same.

My therapist, who I see privately, has told me some horror stories about working in the NHS, and how the system works against the therapist if their client's mood questionnaire answers don't improve (the form is partly based on PHQ-9, the nine-question depression scale).

Each week you fill out the questionnaire before your appointment, with answers given a score, then you hand it to your therapist when you arrive. They log the answers on their computer, and ask you about any dramatic changes when compared to your previous scores.

My therapist discovered that, unless her clients' scores improved during their course of CBT, her boss would blame her. Other therapists would try to manipulate their clients' scores, talking them into changing their answers, so it wouldn't reflect badly on a professional level.

This undermines the point of the client being in therapy: shit happens, and you come to talk to your therapist about it. Sometimes nothing happens per se, but you feel horrendous anyway.

It's not the therapist's fault if your symptoms worsen; it's usually consistent with your circumstances, or just whatever's going on in your head. The idea that you can criticise someone professionally for that is ridiculous.

Cognitive Analytic Therapy (CAT)

Oh, I thought CAT would be the one where they make you stroke kittens to feel calmer. No?

No, it's another acronym. Cognitive Analytic Therapy. Sorry, no kittens.

I suppose you're going to give me the history lesson now.

Well, since you asked so nicely . . . CAT was developed in the early 1980s by Dr Anthony Ryle while working at Guy's and St Thomas' Hospitals in London. Ryle had noticed that although traditional analytic therapy could be effective, it often took a long time to produce results.

This long-term approach was not always practical for those with busy working lives, so Ryle set about devising a type of therapy that integrated traditional analysis with cognitive techniques to get results within shorter time frames.

So he nicked two ideas from other people and stuck them together.

That's a little bit mean. We've already learned that cognitive therapies deal with thoughts and their impact on behaviour. In contrast, the analytic approach deals with past events and discovering reasons why individuals feel the way they do about certain things. CAT combines the two by delving into the patient's history, and then looking for practical strategies for dealing with their problems.

'Practical strategies'? What are they when they're at home?

The therapist will discuss with you what you could be doing differently to make positive changes. What those things might be will vary from client to client, which is why the relationship between the therapist and the client is so important – they must work together to find the best solutions.

You mean there isn't just a checklist of things to try?

No. The way forward is dictated by the client's own individual needs. It's important for them to feel involved, and that the treatment is specific to them.

But isn't that like starting from scratch every time? Surely the therapist should have some tried and tested methods to save messing around.

It actually saves time to tailor the treatment to each client. Humans are complex creatures, and what works for one person might be totally useless to another. By deciding together on an approach that's likely to be effective, you can dispense with all the stuff that won't be.

Therapists will certainly have methods that they know to work, it's just a matter of deciding which ones to use. If the right framework is in place, the patient will be able to continue moving forward after the treatment is complete.

You mean like teaching a man to fish instead of giving him a fish.

If you like. Except less fishy.

You say 'after the treatment is complete', but how do you know when that will be?

CAT is a time-limited therapy, normally lasting for sixteen sessions, but it can be longer or shorter depending on the problems that need to be addressed. The number of sessions will be agreed at the start, after the therapist has assessed the client's needs.

What if they get it wrong, though? What if sixteen sessions aren't enough?

Follow-up sessions may be offered at the end of the programme. It's unlikely that a client will be thrown out if they still desperately need help, but the therapist will structure the sessions to ensure that hopefully doesn't happen.

And is this another one where the client has to do homework, or whatever you call it?

There might be questionnaires to fill in, where you rate your feelings and what you do in response. You could also be asked to write a goodbye letter to your therapist, who will do the same for you.

Your therapist's letter will summarise the progress you've made and what still needs to be done, while your letter will do the same and also reflect on the end of the therapeutic relationship. It's an unusual way to end therapy, but it won't feel like homework, I promise.

Could you just write 'See ya' and sign your name?

If you really wanted to, but the more you put into it, the more you'll get out.

Thanks Mum. Is there anything else I should know about CAT?

One key aspect of the treatment is the concept of traps, dilemmas and snags. Traps are like loops of thinking that are hard to escape from. You might feel, for example, that nobody ever listens to you. As a result, you stop talking about how you feel but this makes you miserable and isolated.

Others might notice this and ask what's wrong, but you don't tell them because you don't think they'll listen, which keeps the cycle going.

Sorry, what was that? I was checking my phone.

Dilemmas are where we feel that we have to choose a certain option even if we aren't happy with it, because we imagine that the alternatives will be even worse. These assumptions may be false, but they can nonetheless narrow our options.

Right. And what was the other one again?

Snags, which can also be thought of as self-sabotage. These are the things we might tell ourselves that stop us moving forward. An example of this would be that you say you'd like to have a better job, but you tell yourself you don't have the skills and it's too late for you to learn them. A CAT therapist will help you to recognise these elements of your behaviour so they can be addressed.

Sounds like a plan. And maybe if CAT doesn't work, I can get a kitten instead?
Maybe.

The therapist: Elizabeth Wilde McCormick

'*So often, people don't get listened to*'

What made you decide to become a therapist?

I was always interested in the mind and how people coped with suffering. I had an early marriage failure and was a single parent for a while. During this time, I joined Samaritans as a volunteer. That helped me learn to sit with people with an open mind.

The most important thing is listening, really listening, because so often people don't get listened to and they don't learn to listen to themselves. The real art of listening, with all our senses, is essential for working as a therapist – and for all relationships, really! It's not a great distance from this to the more contemplative approaches such as mindfulness.

After a while, I got more and more curious about how people got themselves into difficult situations and what could be done, so I then decided to train as a therapist.

Why did you specialise in CAT?

I worked in the private sector in the 1980s and wondered about people who couldn't afford therapy, and what happened in the NHS. I did a two-year training course at Guy's Hospital in social psychiatry, and that's where I met Dr Anthony Ryle, the pioneer of CAT. He came to give us a lecture and it was like, 'Ah! This is a man who really understands human nature.'

He could put complicated psychological theories into ordinary, common-sense language. He invited me to join his new therapy project. I've been part of CAT for a long time and am a founder and life member. I feel very lucky.

What does CAT offer over other types of therapy?

It's collaborative. The therapist and client work together. Tony Ryle always believed that people could learn far more than they were ever given credit for. CAT uses the patient's own words; being a writer, I'm very interested in language, what people say and how much that tells us about feelings.

CAT is also time-limited, which is a relief for many people! It's sixteen sessions and then a follow-up, traditionally. Clients have a map that they can continue to work with and refer back to over and over again. CAT is a therapy that helps to make sense of what often has felt nonsensical, all without a complicated psychological word in sight.

What do you enjoy most about your work?

It's a great privilege to sit with another person and hear their story. To be alongside someone as they make sense of what they've not been able to make sense of before, and even experience healing.

In deciding whether you can work with a client, do you have an initial consultation?

Yes. There would be an exploratory session, for someone to come and see what it feels like to sit with you and vice versa. It's an opportunity to have the therapy process outlined. One of my early supervisors said to me, 'Helping someone find a therapist is like marriage guidance. There's a lot of chemistry and it does need to work.'

Are you careful not to reveal too much about yourself to clients?

Yes. There are times when revealing things can be absolutely spot-on, where you're just being a human being. And there are times when the use of humour is really valuable, but it's a very subtle thing. You have to know the person.

The most important thing is that the person feels safe; safe with you and safe in your professional skills. Safe enough to be vulnerable and afraid, feeling some of those things they've always carried but covered over with their learned behaviours. I wouldn't want to reveal too much – it's too confusing.

Would you accept a gift from a client?

It depends. If someone brought a gift at the follow-up, or at the end of the therapy, something like a flower or a piece of fruit, and it's a genuine and generous offering, then it feels churlish not to accept it.

If someone continually brings something and there's a pattern to it, you have to ask whether they feel that they need to do more than just turn up. Do they need to please you?

You mentioned the use of humour. Presumably you have to gauge that on a client-by-client basis?

Psychotherapy is all about attunement. It's about deeply listening to the other person and really noticing what is happening, in what you're being told or asked, the eye contact, the body language, the tone, the content, the repetition . . . you're noticing every subtle thing and you're attuning to that to find a way to communicate in the deepest, clearest way.

So you would have to feel really comfortable to bring in something levelling like humour, and of course to know when not to. It would have to be absolutely appropriate.

If you knew of someone wanting to try therapy for the first time, would you encourage CAT over other modalities or do you think it's only suitable for certain people?

I think CAT is a very good start. If the person finds that what comes out of it is a desire to look at, in more depth, a relationship with a family member, or they realise that they'd quite like to look more deeply into the nature of their depressed thinking, then they can find another form of therapy after the sixteen sessions. I would always recommend CAT first.

Have you found in more recent times that people are more impatient for results?

We live in a quick-fix, tick-box culture hungry for instant gratification and to move on to the next activity. Human beings are a rich, complex mixture of feelings, sensations and thoughts. There is a tendency now in training therapists to discount the importance of the therapeutic relationship.

In my view, this is where real lasting change occurs: in that intimacy with another person, being respected, listened to and cared for. It's a confidential space, not unlike the confessional, and so for me it has an element of the sacred about it.

I feel very sad when I hear about depressed patients filling in forms and therapists ticking boxes.

Do you think more can be achieved from knowing there's a time limit to the therapy than if it's open-ended?

That's one of the crucial aspects of CAT: the end is on the agenda right from the beginning. What often happens towards the end is that old patterns reoccur, symptoms might return, and there is this opportunity to put the new learning into practice, together with another person.

The other thing is that a brief therapy saves you from having to endlessly search for what is enough! There's the Woody Allen character who's in analysis for forty years, looking for the perfect father and mother, and it saves you from that.

For people who have real difficulty with relationships, the time limit is very important. Sometimes things come out towards the end, *because* of the end, that people wouldn't say if they had another year or so.

If someone got to the end of the scheduled sixteen sessions and felt that they really needed more time, would that be out of the question?

These things are all negotiable within the relationship. Wanting more could be part of what we call a learned procedure and this would be reflected upon in a shared way. It would also be checked again at the three-month follow-up appointment.

If a disclosure of abuse or some other very painful material comes to light right at the end, then it needs to be negotiated whether it's a good idea to stop as planned or whether another month or two months is needed to process feelings. CAT therapists are all in supervision, and this is where these decisions are discussed.

Sometimes people come for extended follow-ups, so after their three-month follow-up they might contact me a year or so later and ask to come back. They might realise they are going over a sore place again and need a bit more input.

You can do that in private practice; it works in a more varied way in the NHS, and depends on who's available.

Have you had contact with people after the follow-up sessions where they've told you how they're getting on?

Yes, it's really nice. Some people decide they want to do something long-term, or work as a couple or in a group, and can be helped with this. The CAT structure, the letters and maps are a good strong foundation.

To someone who is unfamiliar with CAT, is there anything about it that you'd like to explain in more depth?

It's a really well researched therapy. The structure of CAT offers scaffolding for therapists to work in the most creative and appropriate way for patients from different groups and ages, and there are CAT therapists working in many different clinical settings, with children, families, young people and elderly people.

There are therapists working in CAT with music, art or drama – there's space to be really playful according to what suits the client best.

Reformulation is also important. During the first four sessions, there is a gathering together of information that forms a 'reformulation', written by the therapist and read out loud to the client.

It's the therapist saying things like, 'From what you have told me so far, it seems like most of your life you've struggled with this,' and it makes sense of what has often felt chaotic. It also adds what we hope to do together, so it begins to put in aims for the therapeutic work that need to be tailored to what the person can manage. I think the reformulation is a real gift. I don't know of any other therapy that offers that.

The client is encouraged to take part in daily self-monitoring, keeping a diary of their traps, dilemmas and snags, how often they happen and what was happening at the time. Noticing, stopping, revising and trying something new – those are the steps to follow.

Finally, at the beginning of the last session, both therapist and client write goodbye letters to each other. They read theirs, and you yours. Usually, if things have gone well, they're similar!

The letters can be as long or brief as you like. Some people write poems, or a song. I have all sorts of wonderful examples. It's something for the person to have during the three months where they're really on their own, practising what they've learned in the therapy. Then, at the follow-up, you see how they have weathered the gap, and whether they need another follow-up or some other kind of therapy.

Do you think there's enough information about CAT available?

Most people have heard of CBT but not CAT. We worry about that. We don't know if the CBT people are better at promoting themselves than we are. CAT is now on the NICE guidelines for personality disorder and I think for eating disorders as well [NICE is the National Institute for Health and Care Excellence, a UK governmental health body]. I wish it were more widely known about.

How do you think therapists are perceived?

I stopped telling strangers I was a therapist years ago because they tended to say, 'Oh, I hope you aren't going to start analysing me!' There's a sense that you've got some knowledge and are superior. There have been therapists like that in the past, but I think it's all a lot more accessible now.

The client: Ariane Sherine

'She explained that I would never be perfectly loved'

I had cognitive analytic therapy when I was twenty-seven, with a trainee in the NHS. I remember the assessment being unusually aggressive, so it was a pleasant surprise to finally be introduced to my therapist. She was around the same age as me, maybe slightly older, with a gentle demeanour, honey-blonde hair and immaculate clothes, a lazy eye and a ready smile.

I would come into the health centre in Russell Square in the morning, once a week for ten weeks. I was angry and scruffy, wearing my baggy jeans and scuffed trainers, and my therapist would come down to reception to collect me, friendly and affable in her loose smart blouse and midi skirt. She looked as though she had life all figured out. I wanted to be like her.

To start with, I asked if we could work on my claustrophobia, because since being suffocated while pregnant by my boyfriend when I was twenty-four, every situation I was in felt claustrophobic. Even being in a room with the windows and door shut was only just possible for me by that point.

But then I realised that I would have to face my fears and put myself in situations I didn't want to be in, such as lifts and the Tube; and that even when I talked about the incident that took place in 2005, I was back in that dark room in the middle of the night, trapped and terrified.

So I told my therapist that my claustrophobia was no longer impacting my life that much – which was true on one level, because I just totally avoided lifts, planes and the Tube – and asked to work on my relationships instead. I'd figured out by then that, because of my father, I was often attracted to violent and domineering men, older men who were trouble. But the boyfriend I had at the time wasn't like that; he was just immature and silly.

For no reason, he once took his chewing gum out of his mouth, full of spit, and stuck it on my forehead. When I said I was leaving him, he said, 'You can't, otherwise you'll have to tell everyone you left because I stuck chewing gum on your head!' and had a giggling fit. (Ten years on, this incident is still humiliating, and also objectively quite funny.)

My boyfriend would also, whenever we were out walking hand-in-hand, abruptly drop my hand and start walking in the opposite direction. I would switch direction and run after him, sprinting to keep up, asking what he was doing. He would keep walking silently without explanation.

My therapist and I talked a lot about how, because of my borderline personality disorder, I needed relationships to be perfect. She drew a diagram in quadrants with a picture of an eye looking at it (called an 'all seeing I'), exploring the fact that I had a tendency to, as she put it, 'throw the baby out with the bathwater' and end my relationships as soon as they went even slightly wrong.

No relationship would ever be perfect, she explained – I would never be 'perfectly loved', something I felt I needed as a substitute for not feeling loved as a child – but my relationships could still be very good if I overcame this ingrained hurdle of demanding perfection.

I pointed out that my current boyfriend was childish and difficult, and asked her whether she thought I would still be acting out unhelpful patterns if I left him. My therapist shrugged and said that I should leave him if I was unhappy, but consider applying her advice to future relationships.

Though the therapy was directive, I never felt as though I was being told what to do. The advice was there for me to take or leave, and was delivered in such a gentle manner that I felt supported and not admonished. I never quite got my head around the diagrams, but pretended that I did, because I didn't want my therapist to think I was stupid.

Unlike most therapists, my therapist was also not afraid of unobtrusively making her views known. I was very anti-religious at the time, and I told her that I thought religion was dangerously irrational and could exacerbate mental illness. She quietly agreed. When I started writing for the *Guardian* and told her I was planning to start the Atheist Bus Campaign, with its slogan, 'There's probably no God. Now stop worrying and enjoy your life', she laughed hard.

It was so unusual for me to meet a fellow atheist that I felt a real connection with her. She was smart and funny; I liked her genuine laugh, her honesty and openness, her optimism and realism. When I had to write her a goodbye letter, I told her that I would really miss her. That I had been dreading having to tell my endless story again to yet another therapist, but despite all I'd been through, she made life feel as though it could be OK again, even fun.

I thanked her in a very heartfelt way, and she seemed very choked up. She said, 'That's a very good letter,' and wiped her eyes. She read her own goodbye letter to me, saying that she would miss me and my sense of humour. I felt accepted, even loved. I told her that, though I knew we would never meet again, if she wanted to know what I was up to, she could always look me up in the *Guardian*.

I've looked my therapist up a few times in the decade since our therapy sessions ended, and have never been able to find her. Maybe, like a lot of NHS therapists, she uses a different name online, or isn't online at all; or perhaps she got married and changed her name.

It's one of the hardest things about therapy: that, when you meet someone who you think could be a friend, and connect with them, that closeness has to stay in the therapy room. You can't take it away with you into real life. But my therapist helped me greatly, just by being herself. She taught me a lot without wanting anything from me, and made me feel something I had never felt before: likeable.

I hope that, whatever she's doing now, she's happy.

Acceptance and Commitment Therapy (ACT)

CAT, ACT . . . aren't we just shuffling letters around here?

No, the letters stand for something quite different. ACT was developed by Steven C Hayes, a professor at the Nevada Foundation, in the 1980s. It's based on Hayes' own Relational Frame Theory (RFT), which looks at human language and cognition.

RFT recognised that the rational skills that human beings use to overcome general problems in their life were not effective when it came to coping with psychological distress. ACT evolved, with Hayes' assistance, to help individuals change their relationship with emotional pain by accepting it as a normal part of life, rather than trying to avoid it.

It's nothing like CAT then?

No, acceptance and commitment therapy takes an alternative approach. Rather than trying to remove or replace negative thoughts, ACT (which, incidentally, is pronounced as the word 'act' rather than by its initials) is about accepting that bad thoughts and feelings will exist and looking at ways of changing our relationship with them.

Sounds a bit defeatist.

Well, its proponents suggest that trying to eliminate bad feelings only increases them, since they're an inevitable part of our lives. Their thinking is that it's better to accept that they will come and go without overreacting to them.

If people around you are telling you that you need to behave differently, it can be easy to feel that you're letting them down and that you're to blame for what's going on, but those people might not understand your problems or why you feel the way you do. Instead, you learn to manage your feelings in a rational way.

Isn't that more easily said than done?

ACT promotes the use of mindfulness techniques to make it simpler.

Mindfulness? You mean like meditation?

Mindfulness is about living in the moment, accepting and understanding your experience as it happens. You might think of it as stepping outside yourself for a while and letting go of those thoughts and feelings that aren't helpful, while also allowing them to exist, rather than trying to suppress them.

You might also take an interest in the process – not exactly welcoming negative feelings, but treating them with curiosity, as something to be understood.

So it's a bit like analysing yourself.

A little bit, but more like analysing your thoughts. The important thing is to treat it like an experiment and not to judge yourself. You might find yourself feeling or acting in a way that you don't like, but instead of berating yourself, ACT encourages you to try to understand what is making you feel that way, and what the best way of coping with it could be.

Like counting to ten when you feel angry, instead of punching a sheep in the face?

In the sense of stepping back and not reacting, yes.

Well, that's the acceptance part. What's the commitment?

ACT involves identifying the important values in your life to determine what you need to move towards. This is different from setting targets or goals, because values are non-specific; they're just the things in life that you think are important.

These values are therefore geared towards changing how you live your life, because they encourage you to take a long-term outlook rather than setting a short-term goal. The commitment is agreeing to uphold these values in the pursuit of creating a better life for yourself.

When you're feeling distressed, it can help to focus on your values and ask yourself whether the problems you're having are really serious, or just obstacles.

OK, but if it's a lifelong commitment, does that mean the therapy never ends?

ACT can actually be a short-, medium- or long-term process depending on the client's needs, but it's certainly not intended to last for ever! The hope is that by the end of the therapy, whenever that may be, the client will be in a position to move forward using the new skills that they have developed.

I struggle a bit with commitment. I thought about nicking off while you were droning on.

Well we're done now, so don't let me keep you.

OK. I'm off to apologise to a sheep.

The therapist: Joe Oliver

'It allowed me to be kinder to myself'

How would you explain what ACT is to someone who has never heard of it? And who would it be suitable for?

Although ACT stands for Acceptance and Commitment Therapy, it could also stand for:

Accept
Choose
Take Action.

This means that, at its heart, ACT focuses on helping people to build the skills to mindfully step out of auto-pilot, disentangle from thoughts and feelings and consider, in that moment, choosing what really matters. And then take the steps to move in that direction.

ACT is an evidence-based approach that's extremely versatile and suitable for all sorts of issues. It's a model of human psychology and, as such, it's been applied wherever psychology is important (which is most places!).

For example, it's used with people struggling with depression and anxiety, with chronic pain or physical health conditions, and with high performers – athletes, leaders, etc.

Why did you decide to specialise in ACT over all other therapeutic approaches?

There are three main reasons.

The first was a personal resonance with the idea of acceptance. Before coming across ACT, I'd found myself spending lots of time fighting and struggling with negative thoughts or unwanted feelings. The notion that there was an alternative was a real revelation.

It allowed me to be kinder to myself, as the presence of unwanted thoughts and feelings didn't preclude compassion. But also, I found it helped me to be clearer about what was important to me. Thoughts and feelings became less the boss of me and my actions, and I was the one doing more of the choosing. That's a good place to be.

The second was the strong scientific tradition with ACT. The science really matters to the ACT community! This means doing what is effective, whilst at the same time, looking to evolve the practice based on new, emerging evidence.

ACT today is not what it was ten years ago, and in another ten years, it's likely to be different again. This is cool and it speaks to my inner geek, but I also like the fact that the community is willing to be flexible and change the model when the data says the model is not working.

Lastly, the international ACT community (the wider term is Contextual Behavioural Science) is incredibly co-operative. It's like a total 'open source' community. This means ideas and resources flow freely and people work hard to both help each other, and also take care of each other. It makes the journey easier and a lot more fun.

What does a typical session of ACT involve?

ACT is a practical type of therapy, so I'm always thinking about how to help a client learn skills in the moment so they can move towards their goals. But at its heart, it's about building psychological flexibility so that painful, difficult or unwanted thoughts and feelings are less impactful.

This means people's actions can be guided more by their values and what's important to them. To do this, a typical session will be developing three skills, called Open, Aware and Active.

Open is about fostering an open stance towards thoughts and emotions. This means acknowledging emotions and easing up on fighting and struggling with them (aka acceptance). And catching unhelpful thoughts or self-stories and practising unhooking from them.

Aware skills involve stepping out of autopilot and coming into the present moment. This might be practising mindfulness, checking in with thoughts and feelings, or shifting awareness from the past or future to what's going on in the moment.

Right alongside this is the *Active* component. Here I help the client to identify who or what is important to them; the things deep down that really matter to them. And invite the client to take actual steps in this direction.

All of these processes are intertwined and are often going on in each session. I sometimes think that this is like wiggling a cork out of a bottle – pushing on each of the three sides at different points throughout a session to increase flexibility. An ACT therapist sets the scene for the client to safely, creatively, even playfully try out these skills, while offering coaching and encouragement to the client.

What can a client do to get the most out of ACT?

It's an approach that is, at times, counter-intuitive. It asks us to stop fighting with thoughts and feelings, when often that can be the last thing we want to do. In fact, most clients will say to me in the first session they want help getting rid of these experiences. While totally understandable, this obscures the important questions, which ask how they want life to look – if they could choose. So good preparation for ACT is to keep an open mind and be prepared to go to unexpected places.

Along with openness, curiosity about experiences is important. It helps to be interested in thoughts, feelings and emotions, especially the tough ones. Becoming aware of patterns, fluctuations and connections is useful. Developing a mindfulness practice can be one way to do this; or simply starting a journal to make a few notes on these experiences.

Lastly, it's always helpful to read a bit about ACT. There are lots of great self-help books on ACT out there now that tackle all sorts of issues.

The client: Francesca Baker

'It's helped me see that life won't be perfect, but I can still muddle through'

I stumbled across ACT while googling for self-help sheets, and loved the concept. I've always struggled with the idea of acceptance, as though it means giving up. ACT has helped me to see that life won't be perfect, but I can still muddle through and get closer to where I want to be, if I put the work in.

I wouldn't say the mindset has changed my life. I'm still working on it, but I do find it very liberating as an approach, and especially love how down-to-earth it is. It seems to be a kind of softer CBT or more practical counselling. I've recommended it to a few people, and think it's just a helpful approach to life.

Musa Okwonga on the Benefits of Therapy

'I honestly believe that it is never too late to start therapy'

I found my first therapist through a friend. I was at university at the time, in my final year, so I discreetly asked around. I didn't want too many people to know that I was struggling.

I was very fortunate not to have to try lots of therapists before settling on her. She was the first person I spoke to. That's about as lucky as it gets, I think.

I liked her because she was very, very good not only at listening, but at picking up on statements that I made in passing, and asking me to expand on what I meant. I am very guarded about certain issues in my life, and she made me comfortable enough not only to discuss them but to discuss the roots of them.

She was warm, engaging, but not overfamiliar – it was a little like talking to a very cheerful doctor who's going to give you a painful injection. You both know it might hurt, but that the discomfort isn't something you can avoid, and that it will not only be delivered with compassion but will lead to a better outcome.

I would say to anyone seeking a therapist: find someone who not only listens to you but who encourages you to hold up a mirror to how you are feeling and behaving. Someone who patiently and gently allows you to find and examine patterns in your behaviour, and discuss ways to change them.

I have gone to a couple of therapists at different times since then – as a form of mental MOT, a bit like going to the GP to check in, to make sure everything's OK.

Therapy has been immensely helpful. One person I worked with was especially helpful, because he identified one key factor that was affecting me negatively across all my relationships. It was the kind of thing which, once he had pointed it out, I could take plenty of small but effective steps to address at once.

I think therapy is so daunting because people are afraid of the amount of work they need to do to feel better – it can seem overwhelming at times. But I honestly believe that it is never too late to start therapy, and to be free of turmoil.

Dialectical Behaviour Therapy (DBT)

DBT? That's not therapy – it's what you can get on long-haul flights.

You're quite the comedian, aren't you? DBT, or dialectical behaviour therapy, is a form of CBT that was developed by a doctor called Marsha Linehan in the 1980s. She wanted to create a type of therapy specifically for people suffering with borderline personality disorder.

Well I'm borderline falling asleep, so get on with it.

She found that she was getting better results from engaging with her clients more and asking them to stop blaming themselves for their predicament. It was apparent to her that people with self-destructive conditions and suicidal ideation had very negative views of themselves that were being enforced by the reactions of those around them.

By changing this way of thinking and trying to make the clients look more kindly upon themselves, she found that they were better able to manage their reactions, and cope better with the situations that triggered their negative thoughts.

So it's just for people with borderline personality disorder?

No; after some initial encouraging results Dr Linehan used the technique to treat a number of other conditions, and had equally positive outcomes. She has since revealed that she herself self-harmed from an early age, giving her an important insight into the minds of fellow sufferers. DBT has also been used to treat other self-destructive conditions such as substance abuse and eating disorders.

So what makes it different from CBT? I mean, apart from the first letter?

It has the same aim of helping the client to change unhelpful behaviours, but there is much more emphasis on acceptance and understanding. DBT therapists understand that their patients are often criticised for their behaviour, so they focus on helping them to understand why they behave that way and teaching them that it's normal given their circumstances. They then look at techniques that can help them to accept the way they feel but modify their response to it.

Sounds like it might help those who feel misunderstood.

Some people experience emotions very intensely. They can react strongly to situations that others might take in their stride, often to the surprise of those around them. They might be told that they're overreacting, or too intense, and be made to feel abnormal. They can also feel that they're letting down the people around them as a result.

 DBT removes the blame from the client and focuses on how they can recognise these heightened emotions and how to cope more effectively with them. A lot of importance is placed on the relationship between the client and the therapist, as this is the main driving force for motivating the client to change.

I sometimes feel misunderstood. I probably shouldn't talk with my mouth full.

Self-destructive behaviour can be difficult for others to understand, so sufferers can often be made to feel negative about themselves. The compassionate aspect of DBT can be helpful to those people and make them feel less isolated.

Dialectical Behaviour Therapy (DBT)

I'm not thick or anything, but what does 'dialectical' mean?

It means dealing with opposing forces. In this context, it's about finding a balance between accepting unhelpful behaviour and changing it. It's a bit like dissecting the truth from two opposing viewpoints. It's unhelpful for someone to hear that what they're doing is wrong and that they need to stop doing it, especially when they find it difficult to control their actions.

The acceptance element of the therapy is crucial to stop the patient from feeling that they're a disappointment or a failure. It might not be possible to change the things that cause distress to an individual, but simply learning how to tolerate them better can be a big step forward.

Anything else I should know?

DBT doesn't necessarily have to be one-on-one; there can also be group-based skills sessions where people can learn important social skills if their condition makes it difficult to bond with others. It's likely to be in a classroom environment with weekly sessions held by two therapists.

You mentioning classroom environments reminds me – do you have to do homework with this one?

Let's call it helping yourself. Your therapist might ask you to keep a diary or to fill in questionnaires that they give you. It's nothing too taxing, and is an important part of the process.

I'm off to tell people what 'dialectical' means. They'll think I'm dead clever.

So glad you got something out of this.

The therapist: Fiona Kennedy

'I enjoy it when clients have a light-bulb moment'

What is DBT?

It's a therapy aimed at changing behaviour: reducing self-destructive and life-ruining behaviours and increasing skilful ways to handle life's challenges and emotional distress. It doesn't focus on the past or on traumatic material.

DBT does this by first having a period of time when the client and therapist put their heads together and decide whether or not to go ahead. This is called the pre-DBT phase or commitment phase. During this time, we make sure the client knows exactly what the therapy will involve, including committing to a definite period of time, usually a year.

The client agrees to attend individual and group sessions weekly and to use telephone coaching to help prevent themselves carrying out destructive urges. The therapist commits to attending peer supervision, the Consult Group. The therapist uses specific strategies to increase the client's commitment and also honestly considers whether it is right to go ahead at this time.

The therapist ensures the client knows about DBT and if appropriate, about borderline personality disorder and how it applies to them.

The client's Target Behaviour List is laid out, describing all the behaviours the client agrees to reduce, including suicide/self-harm, physical aggression, drug misuse, eating disordered behaviours, etc. Also any behaviours which interfere with the effectiveness of therapy or seriously affect quality of life.

The client and therapist then sign a contract, and DBT begins. The client and therapist meet up individually every week to focus on reducing target behaviours, and the client attends a weekly skills training group to learn mindfulness, interpersonal skills, emotion regulation skills and crisis survival skills.

The client calls the therapist as needed before the target behaviours occur, in order to get coaching on using the previously made plans to deal with urges and do something different instead of the target behaviours.

What does a typical therapy session entail?

A mindfulness exercise, homework review and diary review to check for target behaviours. It can also include chain analysis of a target behaviour, solution analysis, making a plan, troubleshooting the plan, homework setting, and anything on the client's agenda if time allows.

How much do you disclose about yourself in sessions?

Within DBT one is encouraged to use self-involving self-disclosure in order to help the client learn the effects of their behaviours on others. For example: 'When you cry when asked to do something difficult it makes me feel protective of you and reluctant to push you. This could interfere with our progress.' We also use self-disclosure in a validating way: 'I'm so pleased you did that!' Or 'If I were in your position, I might feel the same.'

I would often undertake to do homework along with the client, and report back on my progress next session.

Do you ever get frustrated or exasperated when a client is resistant to change or fails to make progress?

Yes! The DBT Consult Group or peer supervision group meets weekly to support therapists through issues like this, give them the chance to express their frustration and then get back on track to identify and address the client's or the therapist's therapy-interfering behaviours, which might be blocking progress. DBT also has a saying: 'The therapy can fail but the client cannot.'

What can a client do to help themselves during therapy?

Do their assignments. Be open and willing to experience some discomfort, and take risks for the purpose of getting a life worth living. Reduce targeted maladaptive behaviours. Increase skilful behaviours.

What qualities should a client look for in a DBT therapist?

Persistence, courage and optimism. The ability to confront with compassion and a sense of humour. Being nurturing, and possessing DBT skills. The therapist should embody the DBT approach in their own life as much as possible, as well as in the therapeutic relationship.

Are there people for whom DBT isn't suitable? If so, who?

People who are unable to concentrate on and remember the sessions because of substance use (though DBT is great for addictions), or because of hallucinations, delusions or depression. People with moderate to severe learning disabilities. DBT has been adapted for people with mild learning disabilities.

What do you enjoy most about practising therapy?

I enjoy it when clients have a light-bulb moment, when they manage to do a difficult thing, and when they get a life with meaning and purpose for them.

If you could start life over, would you still have been a therapist?

Yes, and a researcher and supervisor and trainer. All of it is endlessly fascinating and always changing, and it's such a privilege to be entrusted with people's inner lives.

What would you have done if you hadn't been a therapist?

Been an actress or been in advertising or charity work of some kind.

The client: Rae Ritchie

'I'm doing far better than I ever thought imaginable'

What first led you to seek therapy?

I'd previously had episodes of depression and anxiety, and had also struggled with PTSD. This came to a head again, and I sought support from my GP. I began taking antidepressants but was rejected by the local therapy services, then my state of mind deteriorated and I became suicidal.

An awesome A&E psychiatrist boosted my meds and involved the mental health crisis team. From that point, I quickly moved into eight weeks at a local outpatient mental health clinic – we were picked up daily by volunteer drivers and spent our time in workshops, holistic activities, etc.

As part of this, I saw more psychologists and was diagnosed with borderline personality disorder. I was put on the waiting list for DBT, and began this a few months later, when the next slot was available in a group, called a Managing Emotions group. This ran for around five months.

How did you feel when you learned you would be in group therapy rather than individual therapy?

I'd have preferred one-to-one therapy but I always knew that it would be a group – and to be honest I was just massively relieved that DBT was even an option. And, while the group was challenging at times (unsurprisingly I struggle with boundaries against others' emotions) I think it was an important learning curve for me.

Plus it was great to meet some other folks with BPD. We're actually arranging a lunch together soon.

What happened in a typical group session?

We'd start with chit-chat and coffee-making, then do a mindfulness exercise (the mindfulness element of DBT was covered each week over the six months). Next, we'd discuss how we'd got on with the homework (an exercise based on the previous week's technique).

After a coffee break, we'd explore a new technique (the first module was distress tolerance, the second was emotional regulation). They'd then outline the homework for that week. It was a very set routine.

Did you do the homework religiously or omit to do it on occasion? Did it feel like a chore, or was it enjoyable?

I'm sure there were weeks when I didn't do it, but I was pretty consistent as I knew that's where the course's value really lay. Just talking about the techniques wasn't going to make the changes I needed.

It felt like an adventure – a challenging one, but ultimately one that was for my benefit. I also made the effort to keep trying out the techniques even when they weren't that week's specific homework, and we were able to share our thoughts about that too.

Did you find that your level of distress in everyday situations lessened after the course, and that you were able to regulate your emotions more effectively?

Yes, I've definitely found that my ability to tolerate everyday stresses has increased since beginning the course. It has really helped. I'm probably more relaxed than ever, although the struggle is still there – sometimes I react then have to pull it back, although that happens much more quickly.

A trigger doesn't wipe out my whole day the way it used to. Likewise, I feel much more equipped to regulate my emotions. It's still a day-to-day work in progress but I'm doing far better than I ever thought imaginable. I'm so grateful that this treatment was available, particularly on the NHS.

Was there any moment in particular where something 'clicked' for you and it all made sense – a kind of light-bulb moment – or was getting better mainly a question of practising the techniques?

There were a number of light-bulb moments along the way. Probably the biggest was recognising my own responsibility – that I had to do this, that no one else could magically make me better. That was a bitter pill to swallow! But I don't think I'd have realised this without the consistent practice of the techniques week in, week out.

Could you outline a couple of the techniques you practise?

The two I use most are 'opposite action' and 'mastery'.

Opposite action, as the name suggests, involves behaving contrary to your inclination. So if you want to stay in bed, you get up. If you don't want to leave the house, you leave the house. It disrupts patterns of thought and behaviour, although it isn't as easy as it sounds.

Mastery involves doing one thing every day to make yourself feel capable and skilled. Nothing too challenging, but a task that pushes you beyond your comfort zone. This helps to develop resilience and builds self-esteem as well as making you feel good with the sense of achievement.

Have you any thoughts on the kind of therapy that deals with your past rather than your present, such as psychodynamic therapy?

I've previously had psychodynamic therapy to deal with one specific issue and found it so useful – to the point where I no longer feel triggered about it. However, I think negative thought patterns and unhealthy behaviours had built up layer by layer to the extent that I needed something 'practical' to help me to function.

It's only by regaining some kind of control of minute-to-minute life, thought and feeling that I feel stable enough to do other kinds of therapeutic work. I'm now awaiting the start of more traditional talking therapy to deal with other traumas.

Other Cognitive Behavioural Therapeutic Approaches

I thought we were done with CBT . . .?

There are some therapies that are closely related to CBT, but that require a little discussion in their own right.

And what do we have first?

First we have cognitive therapy.

For people who already know how to behave?

Very funny. CBT is a widely used approach, and as such it has been adapted to many different forms. Cognitive therapy is still based on the work of Aaron Beck, but focuses solely on the idea that negative thinking can have a serious impact on the potential of individuals. As such, it could be seen as a pure, undiluted sibling of CBT.

Remind me about the negative thinking thing again? I've forgotten.

Negative thinking can work in cycles. If you have a bad experience while doing a certain task, your mind might associate that task with something unpleasant. You might then avoid the task in the future, which serves to reinforce the negative association. Cognitive therapy is about reassessing these thoughts and trying to break the negative cycles.

So if there's a cognitive behavioural therapy and a cognitive therapy, shouldn't there be a behavioural therapy? Ha ha.

There is! That's next.

I was kidding. Really?

Behavioural therapy, as you might expect, focuses specifically on assisting those who want to change unhelpful behaviours.

Like leaving the toilet seat up?

Behavioural change could encompass anything from gambling addiction to phobias. Your therapist could use various techniques depending on the nature of the problem.

Such as?

In the case of phobias, they might try desensitisation or flooding. Desensitisation is when someone is exposed to what they fear in a gradual way, perhaps with relaxation exercises before and after, to make them feel more comfortable with it. Flooding is a more extreme version of that, where the exposure is greater and prolonged.

So if they were scared of water, you'd chuck them in a swimming pool?

It probably wouldn't be that extreme. And of course, the client would have to agree to it beforehand. If you trusted your therapist though, you might surprise yourself with what you are willing to try.

And what if it's not a phobia, but something like the toilet seat thing?

I'm really not sure that would qualify for therapy, but a therapist might try an aversion technique. This is where you associate something negative with the unwanted behaviour. A mild example of this would be applying a nasty-tasting gel to your fingernails to stop you biting them.

I don't want to stop biting my nails.

Well, the individual needs to be motivated enough to make changes to their life. You can lead a horse to water . . .

But you shouldn't throw them in unless they agree. What's next?

REBT, which stands for rational emotive behaviour therapy. It evolved from the work of the psychologist Albert Ellis in the 1950s, and works on the principle that many problems are the result of holding irrational beliefs.

Like believing in the tooth fairy?

Not quite. REBT uses an approach to show the connection between events, beliefs and outcomes that it calls ABC. The A is for adverse event; this is the thing that triggers the unwanted response in an individual. B is for belief, or what the individual expects to happen as a result of the adverse event. C is for consequences, which is how the individual feels as a result. This might be depression, anxiety or low self-worth.

I'm guessing that the therapist doesn't just tell them they're being daft?

The therapy assumes that most people aren't aware that their beliefs are irrational. This is why they can go unchallenged for so long. The therapist will set out to identify these beliefs, encourage the client to confront them and then replace them with more helpful, constructive thoughts.

Easier said than done.

The client certainly needs to be dedicated to making these changes. They may be asked to repeat mantras in order to reinforce new ways of thinking.

Are we done with behaviour now?

Well, the next one is called behavioural activation but was actually developed to deal with depression.

That's confusing.

It's behavioural in the sense that it calls for lifestyle changes and facing things that you might be avoiding. It works on the assumption that when you're depressed, you either have too much environmental punishment or not enough environmental reinforcement.

What, like bad weather?

No, I mean the things surrounding you. Depressed people often avoid doing positive activities and therefore receive less positive feedback.

More negative cycles, then?

Yes. One of the ways that behavioural activation deals with this is to set up activity scheduling, which means encouraging the client to do things they would rather avoid. If they do this and get positive results, the activity becomes less troubling and they are more likely to engage in it again.

What if it's just as bad as they thought it would be?

Things are very rarely as bad as we imagine, especially if we've spent some time thinking the worst. If for some reason it didn't go well, the therapist would examine this with the client and try to assure them that bad outcomes aren't inevitable.

Someone who likes to avoid things is probably going to avoid this therapy.

Behavioural activation requires a lot of input from the client. Agreeing to do the therapy is a great first step and shows a desire to change, but this must be backed up with a willingness to do the activities suggested by the therapist.

Is that it?

There's one more – compassion-focused therapy.

Does that mean the therapist is more sympathetic?

No, they're trying to make the client more compassionate – to themselves, but also to others.

Why would you need to be compassionate to yourself? You already know how you feel.

It's important to go easy on yourself when things aren't going well. There's an inner critic in all of us, and for those who set unrealistic standards for themselves it can be difficult to accept anything less than perfection. We often treat ourselves much more harshly than we would treat anyone else in the same situation.

So the therapist teaches you how to chill out a bit.

Yes, although it's not just self-criticism that this therapy addresses. For example, feelings of shame from past abuse would also respond to this method, because people often blame themselves for things that aren't their fault.

I always get the blame when things go wrong in our house. It usually is my fault though.

Compassion-focused therapy works on the belief that the human brain has not evolved to serve our wellbeing, so it requires a bit of effort on our part. The developer of this treatment, Paul Gilbert, noticed that it often wasn't enough for individuals to understand what was causing their problems. He devised compassion-focused therapy to connect with these people and to help them to feel more at ease with themselves.

Are we finished now?

Yes, that's all for this section.

I didn't understand it all, but it probably isn't your fault.

That's very compassionate of you.

The client: Sarah Graham

'Since we started compassion-focused therapy, I haven't been so hard on myself'

Tell me about your experiences with therapy.

I first had CBT when I was fifteen. I was a stroppy teenager who didn't want to be there! You have to engage with the process, and if you don't it doesn't work. The second time I tried CBT I was twenty-three, and my therapist was a trainee. It was fine, but they weren't very confident and we didn't really click.

As a health journalist, I've written a couple of pieces on how to find the right therapist, and the thing that therapists always say to me is that it's a matter of trial and error to find someone with whom you can have a good therapeutic relationship. All the therapy I've had, except for a couple of sessions, has been through the NHS. The difficulty with that is that you get what you're given.

The therapist I have now is brilliant though – I love her and we really get on. I feel that we understand each other, that connection is there, and she has a personality that draws me out of myself. I'm quite a reserved person, and some therapists I've had in the past haven't known how to do that.

Is it a friendliness or an openness that does that?

It's a bit of both. My therapist is very open about herself and she uses real examples. We were talking about mindfulness and she told me that she finds it difficult but she has turned it into a game that she plays with her daughter; they'll be sat having dinner and might decide to do mindful eating, where they describe the taste and the texture of the food.

She's good at making it real – other therapists I've had have seemed detached, as if there's a wall between you and them and they're delivering the expertise while you're supposed to soak it all up. The relationship I have with my current therapist feels more equal. She'll tell me, confidentially, about examples from her other clients and what's worked for them, so she's very down-to-earth.

What made you decide to have CBT? Was it to overcome something specific?

The last time I had CBT before my current therapist, it was for depression. This time around was after I was in a quite serious car accident. I was referred for talking therapy by my GP and did a telephone assessment where they ask you various standard questions. At the end, they said there were two options – lower-intensity CBT, where they would put me on a waiting list for six weeks, or a higher-intensity CBT which was likely to be more effective but had a longer waiting list of three months.

I decided to go for the more intense option as I was in a position where I could afford to pay for some private sessions in between if necessary. It's specifically trauma-focused CBT, but she mixes in bits and pieces from different modalities – we're doing some compassion-focused work at the moment and we've also done some mindfulness. She's good at drawing on whatever she thinks will help.

So it's kind of integrative?

Yes, I think so, and perhaps that's why I've got on with it better than I did with pure CBT. I've found CBT on its own to be a bit mechanical, so a more integrative approach has helped me. I get on with the CBT better and also get the bigger picture.

How would you describe compassion-focused therapy?

It's similar to mindfulness in that it's about having self-compassion and acceptance, so you're acknowledging your thoughts and then being compassionate towards yourself. It deals with self-care and journals and generally being kinder to yourself. I think it ties in nicely with all the other techniques.

Does it work?

Since we started compassion-focused therapy, I haven't been so hard on myself. With CBT, the emphasis is on challenging your thoughts, so the tendency with that is to tell yourself, 'That's a ridiculous thought, why are you thinking that?' and to be quite self-critical in the challenging of it.

Now I'm better at telling myself, 'I totally get why you're thinking that, it makes sense logically, but let's look at the evidence and try to give yourself a bit of a break.' Having done some psychodynamic therapy also, I think I have a better all-round understanding of myself.

I did psychodynamic having had bad initial experiences of CBT, and got a good sense of what things in my past make me react the way I do, what habitual responses I have and the way I tend to think about things. After doing that I did feel that I could put the CBT stuff into practice a bit more, as if it had filled in a missing piece.

You said you were on a three-month waiting list for the high-intensity CBT. Has that started yet?

Yes, I have my twelfth session next week. Twelve sessions is the standard treatment but she's going to do a couple of extras. I still have good days and bad days, but having got a therapist that I really connect with and having that rounded approach to understanding myself, I do think it's really helped. I have the techniques to challenge the way that I think and look after myself better.

Do you think that women find it easier than men to seek therapy?

Yes, definitely. A couple of the articles I've written have been about men's mental health and how to get men to engage with it. Both therapists and men that I've spoken to both affirm the classic belief that you're not supposed to talk about your feelings, you're supposed to just 'man up' and deal with it.

I think there has been progress over the last few years, and people in general are more comfortable talking about depression and anxiety than they were. Women are more happy to talk about their feelings in general and better at asking for help. Men are useless at going to their GP about any kind of health problem, as a general rule, whether it's mental or physical.

If you could build the ideal therapist, what qualities would they have?

I think I'd just describe my current therapist! Friendly, open, warm and a good sense of humour. Someone who's prepared to be real and honest – not to make themselves vulnerable, but to maybe bring themselves down to your level.

It's important to feel as though your therapist is an actual human being rather than someone who has no experience of life and is just doling out advice from a textbook. You need to feel that you can say anything and they're going to understand without looking at you in horror!

My psychodynamic therapist was a student who was perhaps a couple of years younger than me. She lacked confidence and I didn't feel 100 per cent sure that she was qualified to help me. I didn't know anything about her. Maybe some people prefer that – to have a neutral person who they can just offload onto and not have to think about them as an individual.

I prefer someone who's like a friend, but detached enough that you feel you can say anything to them. Someone who has the expertise and knowledge to guide you, but who has maybe been through it themselves, so they can talk from experience as well as what they've been taught.

Is there anything you feel able to do after therapy that you didn't feel able to do beforehand?

I still haven't driven a car since my accident, but it's something that I feel able to think about as a possibility now. Before, I just felt that I could never drive again. I'm at a point where I can get in the car with my husband if he's driving, and we've talked about times when I might have to start driving again. The idea doesn't fill me with horror any more.

I've had conversations with my mum where I've asked if I'm still insured on her car, to maybe practise and build up confidence again. We've got a new car but it's a lot bigger than the old one; my husband is fine with it, but I just think: 'I can't drive that thing!' – but I can take tentative steps to build up to it.

It can be a long process, often taking many years. I guess that's where the compassion-focused therapy is helpful?

I fractured a couple of vertebrae, which take a really long time to heal. For the first six months I was so frustrated by how long it was taking, both physically and emotionally. There was a point where my spinal nurse told me I could start thinking about gentle exercise, so I would go for a little jog but my back would really hurt after ten minutes. I was getting down on myself, thinking I was useless – 'This time last year I was running ten-kilometre distances, and I'll never be able to do that again.'

The compassion side has definitely helped with that, reminding myself that I was seriously injured and it's OK that it's taking a long time. It's OK that I still feel traumatised by it. It's OK that I still freak out when I cross the road and someone's tyres screech as they come around the roundabout. That's normal and I don't have to beat myself up over it.

Driving can be really dangerous. It's not like being scared of something irrational.

That's another thing my therapist has been really good with. She said that if this had happened to my friend, how do I think they would feel? Did I think it would be normal? That made it feel rational and made perfect sense. It also makes sense for me to be scared of getting in a car again, because accidents can happen completely out of the blue.

My therapist is very good at getting me to compare what I would say to my friend with what I say to myself. You really wouldn't ever talk to anyone else the way you talk to yourself.

I think some people see therapy as a way to fix everything, but it's more a process of giving you the tools to help yourself.

Having had both CBT and psychodynamic therapy, it feels like a cumulative process. It's not something to do once and then you're fixed; it's more like a journey that you're continuously building on. Doing some therapy here and there over the years has definitely given me a better understanding of myself and how my brain works.

Sometimes it doesn't happen during the session – there were some things we talked about a couple of weeks ago, and at the time I wasn't really sure, but when I went away and thought about it afterwards I had lots of gradual realisations over the following few days.

Would you ever consider training as a therapist?

It's something I've toyed with. I don't think I'd ever want to do it full time, but doing it alongside writing is something I'm intrigued by. Perhaps when I've had kids I might retrain and it would be a more stable income, but I could still do some writing on the side. It would inform the writing as well, having that practical experience of working with people.

Psychoanalysis

Now we're talking. This is the famous one, isn't it?

It's probably what most people who've never had therapy think about when they imagine it. It was developed in the 1890s by Sigmund Freud who believed—

That we all want to sleep with our parents!

Slow down, we'll get to that part. The foundation of psychoanalysis is the belief that we all have unconscious desires, and memories from early childhood, that have been either forgotten or suppressed – and that these events shape our development as individuals.

So we need to have them coaxed out of us in therapy to better understand ourselves.

That's the idea. Psychoanalysis can be quite an intense therapy – clients can have up to five sessions a week. You'll also be glad to know that this is the one therapy where there may be a couch, to allow clients to relax and access their subconscious.

Oh great – if there's a couch, I think psychoanalysis might be the therapy for me! But does it work?

It's been used for a long time, and many people favour it. But the approach is not without controversy; many doubt the validity of this kind of analysis.

Psychoanalysis

What do analysts do to uncover the suppressed ideas, then?

One technique is called free association. This is where you're asked to say things as they come to mind without trying to make sentences, just verbalising words and ideas. It might seem like total gibberish, but the therapist will try to make sense of it all.

This is really old-fashioned now, though, isn't it?

Use of psychoanalysis is certainly declining. Newer therapies like CBT are much more widely used and don't have the same emphasis on events from the past, but many people find psychoanalysis very helpful, and it's still available if you want it.

Can we talk about the sex thing now?

Not yet. One of Freud's other big concepts was that of the id, the ego and the superego. These were described as systems in our lives that emerge at different times. The id is primitive and instinctive, and present from birth. Freud said this was responsible for our illogical and irrational thoughts. The ego is what develops over time to tame the id, as we are forced to take account of society's rules and manners.

And the superego?

The superego develops between the ages of three and five and takes on the values and morals that are learned from our parents and those around us. It suppresses the instincts of the id, particularly those that are frowned upon by society, such as sex and aggression. It's the superego that gives rise to feelings of pride or guilt.

So this all helps a psychoanalyst to figure out someone's personality?

Yes, though some people will respond to it better than others. Some might suggest that it's not very helpful to identify things in our childhood that influence us now because they can't be changed.

Others might find it illuminating and useful to make that connection.

Now can we talk about the sex thing?

You seem a bit too interested in this. Fine. Freud believed that a lot of our anxieties and other mental health problems were caused by the fact that our natural sexual urges were being repressed by society. He decided that these urges were unconscious, but that their energy affected our behaviour.

He went as far as to say that we all had an unconscious desire to engage in sexual acts with our parent of the opposite sex, while feeling a sense of rivalry with our same-sex parent. He called this the Oedipus Complex.

Right, you've lost me now. That's just wrong.

It's probably the main reason why people think of psychoanalysis in a negative way.

This Freud bloke sounds like a wrong 'un.

He did have a big influence on psychological thinking and therapy in general, so we shouldn't write him off for the Oedipus Complex alone.

Is there anything less weird that he's responsible for?

A more widely accepted idea of his is that unconscious thoughts can make themselves apparent by unintended methods – slips of the tongue, for example.

Oh yes – the Freudian slip!

Exactly. Have you ever said something you didn't mean to say and then wondered if that was actually the truth?

I don't think so, but this chat with you has been very facile. Sorry, I mean fascinating.

Very funny.

The therapist: Robert Weiss

'Psychoanalysis is not a practice designed to promote happiness'

How would you describe psychoanalysis to someone who has never had it?

There are two essential components of psychoanalysis. First, there's an understanding that our early experiences, particularly our earliest relationships, have a bearing (both direct and indirect) on what goes on for us in the here and now.

Second, psychoanalysis believes in the notion of unconscious processes that play a huge part in how we act in the world. This is useful to consider when we ask certain questions of ourselves, such as 'Why do I repeatedly choose unsuitable partners?' or 'Why am I compelled to harm myself?' The unconscious is a part of us, but is not known by us.

Psychoanalysis wants to think about this in the hope that if we are able to reveal something of these unconscious processes, change can happen.

Psychoanalysis is not a practice designed to promote happiness. There is, of course, a hope that those who come to analysis are able to experience moments of joy, but the notion that, for example, all will be well if only we work out how to banish negativity is antithetical to the practice of psychoanalysis. If there were to be a sign above my door it would read 'disappointment guaranteed'.

This is a joke, of course, but as Freud recognised, all jokes are just ways in which we can make the unpalatable palatable. In this case what I want to point to is that life is full of disappointments, frustrations, unhappiness and suffering. The psychoanalyst's job is not to imagine these things don't exist, but to work out ways to live through them, ways to endure the difficulties of life.

While psychoanalysis can't promise a happy life, it can (and must) allow for the possibility of a good life. The notion of the good life is from Aristotle, and refers to a life that one would want to live; a life in which our modes of enjoyment can be at hand in spite of the inevitable disappointments that life presents us with.

Being in analysis allows for a space where we can think about our lives in a less inhibited way than if we were chatting to a friend or family member. It allows us to try on certain ideas about our lives for size, to see how they might feel: 'What would it be like if I left my partner? What might happen if I leave my job? What would my father say if I told him how I felt about him?'

The ideas can be weighed up and carefully considered, but, crucially, do not have to be carried out, do not have to leave the safe and confidential confines of the consulting room.

At its best, psychoanalysis is a liberating and creative experience, an experience that allows for life-changing moments, both small and large. It is a process whereby we can learn to recognise what we want, and work out ways in which we might be able to get it.

What does a typical therapy session involve? Or is there no typical therapy session?

Well, I'm tempted to say that there is no such thing as a typical session. I don't have a set way of starting or finishing a session, for example, and it goes without saying that what's spoken about is different for each person.

There are, however, some things that remain constant: the room itself, the way it's set up, which doesn't really vary, and the length of the session, which is always around fifty minutes.

What's the best thing that has happened to you in the therapy room, or while practising therapy?

This is a difficult question.

There have been many moments in the therapy room that have been rewarding; moments when the psychoanalytic process has been mutative. When someone arrives in my consulting room feeling unloved and unlovable, for example, and when some time later they are able to have a relationship, say, or have a family. When the unique environment of the consulting room allows them to truly examine and change something in their lives.

But it feels impossible to isolate one instance, something that could be thought of as a 'best' experience. Sorry if that's not quite the response you were hoping for.

What qualities would you say are important in order to be a good therapist?

The ability to sit with someone in distress; the ability to listen in a concentrated, prolonged way; the ability to think analytically – that is, to make connections between signifiers often separated by long periods of time. A good analyst must also have been well analysed. There are other 'soft' qualities that may also be important: compassion, empathy, kindness, etc.

What do you think a client can do to get the most out of therapy?

Well, a client must, in the first instance, be willing to commit to therapy, must want to come for themselves, not, as is sometimes the case, because their partner or parent wants them to. But this necessary desire (which, incidentally, is the same desire as the analyst's – a desire for therapy) must be accompanied by a willingness to change.

This seems obvious, perhaps, but is important. By change, I mean a willingness to give up some or all of the symptoms that might define them. To distil this idea even further: it is necessary in therapy to be prepared to face the disappointing elements of our characters without the myriad ways we manage to repress, disavow or foreclose them.

You're one of the few psychoanalysts I've come across with a profile on social media. How much do you disclose to clients, and are you careful about what you say when tweeting? Or do you feel free to express yourself despite being a therapist?

One of the reasons I use social media is because it is such a very present part of the lives of those who come and see me: from the ways in which they keep in touch with family and friends, to the ways in which they meet sexual partners. It is part of our lives and I feel a need to understand something of it.

I only have a personal account with Twitter and mainly use it to keep up with my interests. I very rarely tweet, although I do, on occasion, retweet. It is inevitable that clients can, by looking at my account, see my political allegiances, the football team I support and other activities that I might enjoy in my spare time.

While I don't want to impose my views on my clients, I also understand (and am fairly sanguine about it) that a web presence of any sort means that clients will be able to investigate aspects of my life.

Do you ever feel frustrated with clients, or with the process, when you see them repeating the same problems and bringing the same issues into the therapy room without dealing with them?

What you describe is what shrinks might call resistance. Analysing the resistance is a key part of the psychoanalytic process, and any frustration I feel (which is, at times, inevitable) tends to get in the way.

Someone once said that resistance is on the side of the analyst; that is that when resistance is noticed, it may be because something remains unanalysed, or left without interpretation by the analyst. With that in mind I would answer your question by saying that, rather than feel frustrated, I try to be more analytical when I observe a client not addressing a particular issue.

Lastly: if you hadn't been a therapist, what else do you think you might have done?

I've always wanted to write and, although I get to write and edit theory papers, I can't quite lose my infantile desire to be a novelist or even a poet.

Connected to this infantile wish is the fantasy that being a postal worker would allow me to have time in the afternoons to sit at my desk.

The client: Cosmo Landesman

'He didn't think I would always be a big blubbering mess. Which I was'

How did you find your therapist?

At Christmas in 2016, my ex-wife gave me a pair of socks and the number of a good therapist after finding me weeping in bed on Christmas Day.

Did you try several therapists before settling on yours?

No, he was it. The previous time I went into therapy – over twenty years ago – I picked a therapist whose practice was near to me.

What did you like about your therapist?

I didn't feel I had to impress or perform for him. He was smart but not a show-off. He didn't pretend to have all the answers, and would mock his profession. Plus he was also not afraid to offer a moral point of view.

What qualities made you decide to stick with him?

He was easy to talk to. I also liked his consulting room, which was like something out of the 1940s. Plus he never had a box of tissues placed within easy reach. I liked that because he didn't think I would always be a big blubbering mess. Which I was.

And what would you advise other people to look for in a therapist?

I would advise you to pick someone like my therapist. Someone who can focus on the things you want or need to talk about. In therapy, you can drift along for ages, going nowhere. I think it's important that at times you set the agenda for what goes on in the room.

Do you know what type of therapy your therapist practised?

He was a Bowlby-Attachment based [psychoanalytic] therapist.

How has therapy enhanced your life?

Therapy hasn't made me any happier or more content with my life. I'm still a miserable, self-loathing bastard, but therapy has helped me to understand why that is.

The client: Dolly Alderton

'Therapy is the best decision I ever made'

I found my therapist through a friend's recommendation. She had been seeing the therapist for a couple of years and the change in her was so dramatic and positive it was enough to make me finally make the call.

She was the first and only therapist I've tried.

Every therapist is different – mine is ruthlessly honest. She doesn't ask leading questions or help me get to a conclusion on my own over a period of sessions – she gives me her opinion on everything I present to her. She doesn't hide her emotions and she doesn't beat around the bush – if I've done something really stupid she tells me. I needed that. And I needed someone tough. She wouldn't be for everyone, but I am lucky enough to have a wonderful support network of friends and family in my life who can hug me and make me tea and tell me everything's going to be OK when that's what's called for. What I needed from a therapist was someone who could tell me in a black-and-white way where I had to take responsibility for things going wrong in my life.

My therapist is Freudian [psychoanalytic], but I didn't know that before I started seeing her. At first, I found it difficult because I felt the obsession with childhood and family to be sort of irrelevant. I was much more concerned with the here and now and, naturally, I didn't like hearing any analysis or criticism about my upbringing or family, because I love them.

But slowly I've come to realise that the first eighteen years of our life really forms the entire context from which we enter into the world, and everything in the here and now relates to it. It doesn't define us, but it certainly explains us. And contrary to popular belief, therapy isn't about the blame game – it's about understanding that context, and your parents' context, and that first chapter of your story, to explain your habits, behaviours, fears and hang-ups. And then, crucially, it's about finding practical ways to change.

Therapy has changed everything in my life – it's improved my relationships, it's helped me control and understand my anxiety, it's dramatically changed my historically unhealthy coping mechanisms including alcohol, drugs and sexual validation. It's helped me understand that everyone has a context from which they enter the world, and to be more compassionate and patient while keeping that in mind.

Most importantly, it's allowed me to be vulnerable both in my sessions and then in my relationships and day-to-day life, by helping me understand who I am and being comfortable with presenting that, alongside the imperfect bits, rather than performing for approval. It's the best decision I ever made.

Psychodynamic Therapy

Haven't we already done this one?

No, this is different from psychoanalysis – although it developed from it. A German scientist called Ernst Wilhelm von Brücke is credited with introducing the principles of psychodynamic therapy in 1874 in a publication called Lectures on Physiology. Freud was his student, though he only took on Brücke's 'dynamic' idea after he'd invented psychoanalysis.

So what makes it different from psychoanalysis?

The old psychoanalytic format of multiple sessions a week was clearly too much for some people as their lives became busier. Psychodynamic therapy was devised to provide a shorter, less intensive form of psychoanalysis with a greater focus on current problems that the individual might be experiencing.

Is there a fixed time limit, then?

No, it's still open-ended, but clients should expect to see results in a shorter time frame. There's also more emphasis on the relationship between the therapist and the client, so you're probably going to be talking face-to-face rather than lying on a couch with them behind you. The structure will also be more similar to other forms of therapy – that is, one or two fifty-minute sessions per week.

But they're still looking at unconscious behaviour?

Yes, that's at the core of it. You might still be asked to use techniques from traditional psychoanalysis, such as free association, and you'll certainly be talking a lot about past events, but the emphasis will be focusing on specific things and getting results.

What sort of problems can psychodynamic therapy help with?

Studies have shown that it's more effective at treating anxiety disorders than other problems, but it depends on the individual. It makes sense that it would have more impact on problems with a clear link to the past, such as phobias, but there are no rules here.

What about relationship problems? Just curious.

It can be used with individuals, groups or families, so yes – it might be able to help with that.

Anything else?

There is one concept in psychodynamic therapy that I haven't mentioned, and that's transference.

Is that when you pay the therapist directly from your bank account?

No, transference is the idea that you project feelings about someone else in your life onto your therapist. The therapist will use this concept to look for clues about what might be troubling you. If you're distrustful of your therapist, for example, that could be interpreted as transference of your mistrust of somebody else in your life.

But even if you don't trust them, you still have to pay them, right?

Right.

The therapist: Veena Ganapathy

'We need the light to better cope with the darkness'

How would you describe psychodynamic therapy to someone who has never had it?

Psychodynamic therapy values the connection between the part of us that is conscious and thinking on the one hand, and the element in us that remains at a deeper, often less known level. This deeply embedded layer of inner life is considered by therapists and analysts to be where unconscious processes originate and are given life.

This less cogent, more emotion-led aspect of the inner self can have powerful and far-reaching effects on all aspects of our lives. Often, a way into better understanding of this unconscious aspect of the self is by exploring one's formative years and experiences and giving thought to how they may have shaped us.

As Freud discovered, engaging with and acknowledging the pain – real or perceived – that is inherent in the human condition can be profound, and relieve both psychological and physical symptoms. For many people, there is an understandable ambivalence about exploring less known or understood aspects of the self. This is often accompanied by a fear that they will not be able to cope with what they may learn about themselves.

I believe therapy can offer a safe space in which these fears can be articulated and survived. Individuals often come to feel over time that it is more exhausting to live in a defensive and fearful way than it is to acknowledge and grow from emotional pain and trauma. Engaging with psychological difficulties can lead to a powerful sense of acceptance and healing.

How does psychodynamic therapy differ from psychoanalysis?

I conceptualise them as rooted in the same understandings. Both consider the importance of the conscious and unconscious parts of the self and invite a deeper engagement with the unconscious, perhaps through free association or dream-work.

Perhaps analysis does this more frequently as sessions occur several times a week. Psychoanalysis and psychotherapy also actively consider the ways a client may relate to the analyst or therapist, and how that may reflect their broader ways of being in other relationships.

Ultimately, both therapy and analysis are committed to helping clients better understand and articulate the internal world, so that life can be lived more congruently, and with a greater integration of different aspects of the self.

What happens in a psychodynamic therapy session?

In content and dynamics, each session is unique, and primarily led by what an individual brings when they arrive for their session that day. What is uppermost in someone's mind can give a clue as to what may be preoccupying them at a deeper level. Therapists are inclined to be attentive not only to the words our clients use to express themselves, but also the emotions evoked by their narrative.

Psychodynamic psychotherapy attempts to offer a safe, containing and calmly reflective space. Keeping to a clear time structure – a 'therapy hour' is usually fifty minutes in length – is an important feature of the 'therapeutic frame'.

What can a client do to help themselves during therapy?

Therapy of this nature can – and often does – unfold over many years. The process of self-exploration and engagement with one's psychic pain can be challenging and demanding. It is important for a client to look after themselves emotionally and physically. This may partly include considering one's choices and their impact in the therapy itself.

Balance is vital too. Yes, at times it may be helpful to connect with one's difficulties and areas of struggle. At other times, however, there is equal validity in taking a break from this rather intense pursuit and indulging in something more light-hearted. We need the light to better cope with the darkness.

It can also be helpful, whilst one navigates the landscape of the inner world, to keep in mind that therapy can evoke strong and difficult feelings and memories. Having some trust in the process and one's capacity to cope and grow can be anchoring.

In the work itself, it is always more fruitful to the therapy for a client to speak freely and without self-censorship. Although I appreciate this is much easier said than done on occasion, an 'unfiltered' narrative can offer a much greater insight into the internal world and the nature and source of inner conflict and challenges.

What qualities should a client look for in a therapist?

I would say it is essential to go with one's instincts when looking for a therapist. For those whose struggle to find their inner guiding voice is part of the work, it may be pertinent to consider whether they would feel safer working with someone of the opposite gender, for example, or a therapist from a cultural background different to their own.

You need to feel you can trust your therapist, and that they have your best interests at heart. Therapy may be the first time that an individual feels safe and supported enough to engage with painful and troubled parts of themselves. Having a therapist who can attend to what you bring without judgement, while also inviting you to connect with certain defensive or unhealthy patterns of thinking and behaviour, can feel profound and reparative.

Having an expectation that your therapist will be professional – including having the necessary qualifications – and reliable in their way of working with you is important too.

Are there people for whom psychodynamic therapy isn't suitable? If so, who?

Openness to encountering one's own psychological self is understandably key. Some capacity to manage the strong feelings that can emerge in therapy is helpful but not essential; resilience can grow and be enhanced by the therapeutic process itself.

I think those who are acutely mentally unwell may need psychiatric support before they are in a safe enough psychological space to think psychodynamically. I think a combination of medication and therapy can be powerfully beneficial to some people. For others, the duality of interventions may feel too intense and destabilising.

If an individual is uncertain whether psychodynamic therapy may be suitable, I would suggest they explore this with a therapist and/or psychiatrist. It may be that this form of talking support is not the 'best fit' for them at this point in their life but could be worth revisiting in the future.

Someone with a single, very specific difficulty in their life who would prefer a short-term method of engagement may be better served by a more solution-focused approach.

It is generally a good idea to arrange an initial exploratory session with a therapist, so that such issues and considerations can be talked through and thought about. Generally, some kind of recommendation can be offered to address an individual's situation at the time and what might be a helpful source of support for them.

What do you enjoy most about practising therapy?

I think it takes enormous courage to engage with oneself in the authentic and open way that psychotherapy invites. It is a privilege to be invited to share the inner world of those with whom I work and to be asked to bear witness to people's personal exploration of themselves. It can be profoundly moving and affirming to 'be alongside' someone discovering aspects of themselves, perhaps for the first time.

On a personal level, as a woman of colour in the changing social, cultural and political climate of today, I find it valuable to be in a role that intrinsically challenges stereotypes and realities of psychotherapy. This form of talking therapy has often been seen to explicitly and implicitly exclude those from minorities – for example in relation to race, gender, sexuality or socio-demographic background – both as clients and therapists.

I think the beauty of psychodynamic therapy is that it offers all individuals the possibility of feeling their stories can be heard and made sense of in a sensitive and thoughtful way that, paradoxically, keeps in mind both the uniqueness and the universality of their experiences.

How much personal information do you disclose to clients?

Psychodynamic psychotherapy considers the client as being at the centre of the work. The therapeutic space – both concrete and symbolic – is theirs. It is a realm in which dreams, fantasies, memories and associations that may have previously been nameless and nebulous can be given words and form. It naturally follows that therapists, although attentive and actively engaged, do not intrude into the space by sharing personal information about themselves.

If you could start life over, would you still have been a therapist?

Yes!

What would you have done if you hadn't been a therapist?

In the spirit of keeping personal disclosures to a minimum, I'll leave that open to interpretation!

The client: Megan Beech

'I think the ideal therapist probably doesn't exist'

What led you to seek psychodynamic therapy?

I came to my current therapist at a moment of profound crisis. I'd had a period of three or four months where my normal depressive level had plummeted to a state where I was unable to sleep, barely eating or functioning, which led to me not getting the grades I needed to progress to my Ph.D.

I crawled into bed and hoped never to crawl out. After a week or two of not moving very much at all, I had to catch a flight to visit my best friend in Boston. I was still going through a very complex appeals process related to the Ph.D., and had been without a proper treatment structure for my depression for quite some time.

Thankfully, not only did my friend help restore me somewhat, but her parents are both psychiatrists, so they set about finding me a clinician in the UK who they felt would be able to help navigate me through this difficult time. I ended up in a pattern of seeing this clinician twice a week for psychotherapy. My therapist is a psychotherapist, psychoanalyst, clinical psychologist and professor of psychoanalysis at a leading UK university.

It was such a relief to find someone who I felt I could work with and talk to openly. Prior to entering this treatment, I'd sporadically seen counsellors through my various universities (in London and Cambridge) and these had felt like unsatisfactory encounters really. The strain on services is so great and the resources can't keep up. I was only able to see my counsellor once every fortnight and it didn't feel like I could really explore and improve my illness through this level of work.

I have been taking antidepressants for most of the past five years in addition to this care, and continue to do so. I felt that entering psychodynamic psychotherapy really suited the way I wanted treatment to develop, through trust and collaboration, strain and failure – a proper sustained connection with a single clinician.

For me, intermittent counselling (though one counsellor had been particularly brilliant) hadn't been able to offer this sufficiently due to the time and resource constraints, and it could often feel infantilising, simplistic or reductive (in some of the iterations I encountered).

The new therapy I entered felt like it wasn't any of these things. It was a supportive and collaborative environment where I found my voice and my ability to truly talk about the experiences and conflicts I was having within my illness.

A few people have told me that they find psychodynamic therapists austere, opaque and off-putting.

I don't find that that is the case with my therapist. I am lucky to work with someone who is both a leading researcher and a highly regarded clinician and her research is very much focused on issues of attachment and the relationships encountered (first between mother and baby, later with therapist and client) and I think that makes a huge difference. Of course, you will not know the details of your therapist's life exactly, but I think that is not to say that you don't establish a rapport or relationship between you.

It is a kind of indescribable relationship, unlike any other in your life and even though of course you are the focus of that relationship, by the same token it is not the case (or it shouldn't be) that the therapist is the austere, cold person you describe, or a 'reflecting machine' (simply reflecting back what you say opaquely and austerely).

Analysts are people, and in fact people who have devoted their life's work to thinking about other people's suffering, so there is a lot of humanity there and necessarily so. We don't get better by talking to automatons. We get better by being seen and recognised and held within a (not unproblematic and sometimes uncomfortable) human relationship and learning from it who and how we are.

Having had therapists where there has been no common ground, no connection and no ability to develop a working relationship, I think it matters hugely who our analysts are as people, as well as analysts, and I think clinicians who care about the therapeutic relationship and invest in it with care and humanity, as well, of course, as boundaries, will likely be more trusted by their clients – and at least from a layman's perspective, achieve better results.

How would you say therapy has changed you, or the way you view your-self and life in general?

I think therapy is about a process. Its benefits aren't necessarily easy to pin down into exact changes. I think it's about a gradual improvement. Therapy has definitely changed my ability to think in different ways about situations.

While I still really struggle with negative feelings, therapy has helped me to be more questioning of those feelings. I don't always view a bad thought like 'No one likes me' or 'I'm a horrible person' as a fact so easily. Instead, I think that it's possible that this is just a bad thought and not a fact.

I feel that although I am not 'transformed' or 'fixed' or any of those things we might romanticise that therapy can magically, instantly do for us, I feel more positive about life, and hopeful that elements of my negative thinking and depressive illness can change and evolve over time.

If you could build the ideal therapist, what qualities would she or he have?

I think the ideal therapist probably doesn't exist, and a therapist who is aware of their failings and the breakdowns in treatment that sometimes happen is probably the best kind. Seeing as it is very common to over-idealise one's therapist, I think it is good to dispel the myth that there is an ideal therapist or a perfect person to see, particularly because different things work for different people.

However, it really does matter who we see. Researchers like Professor Mary Target and Peter Fonagy have done a lot of important work about what makes an effective therapist, and what shows up a lot is that whilst it makes a huge amount of difference who your therapist is, often therapists and analysts are not the best judges of their own effectiveness. There's this amazing study by Dew and Riemer ('Why inaccurate self-evaluation of performance justifies feedback interventions', 2003) that showed that 66 per cent of therapists rated themselves in their jobs as A+ or A, and none of them rated themselves below average!

From a client perspective, as someone who has seen multiple therapists and has made much better progress through finding a very good therapist, I think it certainly makes a difference what qualities the people who treat us have. For me, a good therapist would be someone who is enquiring, sensitive, empathetic and open.

It is unavoidable that treatment will be challenging at times, and someone who is both empathetic but questioning also, someone who challenges the very real representations of the world you have built for yourself in depression, who loosens your grip on those immovable beliefs – that's the kind of person I would like to treat me, someone who takes their vocation seriously and truly cares about their work ethically and emotionally. I am lucky to be working with someone with these qualities.

Why do you think it is that psychodynamic therapy suits you better than, say, CBT?

I believe CBT can be a great thing, and offer great short-term problem-focused care, but for me, I had been caught in a lot of short-term treatment for a while and I just truly felt that I needed (at this point in crisis mode) some more sustained long-term person-to-person focused treatment – and for me, psychodynamic therapy was able to provide that.

I don't even have intensive treatment [intensive is traditionally defined as four to five sessions a week] but to have two sessions a week has completely changed my life and my belief in treatment.

I think the most important factor to discuss around psychotherapy, though, is access and privilege. I am lucky that I can use my Ph.D. funding to pay for therapy. Studying gives me a flexibility of time that many in nine-to-five working environments don't have and that gives me better access options to this kind of therapy.

There are wonderful charitable and research organisations such as the Anna Freud Centre which do provide long-term child psychotherapy, as well as brilliant researchers such as Peter Fonagy, Mary Target and Anthony Bateman who have spent the whole of their careers researching and advocating for the efficacy of psychotherapy in long-term results and outcomes and arguing for a greater investment in psychotherapy in the public sector.

It really should not be the case that long-term psychotherapy is something only available to those who can pay for it. I truly believe that the value of that space and time to work with one person on your problems and yourself is just invaluable.

Do you think there will ever be a point when you feel you don't need therapy any more?

I think the work I am doing in therapy at the moment is at the centre of my life, and something I commit myself to fully. I can't see the point in my near future where it won't be necessary. But there is also in the back of my mind that Nietzsche quote, 'One repays a teacher badly if one always remains nothing but a pupil.'

Not that I think that is the exact dynamic of therapy, but I think both clinicians and patients feel that if at some point the encounters between therapist and patient cannot generalise to outside life, then therapy has failed.

In other words, if the relationships outside of therapy, the inter-personal struggles that might have brought you into therapy in the first place, don't improve in your day-to-day life and ideally allow you to be less dependent on therapy, then you can never move on with your life.

I think I am a long way from ending my current treatment, and I'm also acutely aware (as I think many are with long-term mental health problems) that relapses can often be indiscriminate and we are always encountering new challenges and life changes which can contribute to a change in feeling. So I don't think anyone can say that they will never need the assistance of a therapist in the future.

I think when I have moved into a different phase of my life I won't be afraid or ashamed to seek therapeutic assistance, should I need it again. I think that for many different stages of life and development, it can be helpful and incredibly valuable for people.

Person-Centred Therapy

Isn't all therapy person-centred? I'm worried that there's going to be a dog-centred one coming up later.

There isn't. Person-centred therapy was developed in the 1950s by an American psychologist called Carl Rogers. He believed that people had an innate ability to make the best of their lives if given the chance to recognise and acknowledge their own value. This idea was pretty radical at the time, as most people up to that point worked on the assumption that the therapist was the one with all the answers.

So therapists don't *have the answers?*

Rogers believed that, instead of telling the client what they should be doing – being directive, in other words – therapists should help the client to find their own answers by asking questions and making suggestions about why they might be feeling a certain way. After working through a problem, the client could have one of those light-bulb moments where things suddenly make sense.

Hmm. It doesn't sound as if the therapist is doing much except taking the client's money.

You're ignoring the relationship between the therapist and the client. There are three core conditions in person-centred therapy that Rogers said were necessary to achieve results: congruence, unconditional positive regard and empathy.

Eh? I think I'm in need of one of those light-bulb moments.

'Congruence', in this context, means that the therapist must be genuine. There has to be a bond of trust and a belief that they have your best interests at heart. 'Unconditional positive regard' is providing a totally non-judgemental atmosphere where the client feels valued and able to discuss whatever is on their mind without meeting disapproval or negativity. 'Empathy', as you might expect, is the therapist trying to see things from the client's perspective and understanding their position.

So if you don't have all those things, it won't work.

Right. But if that was the case, it might just be that the therapist isn't right for you rather than the approach being wrong. Remember, the therapist's job here is to provide the right conditions for the client to help themselves. The relationship is regarded as equal, rather than the therapist being the expert sat on a pedestal. If you don't feel comfortable with the relationship, you might just need to find a different therapist.

Does the person-centred approach help with specific problems, or is it a bit woolly?

It can certainly be focused on specific problems, but because the aim is to promote self-awareness and better self-regard, it should also translate into a better approach to other aspects of your life. You should end up with a better understanding of your behaviour and the patterns that you tend to fall into.

Is it short-term or long-term?

There's no rule on that. It can be as long as you need it to be. It's not a structured therapy; you'll just be talking about whatever you feel like discussing at that particular session. You're in the driving seat. The lack of structure has drawn criticism from some other branches of therapy, but there is plenty of evidence that it's effective.

I'm wondering if it might be a bit lightweight. Surely there's a limit to what problems can be sorted out with a handful of observations from the therapist?

You might be underestimating the value of having a safe, confidential environment where you can discuss anything at all. For many people, having that outlet – especially if they find it difficult to talk to friends or family – can go a long way to getting them back on track.

But they need to do some of the work themselves.

Yes. You're unlikely to be asked to keep diaries or anything like that, but it's not entirely passive either. You might gain new insights into why you think or behave the way you do, but it's still down to you to do something about it. As person-centred therapy is non-directive, your therapist isn't going to step in and take the reins.

They might be very frustrated if you keep coming back week after week with the same complaints, but they can't do much more than gently point this out to you. You need to be ready to put your new insights – or 'self-actualisations' – into use. You can find out more at the British Association for the Person-Centred Approach (see page 310) which also has a list of therapists in your area.

And no dogs?

No dogs.

The therapist: Jonathan Izard

'People often tell me things they've never told anybody before'

You're a private therapist, so it must be helpful to feel that you're not wedded to an institution whose values you need to uphold . . .?

In a way that's a freedom, because I run my own business and make my own decisions. Nobody tells me what hours I have to work, or how much I have to charge. But on the flip side of that, as we know existentially, with great freedom comes great responsibility, and so there's no colleague for me to ask, 'What do you think? Is this right or wrong?' It's entirely my choice.

How does it compare to your broadcasting work?

It's really odd that this has come about. One of the other major parts of my working life is broadcasting at the BBC, and it's an odd but balanced existence – in the morning I might be listening to an individual, or series of individuals, then in the afternoon or evening broadcasting to millions of people. It's a weird kind of balance. I don't combine them at all – there's very clear blue water between the two.

I think of you as quite extrovert. The therapists I've had have been quite introverted. Perhaps being a journalist balances the fact that it's quite a solitary profession?

I think I agree with you that I'm an extrovert, but I think there's a way of being with a client where I'm quiet and listening and very much waiting to see what they fill the space with. I provide the space and they start unpacking something, then we look at what they've unpacked.

I don't think that makes me an introvert, though, because in that process we can have a lot of laughter and tears. They can share some extraordinarily painful things and I can be touched by that. There's something about engaging which feels more extrovert – it's not that I need to fill the space, but I feel that I can match where they are.

There are other therapists who want to remain as if behind frosted glass. I'm absolutely not like that. I'm present, available and committed. That's not to say that I dominate it, but that I'm involved and not distant. I don't want it to be watered down.

Maybe I'm an extrovert in that I'm comfortable doing large things, but I can be equally comfortable being quiet, listening and waiting for the point where we engage. That engagement might be a quiet, delicate and painful thing, but it might include humour and anger.

It's hard to write about the different modalities and remain balanced. It strikes me that every therapist must think that their modality is the correct one.

I can't speak for others, but I know that there are some people who train in one modality and think that it's fine, but later they're more interested in something else. I can imagine that happening. I'm interested in other ways of working, but I don't want to work in those ways. I hope to be totally person-centred and I'm passionate about it. I believe in it, I care about it, I think I understand it and it fits for me. If it didn't fit and I were tempted by other areas, I would explore them. I'm aware of them but I don't feel the need to incorporate them into my work.

How was the training to become a person-centred therapist? Were there times when you wanted to give up, or did you know this was the route for you?

I never wanted to give up. Giving up would have denied me the challenge, the confusion, the frustration, the learning and the growth that happened over that process – and of course it doesn't stop. I hope I'm still learning and growing with every hour that I spend with a client. It can still be frustrating and confusing but I never wanted to quit.

What do you enjoy most about your work?

I feel a real sense of privilege that somebody who is in confusion or distress has chosen me out of all the therapists available. They then start to unpack things that have probably been withheld and locked away for a long time and they trust me to witness it, share it, and acknowledge what's there. It's an incredibly touching, moving and powerful experience. At its best, we're working at relational depth.

People often tell me things they've never told anybody before, things they can't even share with their partners, and even when they're speaking they might not realise they feel a certain way until they say it out loud. It's freshly minted, and an extraordinary honour to witness that and help that to emerge.

Those changes can be big, significant things in just a few words. There can be a moment of realisation, or something that they've known for a long time but never had the courage or the circumstances to say before. To be able to give someone that space, to witness and affirm them, is a real honour.

Therapists are walking repositories of other people's secrets in some ways. You must get a great insight into human nature from it.

I get insight into myself as well. I can't help but admire a client for some of the qualities they have that I don't, in the same way that I can acknowledge that I perhaps have a confidence or strength that they don't yet have. I can see that difference between us but the common humanity overlaps, whatever the gender, race, sexuality or background. The two of us are committing to trust in this psychological intimacy and that's so valuable.

Do you ever lose focus during sessions? Are there some clients who are just incredibly boring?

If I'm feeling bored then I will be trying to monitor what's going on with me. Some years ago I was working with a client who I would see intermittently; he'd come in to resolve various issues about his personal life as they arose. There was one session where I was feeling light-headed and disengaged. It was persistent and I was monitoring it, asking myself whether I'd slept well the previous night, had I seen too many clients that day or was I coming down with a bug? I couldn't find a reason for it but it remained present and oppressive.

Being authentic is one of the ground rules of this work, and I realised that I needed to say something, so I told him that I felt we were in a holding pattern and hadn't landed. I asked whether he agreed, and did he think there was a reason for that, if there was something he wanted to say but hadn't?

He then told me the most extraordinary fact about his own childhood. He didn't think it was particularly relevant to his current relationship problem or his work crisis, but we discovered it was this enormous event that had clearly cast a huge shadow over his entire existence.

We then had two or three more sessions after that of looking at this process in his life and what it meant to my client. It was a painful but healing process for him, bringing him insight and understanding. If I hadn't taken the risk of voicing my own feeling about being in a holding pattern and inviting him to land upon this information, I wonder if he ever would have done. It proved so fruitful. I can't imagine that happening in any other context.

So, to answer you: yes, sometimes I'm bored and I try to understand why that is and, if helpful, find a way to share that feeling with my client.

I often think that therapists can say things that friends can't. There's something about that relationship that means we can accept comments that we wouldn't accept from our friends.

It's a very different relationship and that's the benefit of it. If I go to see my therapist, she's not my mother, colleague or friend and there's something about the fact that we've come together for that very specific purpose in a therapeutic relationship. It's a contract, an agreement – that's why money changes hands. One person is in distress and the other person is there to help them in whatever way they can. That's the deal.

Somebody might think, 'I'm in great distress, but I'll wait until Thursday at six p.m. to express it to that person. I don't need to scream at my partner because when I see my therapist, that's when I have the freedom to let it out.'

I remember you said that therapy wasn't directive. Have there been times where you've seen somebody making an absolute mess of their life but you've found yourself unable to intervene?

Certainly person-centred therapy isn't directive. I haven't trained in other fields so I wouldn't speak for those. I'm sure I've had those thoughts and I suppose in extremis I might offer alternatives, such as 'If not this relationship, how would you like it to look? If not this partner, what kind of qualities would you wish for?' It's offering an alternative and seeing if that's appealing or is rejected. It's extraordinary how people move goalposts.

The most dramatic example of that was somebody saying that her partner had burned her arms, but it was all right because he had only burned them at the top so her blouse would cover it. For somebody to have shifted their perspective that far, to say that that's OK, is incredible.

When bells ring that alarmingly, if that was something in the present, I would need to explore what alternatives there were in that situation and to think about intervening if a client's life was in danger. I also might tell a client that I'm scared for them, that I worry they're not safe and seek their reassurance. I would want my response to this person to be as authentic as possible.

If someone is talking about ending their life, or that their life isn't worthwhile, then we put things in place. I ask if I need to be concerned about them and what we can do about that. I'm looking for a shared process. I have a responsibility to the client but I'm not responsible for them. If they don't come up with anything then I'll make suggestions such as texting me first thing in the morning to let me know they've got through the night, or calling me during the night if they're in great distress.

My phone won't be on if I'm asleep, but they can leave a message and I'll call back as soon as I can. Sometimes knowing that's possible is enough to create reassurance. I also make sure with a client in this situation that they have Samaritans' number in their phone. I feel I have a duty to be as open with clients as I possibly can be.

They're coming to me with fragile, delicate things and I don't want to just sit back and say, 'Well that's very interesting, how do you feel about that?' Instead I may well say, 'My goodness, that sounds horrific', or 'I'm really touched by what you say'. I feel it's important to be honest.

One question that people often want to know about therapy is whether you reach a point where you're fixed, and if not, can therapy be said to be effective?

I know that I've been in therapy at certain times in my life, and I've really needed that, but for a lot of the time I'm not in therapy and I'm not at the moment. I recently finished twelve months in therapy to work on a particular crisis.

'Fixed' is not a word I would use. With long-term clients I will often try to build in a catch-up where we talk about how we're doing and whether they're finding it useful. Are we on course? Are they getting what they need?

You wrote a book about a very bad therapist: Mel Pepper and the Meaning of Wife. *Was it cathartic to write about all the things you can't do in a therapy session?*

I never thought about it like that, but I suppose it was. I went on a training course once on a residential weekend and we would play at being bad therapists as a joke. Somebody might look up and say, 'Good heavens, are you still here?' or mistake the client's son's name for that of their dog! It was great fun as a game, and this book is completely fictional, but I wondered about how hopeless a therapist could be.

The only thing of my own experience that's in there is getting a client's name wrong, which I did on my very first placement. It's stayed with me, how awful that was, but it's the only thing I've taken from my own career. The rest is purely fiction, I promise! Anyway, Mel's lack of skill in her job is only a part of the narrative; the main issue is the struggle she has to feel love for her husband and her relationship with her parents. Of course.

Have you ever been propositioned by a client?

There's sometimes a lot unspoken, such as the sexual attraction in a therapy room, a lot that isn't named. There was a female client who would ask me pointed questions, such as 'Lovely flowers – did somebody buy those for you?' or 'You went to the opera – did you go with somebody special?'

After a few weeks of this I did ask what was behind the questions and she said that she wanted to know if I was gay. We then spent a couple of weeks touching on the subject of what was important to her about that question and the possible answers. There are a lot of different answers to that, including maybe me declining to answer, and I wanted us to explore how she would react to them and how it would impact her and our work.

Eventually we talked through all that and got around to actually answering the question, and the answer was 'Yes I am'. She could have asked me directly five sessions earlier, but she wasn't ready to name it. We then talked about how she had been sexually abused by a man when she was a teenager and that she'd only started working with me originally because apparently I had a pink shirt on the day she met me; she'd taken that as a signal that I might be gay, and if I was, then it was safe to be in a room with me.

So it was all tied up with the abuse and her needing to know that I was safe, although we'd been working together for a long time before that. She wasn't propositioning me, in your words, but there was a sexual curiosity about how we related to each other.

Another extreme example would be the male client who went into great detail about the fantasy he had about our relationship and the things he wanted us to do together sexually. It felt very freeing for him to be able to say those things in a way that he knew would never happen. In that situation I can say, 'I'm not your boyfriend, we're not going to do those things, but if it helps you to talk about them it's OK.'

It led on to a discussion about his relationship with his father and the disappointment he felt at not being cuddled by his dad. So it was a very fruitful place to go even though it felt a bit awkward at the time. That element of risk is an important part of the work for me; when there's safety and trust, then we can risk something. That risk might be from the client, or it might be me asking a direct question or noticing something.

There was one client who liked to hug at the end of a session, but he also said that he was really scared when he let go of the hug that I wouldn't be there any more. That physical contact meant a huge amount to him, so we would work on how to make it OK. It takes a lot of courage to address those things, but with that risk comes huge emotional intimacy.

We don't hold up our hands in horror and say, 'Oh, I can't talk about that.' Instead we say, 'OK, where does that take us? Are we OK here, is this all right?'

With the client who didn't want the hug to end as he thought our relationship would end with it, by addressing his deepest anxiety about that moment, it opened up the subject for us to examine the meaning and what he might be able to do differently so that his future could be better than his past.

Do you ever dwell on disturbing things that clients have told you, or are you able to switch off?

The work takes place in the session and there's an agreement that we will meet again and either continue talking about that or move on to something else. Once I've written my notes up I tend to put it away; the notes and the issues tend to go away, and I think that's important because I've then got my mind free for the next client and the next day. I don't feel like I switch off, because I know it's there, but it feels as if it's gone somewhere safe. If it doesn't feel safe then that comes up in the session, and that's when we talk about what else we need to do.

If there's something that's really pressing and alarms me or frightens me, then I will get support for that. I would contact my supervisor and ask if we can talk, or if it was something else I might phone the BACP and say there's a legal or ethical issue here that we need to talk through. That's very rare, though. We do what is necessary so that I don't have to wake up in the night thinking about it, and we know it will be there next week when we look at it again.

You're one of the few therapists I know who has a social media presence. Do you have to be careful what you tweet, knowing that clients might be reading it? There was a photo of you topless at Gay Pride, for example.

I didn't actually make that public. Other people have been putting pictures in places over which I have no control. What I did was go out on the street, dressed the way I wanted to dress for Gay Pride, and did what I wanted to do.

Although I was with a group of people from the BBC, I wasn't identified as BBC. I wasn't there with a group of counsellors, I was there as me saying that I'm proud of myself and my sexuality, which felt important to me. Other people took photographs and put them online.

I did wonder if it would be reasonable for me to say that I didn't want those photos to be shared on the internet – but that would be a bit like going on a naked bike ride and then asking people not to look at you because you're shy. I'm comfortable with people taking pictures. I might look at them and wish I'd held my tummy in that day or whatever, but I didn't – that's what I look like and that's who I am. Again, there's something about being authentic.

During the 2015 election I was doing some phone bashing for the Labour Party and I put up a picture of me. A client of mine saw it who was in training to be a therapist, and she said it made her realise that therapists could be real people too. I thought that was interesting.

Since then, I've decided to be a bit more visible. What I put up online I hope is either witty, or relevant, or in some way worth sharing. When I do it I think, 'Oh, this is worth saying.' It's something to do with politics, or art, or therapy, or something silly perhaps.

Clients will see that I'm gay, that I'm left-wing, that I'm a Labour Party member, that I'm an atheist, a humanist, anti-monarchy and a Remainer. I'm very happy for anybody to know those things about me. They might choose to work with me because of it, or choose not to because of it. And if it creates any issues for them, we can address those face to face in our sessions.

I have a client with a deep faith who knows I'm an atheist. We talk about her faith and she knows she's talking to an atheist. In some ways perhaps it's not an echo chamber for her, it's somebody she knows doesn't agree. We don't have to agree; we can talk about the music that she sings and plays, and how that moves me to tears, not because of the words about God but because of the sound of it, in the same way that I can go to the opera and be in tears despite not speaking Italian.

There are plenty of things about me that I don't want people to know, things that only my therapist knows about, and I wouldn't put those things up. Private, not secret. I think there's a balance of having a profile, but then managing it in a certain way.

Do you ever turn down clients if you feel you can't help them?

Yes, I do. In my experience what's tended to happen is that it's often a practical thing. If someone contacts me I'll say, 'Let's not speak on the phone, let's meet for half an hour, free of charge, and see where we go from there.' I'd rather have a conversation face to face.

In one example, I had a conversation on the phone with someone, and when he came in he said that he recognised me from somewhere. Then he pointed out that we sometimes see each other in the showers at the gym, and one of us is saying, 'Your shoulders are looking good, mate!' That was not going to work . . .

Or it could be that someone was bringing in grief, and if I had recently been bereaved I would say to them that this is not a good working relationship. I would be honest about why. I always hope that somebody is shopping around and that I'm just one of the people they see, because it's a very personal relationship.

If someone is looking for help with something like an eating disorder, or something else that I don't have much experience with, I might tell them that I'm happy to work with them but there's also someone else I'd like them to see.

The client: Graham Nunn

'Men are allowed to talk about our problems. It really helps to do so'

My best friend was losing patience with me. 'You need to see a therapist!' she would plead down the phone as my low mood made me increasingly unbearable to talk to. She had long been an advocate of psychotherapy, but I always had an excuse to avoid it – I just didn't see how it could help me.

Therapists, my friend explained, weren't there to offer advice; they just asked questions and allowed you to find your own answers. That sounded a bit hokey to me. I made a tentative enquiry as a sop to my friend's badgering, but eventually I took the macho approach of hoping my problems would just go away.

Statistics on suicide reveal an alarming reluctance among men to seek help for mental health issues. From an early age, we're imbued with the belief that emotions betray weakness and that real men just puff out their chests and get on with it.

I remember a conversation between several boys at my school where each was boasting about how long it had been since they last cried, ended by a demonstrative 'Well I've *never* cried!' as somebody's unconvincing mic drop.

I first started feeling depressed at the age of fifteen, and it has been an intermittent problem ever since. Because it tended to come in cycles, I was always more inclined to ride it out than to seek assistance; one unsuccessful spell on an antidepressant did nothing to convince me that medicine had the answers. It felt like something I just had to put up with.

I also have social anxiety, which means I tend to avoid invitations to go out with others; this, of course, only feeds the problem.

As the gloom showed no signs of lifting, my best friend was once again trying to cajole me into doing something about it. Having met with my usual resistance, she became exasperated: 'Well if you're not going to contact a therapist, I'll do it for you!'

She then wrote to a selection of therapists in my area asking if they could help, and I was relieved. I knew something had to be done, but I needed that push to get things rolling. I also promised to make an appointment with the doctor.

Four therapists emailed me back, and I made appointments with three of them. It was important to find someone I felt comfortable working with, so 'auditions' seemed like the best way to go. They were all within four days of each other, so I dubbed it Therapy Week.

Monday was Clive*. Our appointment was at his house soon after I finished work, and I was running late. It was the last week in January and a thick fog had descended, extending my anticipated journey time. My anxiety was ramping up:

Clive's going to think you're not coming. He's going to think you don't care enough to get there on time. You've messed this up before you've even started.

Thankfully, my fears were unfounded as I pulled up on his drive with seconds to spare before our scheduled appointment.

I approached the front door, shaking. A sign next to the doorbell warned visitors that the door would not be answered during appointments. I pressed it and waited for what seemed like a full minute. Had I got the time wrong? Was he seeing somebody else?

Then a figure appeared behind the glass and opened the door. He shook my hand and ushered me into a small room off the hallway, taking a seat in a large leather chair and gesturing me towards a small, threadbare two-seater sofa.

The room was full of books and ornaments; it smelled damp and musty. I realised I had been expecting a large drawing room with a grandfather clock and a chaise longue, so that was one illusion shattered.

Next to Clive was a small table on which sat a transparent cash box with several hundred pounds inside. *Takings*. It seemed a bit unnecessary to have it on display. The room wasn't cold but he wore a scarf looped tightly around his neck, which seemed a bit odd. Perhaps he had love bites.

Clive invited me to tell him what I needed help with, so I explained about the depression and anxiety, despite the latter being fairly evident by my inability to stop shaking. His website said that his approach was 'person-centred', which I didn't really understand; wasn't all therapy person-centred?

As the session developed, it was clear that he wasn't really interested in my past. I knew enough about therapy from my best friend to know that it wasn't all in the Freudian mould, but I'd been expecting more questions about my childhood and family life.

Instead, Clive explained that anxiety and depression worked in balance; whenever the anxiety threatened to get too high, the depression would pull it down so the sufferer would feel it as a numbness. It kind of made sense, but didn't really help. The rest of the session went by in a blur; I remember him talking more than I did. It felt very much like an introductory session rather than one that would give me any lasting insights.

He concluded by telling me that he'd suffered with depression all his life and felt that it was possible to manage it, before announcing that time was up. Bewildered, I handed over my cash, which was added to the transparent box, and told him I would be in touch if I wanted another appointment. I was pretty sure I wouldn't. The fog was thicker than ever on my way home.

Wednesday was Kate, another person-centred therapist. She had moved our appointment twice already following a mix-up with another booking, which hadn't made a good first impression, but as I parked up at the end of her drive she was there to meet me and show me to her modern conservatory.

Again, my Hollywood-infused image of a therapist's office was shown to be wide of the mark as I took a seat in a small red chair and forced a smile. I was shaking even more than I had with Clive, convulsing almost, and found it difficult to speak.

Kate made notes on a clipboard, explaining that this was just something she did on a first session. She told me that everything said was confidential unless she felt that I was in danger of hurting myself or anyone else.

Straight away she began to ask about my family and the relationship I had with them, about my childhood and my experiences at school. This was more like it. Her questions felt relevant and her comments were insightful. There were no forehead-slapping revelations, just the gentle reframing of viewpoints to make me consider a different perspective, a fresh light.

Kate taught me some breathing exercises to manage the anxious shaking. She was straightforward and professional. The session seemed to be over in a flash, which I have since learned is a good sign, and I felt confident enough to make a second appointment even though I still had one more therapist to try.

Thursday was Sheila, an integrative therapist. She opened the door as I approached, beaming widely as she invited me into her large, modern home but warning me to be careful of all the steps on the way to the lounge. She had an accent that didn't seem to belong anywhere and a demeanour that felt unnaturally friendly. I took a seat on the sofa opposite her, shaking uncontrollably once again, and began to answer her questions.

Like Kate, she asked about my past but had a habit of staring at me and furrowing her brow before scribbling notes on her pad. It was like she was trying to actually see inside my head.

She was pleasant enough, but a few of the things she said put me on guard. When I told her I was wary of antidepressants, she gave me the name of a herbal remedy for anxiety that she claimed 'absolutely works'. I'm not a believer in alternative medicine, and for a therapist to endorse it so vehemently rang alarm bells.

Sheila then observed that I was a visual thinker because I looked up to my right when recalling a holiday experience. She also wanted to spend rather too much time discussing an old friendship that didn't feel that important to me. It felt as though she was digging in the wrong place and wasting time.

As the session ended, she leafed through her diary. 'I'm not really taking on new clients at the moment,' she declared unhelpfully. 'I might be able to squeeze you in again next week if someone else cancels . . .' But I had already decided that I wouldn't be seeing Sheila again.

I kept my second appointment with Kate and continued to see her weekly for a couple of months. I'm glad I tried three different therapists before making my choice – I could easily have assumed that Clive or Sheila were representative of all counsellors and stayed with them despite not feeling entirely comfortable. I also kept my appointment with the doctor, who prescribed citalopram.

While talking things through with Kate, it became clear to me that I had feelings for my best friend that I wasn't acknowledging. Kate would press me on the subject, clearly sensing that I wasn't being entirely honest, and eventually I told my friend.

Thankfully, she felt the same way! Within a couple of weeks we were planning our future together. It didn't feel like rushing; if anything, it felt long overdue.

I had gone from feeling hopeless and depressed to happy and excited; all the problems I'd sought therapy for had disappeared. I told Kate that I didn't feel I needed her help any more and that I would like to end our sessions. She seemed genuinely happy for me. Before I left for the final time, she told me that she'd rarely seen anyone's fortunes turn around so quickly.

A year down the line, I have stopped taking citalopram and don't miss it. I'm not sure that I can attribute this entirely to therapy, but the process certainly made me think about what was important to me and helped to order my thoughts.

If I had the opportunity to speak to my cynical self from the past, I would definitely encourage him to try therapy; it turns out that men are allowed to talk about their problems after all, and it really helps to do so.

Therapists' names have been changed in this interview.

Gestalt Therapy

Gestalt? What on earth is that?

It's a school of thought that looks at human perception. Gestalt is a German word that means 'shape and form'. It was developed into a therapy by Fritz Perls, Laura Perls and Frank Goodman in the USA in the 1940s. They wanted to look at the benefits of self-awareness.

Are you aware of what those benefits are?

The idea is that individuals can be understood best in relation to their current situation and how they experience it.

You mean, their perception of it.

Yes. Which might be totally different from how another person would perceive it. The focus is very much on living in the moment rather than dwelling on the past or worrying about the future, but in a way that deeply acknowledges the emotions and sensations as you are experiencing them.

It's about engaging with the here and now, rather than passively letting it happen. This, according to Gestalt proponents, is the key to personal growth.

So all you have to do is think about what's going on right now? Sounds like a doddle.

There's a bit more to it than that. Your therapist will try to identify what's preventing you from fulfilling your potential. This might be negative thoughts and feelings, or conflicts in your personal relationships.

And how might the therapist deal with that?

There's an exercise in Gestalt therapy called the empty chair technique.

Is that where the therapist nips off for a cup of tea?

The client is asked to sit opposite an empty chair, then imagine that someone is sitting there. It might be someone they're having problems with, or someone they find it hard to talk to. They would then be encouraged to talk to that person, engage and interact as if they were really there.

It would be a rather one-sided conversation though.

Not necessarily, because the client may then be asked to swap chairs and imagine that they are the person they've just been talking to. They can imagine that they're now talking to themselves, seeing things from the other person's perspective.

I still think it sounds like having a pretend friend.

The aim is to help the individual see how they present themselves to the world and gain a better insight into how others might see them. Gestalt places great value on relationships, both with others and with the self. It's seen as the key to being a complete, rounded person. The relationship between the client and the therapist is equally important.

Are there any other weird techniques?

Body language is seen as being very important in Gestalt therapy. The therapist will be looking for subtle signs while they're talking to you, and might point them out to you when they spot them. You might even be asked to explain what it means to you – if you fold your arms, or clench your fists, for example.

What if it means they're about to punch the therapist?

Let's assume the client–therapist relationship is a bit better than that. The client might be asked to repeat the action and exaggerate it, with a view to revealing the hidden meaning behind it. It's more self-awareness, you see, and helps maintain focus.

Right. Acknowledging the present moment. So how many sessions would you typically have?

Gestalt can be either a long-term or a brief therapy, so there's no typical scenario; it depends upon the client's needs, and the problems they have.

What problems can it help with?

A wide range, from anxiety and depression to addiction. The focus on self-awareness can help to improve the client's self-confidence and make them more at ease with themselves, which goes a long way to helping with a number of issues.

My awareness of the present moment leads me to believe that we're finished here.

Very good.

The therapist: Candice Johnson
'It's a safe, non-judgemental "laboratory"'

How would you describe Gestalt therapy to someone who has never had it?

One of the reasons I chose to be a Gestalt therapist was because it is a relational therapy. This means that the therapist is present and available, in dialogue with you, the client, and open to sharing their experience of being with you, when appropriate and with your best interests in mind.

I, as the therapist, am not a closed book, nor indeed am I the expert on you. You know your experience and will always know this more fully than I will. A Gestalt therapist is there to actively listen to your experience, help you see your part in a situation and help you to identify any repeated patterns. The therapist is certainly not there to tell you what to do, or dole out advice about what you 'should' be doing.

As a Gestaltist, I truly believe that we all have the potential to fully access the whole of ourselves – mind, body, emotions and spirit – and one of the aims of this therapy is to help you grow towards integrating all of these parts of yourself.

In Gestalt therapy we work very much in the here and now, not the there and then. We do talk through past experiences but always bring them back to how they might be impacting you now because that is the moment you are in.

What does a typical Gestalt therapy session entail?

A therapy session typically lasts for fifty minutes and is on a weekly basis. A client may have something they specifically want to 'bring', talking through a situation that is currently troubling them. The therapist's role in this is to help the client heighten their awareness of their experience, their contribution, what might be familiar, what might not be being said.

This happens through active listening on the part of the therapist and dialogue. Sometimes, this may lead towards creative experimentation: role play, drawing, storytelling or body work, for example. However, this only becomes a part of the session if it's useful for the client, if the client is willing (which needs to be thoroughly explored), with the therapist holding no agenda or expectation of the outcome.

It's a safe, non-judgemental 'laboratory'; we just see what happens, allowing time afterwards to discuss what occurred and the learning that has come out of the work.

What can a client do to help themselves during therapy?

A client can help themselves by being open and willing, allowing themselves to trust enough to do the work they need to do. I say 'enough' because for some people, trust is a very difficult thing. In fact, the whole of their therapeutic journey may be about learning to trust their therapist.

A client needs to feel safe enough to do the work, while also being at the edge of their comfort zone at times in order to stretch themselves further and allow for change to come.

What qualities should a client look for in a therapist?

One of the key considerations when looking for the 'right' therapist is finding the right therapist for you! The fit between you is essential to the work. The healing in therapy takes place within the relationship between the client and therapist, so it is vital that the client feels safe enough, not judged, and able to share their difficulties.

I believe it's a huge privilege for people to come to me and tell me, perhaps saying it for the first time in their lives, what they struggle with most in the world. It is crucial, therefore, that you as a client connect with the person to whom you are trusting this part of yourself.

I personally believe that it is also important to find someone who is qualified and accredited, someone who has been through the rigours of a thorough training and personal therapy, and has regular supervision.

Are there people for whom Gestalt therapy isn't suitable? If so, who?

If you are someone who wants a highly cognitive approach with weekly techniques and strategies then I don't believe Gestalt therapy is the modality for you. As one of the aims of Gestalt therapy is to integrate all parts of ourselves, focusing on the mind so fully does not support this.

What do you enjoy most about practising therapy?

I enjoy being with people in a one-to-one, authentic, supportive and also challenging setting. As I mentioned earlier, I feel it is a huge privilege to bear witness to people's innermost fears, beliefs and hopes.

Building a relationship with a client and seeing their shifts, growth and transformation is hugely rewarding. I find it utterly remarkable to sit alongside a client in their journey of change.

I enjoy meeting someone in a horizontal relationship, whereby the boundaries are clear, neither party is the 'boss', and I am fully present to what happens in the room.

It's a very exciting, dynamic process based on a genuine connection. There aren't any other professions I've worked in that offer that opportunity.

How much personal information do you disclose to clients?

I will disclose personal information to the client if I feel it may be of service to them. I would never share something irrelevant or that is not conveyed with their best interests in mind. It can be really helpful to a client to hear something of their therapist's experience when it relates to something they know about too.

Equally, if you overshare it can be very unnerving for some clients who may struggle with trust, for example. So as the therapist it's important to be sensitive to this and calibrate your sharing appropriately.

If you could start life over, would you still have been a therapist?

I would.

I chose to be a therapist after my own transformational journey with a wonderful therapist when I was thirty. I felt that if I could help just one person in the way my therapist had helped me, then my life would be worthwhile. I still believe this and feel so grateful that I have had the opportunity to be a part of my clients' journeys over the last seventeen years.

What would you have done if you hadn't been a therapist?

Well, for fifteen years I worked in the retail, marketing and publishing worlds, all of which taught me a lot in different ways, so I imagine I may well have continued in that vein.

At thirty, when I chose to retrain, I was working in publishing so I believe I would have stayed in that world and worked my way up the corporate ladder. Who knows where that might have led!

The client: Katy Georgiou

'It allows for creativity and playfulness and curiosity'

I found my Gestalt therapist myself, through my own research online. When I began training to be a Gestalt therapist, one requirement of the course was that we needed to be in therapy ourselves with a very experienced Gestalt therapist. I had seen Gestalt therapists before who were also excellent, but as I was starting afresh, I wanted to start with a new therapist.

I'd tried out a few other therapists previously, but I felt more of a rapport with this one. He also lived very close to me, which played a big part in it. I knew from experience that when you're going through therapy, sometimes it's tough, and if the therapist is far away and the weather's cold it can be very easy to just not want to go. I didn't want to fall into that trap.

I trusted my therapist. I was also interested to have a male therapist, as my previous therapists had mostly been women. I wanted to understand my relationship to men a bit better.

My advice is to really take note of what your gut is telling you. If something doesn't quite feel right, that is going to nag at you and will get in the way of your therapy. It isn't so much about whether or not you 'like' your therapist or they like you, it's more about whether they have integrity.

Therapists are human too and might well slip up on occasion or get things wrong sometimes, but do you have a sense that they've got your interests at heart? Are they a therapist for the right reasons? I believe you can tell these things very early on.

I was attracted to Gestalt therapy as I find it to be very diverse. It allows for creativity and playfulness and curiosity and I think those are the aspects that really drew me to the approach. I like that it's not just about the things you say, but what you're doing while you're speaking, and how our bodies give us vital clues to our emotional experience.

I remember a video in which founder of Gestalt therapy Fritz Perls described Gestalt as like an artist drawing out a painting from a blank canvas. I loved that as an image. It really encourages curiosity about the self.

Having therapy has made me a better therapist. I made a decision to keep having therapy while practising as a counsellor, because I really believe that we never stop learning about ourselves and it's important for me as a counsellor to have humility and not think I have all the answers.

It's dangerous to fall into complacency, so I feel that having therapy keeps me on my toes. In my personal life, it's given me an outlet to explore who I am without fear of repercussions, and it's supportive.

Psychosynthesis

I know about this! It's where plants use sunlight to grow and stuff.

Er, that's photosynthesis. *Psycho*synthesis is a type of therapy developed in the early 1900s by a man called Roberto Assagioli; it has roots in psychoanalysis but is rather different.

Roots? Are you sure this isn't about plants?

Quite sure. Assagioli believed that the key to personal development was combining the best parts of ourselves – synthesising, in other words – into a complete, harmonious being. He devised a therapy to help people use this concept for self-healing and personal growth.

Growth? Like plants?

Can you drop the plants thing please? The idea is that most individuals only achieve a small amount of their true potential, but everyone has the ability to access more. Psychosynthesis uses the concepts of self-actualisation and self-realisation to raise consciousness to a higher, spiritual level in order to achieve this.

Self . . . what?

Self-actualisation is the process of gaining control over your own inner powers of healing by becoming more attuned to your needs, beliefs and desires. It's about overcoming obstacles by having a better understanding of who you are as a person. Self-realisation is taking that a step further to achieve your full potential.

So if it's all about self-healing, what's the therapist doing? Watering the plants?

In psychosynthesis, the therapist might refer to themselves as a guide. Their role is to help the client unlock the potential within them by establishing a safe setting where trust is paramount. They won't offer specific advice, but instead try to encourage the client to find their own answers by nurturing a better sense of self.

But how do they actually do that?

You would be asked to be open about your feelings and thoughts to reveal inner conflicts. The therapist would teach you how to be more aware of these sensations, and connect with the idea of self-healing. You can't always control the things that happen to you, but in psychosynthesis the challenges of life are seen as opportunities for transformation and development.

It sounds quite different to other therapies.

It's fair to say that it's not for everybody; you'd have to be open to its core idea of connecting with your inner self to get anything out of it.

And assuming you get on board with all that, what kind of problems could it help you with?

Since it deals with improving self-worth and confidence, there are a number of things it could help with: depression, anxiety, trauma and anything else that might be affecting somebody's personal wellbeing and enjoyment of life.

So you might say that it could bring some sunlight back into their world.

You just won't let it go, will you?

The therapist: Sandra Ballester

'Be honest with your therapist'

How would you describe psychosynthesis to someone who has never heard of it?

Psychosynthesis is a way of viewing the whole person. It doesn't just look at what you feel is 'wrong' with you, it also takes into account your strengths, your creativity, your values, and what gives you a sense of meaning and purpose.

The therapy gently examines your childhood and your feelings about things that have happened in the past, and helps you to see how problems you have today may have their roots in your history. These things often take time to work with and overcome, but they do not need to hold you back.

The therapy goes further than this, though. As personal issues start to heal, you may find yourself thinking and acting more creatively. Psychosynthesis encourages you to explore your creative potential as it emerges and to reflect on what you may feel 'called' to do with your life.

Psychosynthesis is structured like this because its founder, Roberto Assagioli, started off as a psychiatrist similar to Freud, but he felt something was missing from traditional psychoanalysis. He believed the whole human being includes their creativity, their morality, their sources of inspiration and so on, not just their hang-ups, so he developed a form of psychotherapy which reflects this.

Today, most clients see their psychosynthesis therapist for one hour a week, with both of them sitting in chairs facing each other and talking. The therapist usually guides the client through an exploration of childhood and present-day problems, and weaves in a search for the client's sense of meaning, purpose and creativity.

This psychological journey unfolds over a period of time and there is no expectation of where the client ought to end up. The client discovers that for themselves.

What does a typical session involve?

The first session is usually spent talking about whatever has brought the client to therapy and taking a history of the client's life. Childhood, family relationships, work life and present-day relationships are included in this.

The therapist may also ask about the client's sense of meaning and purpose, and what makes them happy. The client should feel understood and that the therapist empathises with them in their situation.

Later on, therapy can feel a bit challenging at times as we learn to see things differently, so it's important the client feels supported and able to tell the therapist what is really on their mind. The quality of the relationship between client and therapist is the best predictor of a good outcome, and this is built up over time.

Lots of different psychosynthesis therapists use lots of different techniques, but it is all still psychosynthesis. Apart from the first session or two, most sessions are spent talking about whatever is troubling the client most at the time. Occasionally the therapist may suggest an exercise such as a visualisation, a meditation, drawing a picture and so on, which the client does not have to do if they are not comfortable with it.

There is no criticism, no judgement, no pushing the client into anything they are not happy with. It should be basically a positive experience even when it feels challenging. Sessions can sometimes be a lot of fun!

How much do you disclose about yourself in therapy?

I generally disclose very little about myself in the therapy room, but I'm not rigid about it. Clients tend to make up stories about their therapist, imagining them to be like this or that, and this is useful to work with because it tells you something about them that is usually unconscious.

But when I am asked a direct question about myself, I don't like to block it completely because that's a bit inhuman. Usually I'll say,

'I'll answer your question soon, but first I wonder if you could tell me what's behind you asking me that?' We work with their answer to my question before I answer theirs.

Occasionally I do disclose something about myself, if I think it will be helpful. For example, I tell most of my clients how important it is to do some meditation or relaxation exercises, say for twenty minutes twice each day. Without this, it's hard to become emotionally settled or even to make much progress in therapy.

Usually there is resistance to doing this, as people seem to assume it should not be necessary, or that it's only a temporary measure. They look at me sceptically when I'm saying this, so I'll often disclose that for the last twenty years I've meditated two or three times a day because otherwise I might not feel good and can't function so well. They seem to take it more seriously after that!

What is the best thing to have happened to you as a therapist?

I'm not sure there's one single best thing that's happened to me as a therapist. But the best thing for me about being a therapist is seeing my clients become creative when they begin to be relieved of unnecessary suffering caused by their history, usually from childhood.

For example, seeing an artist who hasn't allowed herself to create anything for years begin to experiment again with her work now that she values herself more. Or a businessman relaunching his business now that he's freed from his troubled thinking.

I became a therapist so I could use my own experiences, skills and psychological journey in service of others' wellbeing. When I see my clients benefiting from this I feel deeply content.

What can clients do to help themselves get the most out of therapy?

There's a lot that clients can do. The sessions exist purely for your own wellbeing, so attend them regularly and engage with the process as much as you can. Everyone has some resistance, and if you talk about how you feel resistant to engaging you can work to overcome it.

Be honest with your therapist and you will speed up the process. Self-care is extremely important too. If you are exhausted, hungry, hungover or overworked you will struggle to attain emotional balance and if this is how you spend most of your life it will be very much harder to get benefit from your therapy.

Regular meditation or relaxation together with physical exercise will also benefit your emotional health massively.

I'd also say make it a goal to be your own best friend. You are the only person you spend every minute of every day with, so be compassionate with yourself. Many clients have spent a lifetime telling themselves they are no good, not normal, not worth the effort and so on.

They have often put their own needs, especially their internal, emotional ones, very last on their list of priorities, giving preference to everyone else's needs except their own. We would be outraged to see someone treating another person like this but it's too easy to overlook how we treat ourselves. Then we wonder why we're miserable.

Are there some people for whom therapy isn't suitable? If so, who?

It kind of depends what you mean by therapy. The words psychotherapy and counselling are often used interchangeably which can be confusing. As a general rule, psychotherapy probes deeper into our unconscious patterns – things we are not aware of in ourselves but which influence our lives.

So you might look at how you unknowingly contribute to painful situations in your life, for example, even when it appears that other people are to blame. This usually means challenging your ideas and beliefs, so you need to be up for this and keep your balance as you go through the process.

However, if you don't like the sound of examining your internal processes to this extent you may benefit more from supportive counselling or other types of therapy that are not so challenging. There's so much to choose from, and most people can find something that is helpful to them.

If, on the other hand, someone doesn't really want therapy, it is unlikely to be helpful, whatever sort of therapy they go for. If you're going because someone else wants you to go then it's probably going to be a waste of time. You get out of therapy what you put in, so if you are a very reluctant client just going through the motions you won't get much benefit.

Also, if you want the therapist to 'fix' you, fix your problems, or fix the people in your life, you'll be disappointed. All types of therapy ultimately require you, the client, to resolve your issues. Of course, you need your therapist's help, guidance and support to do this, but the hard work always comes from you. If you're unwilling to do any work yourself, you won't benefit from therapy.

The client: Atalanta Kernick

'Therapy has helped me enormously'

I found my psychosynthesis therapist through a friend who had been seeing her for a while. I had seen several therapists before from different backgrounds and practices, since I was about eighteen.

These included a Freudian therapist recommended at my university, who said everything was connected to my mother; a Reichian who listened to my stomach with a stethoscope, but with whom I had a panic attack when she did the hands-off healing; and a person-centred therapist who seemed anything but! She sat quietly in the corner of the room and complained when I approached her to show her something.

The quest for a therapist I could connect with was important, and I put a lot of effort into it. I had felt that I needed to see someone for the whole of my adult life.

There was a lot that I liked about my psychosynthesis therapist. I had a very positive relationship with her and have used it as a blueprint for my future therapists.

She made me feel confident about seeking a therapist in future because I could 'do therapy'. She was very friendly, practical and down to earth. If she felt uncomfortable about something, she would tell me – and she wore leopard-print leggings!

I would advise people to choose a therapist that they feel comfortable with, as much as possible. It's a bit like choosing friends – if you want one that talks and is forthright, then say so. Research the different practices and decide if there are some that suit you. And don't be afraid to leave a therapist if they aren't right for you.

My psychosynthesis therapist actually practised transactional analysis (see page 166) too, which was very much about our relationship and the here and now. It was also about giving clients a 'toolbox' of skills to use in future. I remember her giving me positive affirmations to do.

She had practised psychosynthesis exclusively in the past, but had chosen to combine it with other techniques. I think I was initially drawn to psychosynthesis because I felt quite fragmented and was very dissociative at the time.

This therapy, which I had for two years, plus two other six-month bouts of Gestalt therapy, helped me enormously to the point where I would say they were life-saving. I had bouts of severe low self-esteem, depression and suicidal thoughts, due to a very abusive relationship and abuse as a child.

I had little to no concept of my boundaries, emotional intelligence, self-care and self-esteem. I couldn't identify many feelings or didn't have them, couldn't cope with conflict and didn't see why boundaries existed because you couldn't make people respect them.

So therapy has helped me enormously. It has helped me to take care of myself, form healthy relationships with friends and partners, identify abusive and unhealthy behaviour in others and protect myself from this.

I can now identify and counteract negative thought patterns and behaviours in myself, plan and achieve my life goals and maintain positive, supportive feelings about myself. I feel that therapy has been vital for me in getting me 'back on track' with my life.

Integrative Therapy

This one must be for people who want to fit in.

It may sound like it, but it's actually an approach that uses elements from different types of therapy, ideally creating a bespoke therapy that better suits the client's needs.

Like picking out all the best bits?

Not necessarily the best bits, as that's very subjective. It's about assessing the individual client and choosing methods that are likely to work best for them. The idea is that no single modality has all the answers, so borrowing from different approaches gives a more rounded treatment without being restrictive.

But how does it work? Do you see one therapist one week and another the next?

No, your therapist will be familiar with various modalities and be able to apply techniques from them as necessary. What they use for each client will vary considerably.

I'm not sure about these people who don't specialise. I hired a builder once who claimed he could do everything and I ended up with a wobbly fence.

That's the criticism that other therapists might use. They would say that although it sounds like the perfect solution, an integrative therapist is unlikely to have the level of expertise that a specialist would have. On the other hand, it gives the client a chance to try different approaches without having to change therapists – which is certainly more convenient.

I still worry that it wouldn't go into enough depth.

Let's not underestimate the integrative therapist. It takes skill to successfully combine a variety of styles into a workable programme; not everything will work together, and they need to understand their clients' needs.

Haven't we already seen therapies that combine different methods?

Yes – we saw, for example, that cognitive analytic therapy blended techniques from CBT with those of psychoanalysis. This is certainly an integration of sorts, but since CAT has its own name and structure it isn't considered to be integrative therapy. Real integrative therapy is more flexible and likely to touch upon more styles.

I'm imagining that integrative therapy is like a rogue state, despised by all the other therapies. Would using it harm your chances of seeing a specialist later?

It's really not like that. Therapists do what they do because they want to help people, so the chances are that they will welcome you if approached and help you find someone else if they're not right for you. You might find that some integrative therapists don't even draw attention to the fact – they'll just offer therapy and explain what they do after you contact them.

A covert operation! Sneaky.

There's nothing underhand about it. It's just another equally valid option among many.

I might have known you'd sit on the fence. Just don't sit on mine, it wobbles.

The therapist: Graham Thomas

'It can feel almost counter-intuitive to let your guard down and to be open and honest'

How would you describe integrative therapy to someone who has never had it?

Integrative therapy combines different approaches to psychotherapy and does not restrict itself to one school of thought. Different integrative therapists will have their own unique way of defining how they work. For me, therapy is a bespoke endeavour based on a notion of shared exploration. The enquiry, which is both supportive and challenging, is unique with each client. Nothing arrives off the shelf pre-packaged or pre-configured.

What does a typical integrative therapy session involve?

I hate the idea that there might be a typical integrative therapy session; it sounds too formulaic, too protocol-bound, too known. I'm sure I'm not on my own in having chosen this career due to its very individual joys and challenges. Every client, every session, every moment is new.

Having said that, there are commonalities across most therapies, including the therapeutic hour, which lasts for fifty minutes, an invitation to speak without judgement, comfortable chairs (and sometimes a couch), and a handy box of tissues.

Different therapists do it differently, of course. Where a strictly psychoanalytic therapist may take on a more observing role, with occasional interpretations, which may sometimes be misinterpreted as cold and distant, other therapists, working from a behavioural perspective, may be very actively present, suggesting experiments, tasks and even homework.

There are two main divisions within therapy: the problem-focused, solution-finding enquiry, where the therapist may adopt a more directive approach; and the idea that therapy is an accompanied exploration, where an opening up of understanding occurs through shared reflection. The integrative therapist may decide to move between these two positions.

What can a client do to help themselves during therapy?

It's not always easy starting therapy for the first time. In a buttoned-up world, with daily pressures, and multiple roles to perform, it can feel almost counter-intuitive to let your guard down and to be open and honest.

We are taught to hide our vulnerabilities, to secrete away our individual hopes and fears. Family, peer, societal and cultural pressures accrue and calcify around our individuality, leaving us sometimes feeling that we are required to play a game that we never asked to join. Good therapy deals with that and says: 'Come as you are.' Dare to be open.

What qualities should a client look for when choosing a therapist?

Make sure your therapist is professionally registered with the UKCP, BACP or BPS (see page 309). Don't be afraid to ask questions before you commit and read what they say about themselves on their website. What resonates for you? Choosing a therapist is a very personal decision.

Some people will be looking for a guru, a top expert, a holder of all perfections. If your therapist is claiming to offer any of these, my suggestion would be to walk away. Personally, I would rather find someone who offers warmth, humour and intelligence.

Are there people for whom integrative therapy isn't suitable? If so, who?

People who have a very specific issue that they want to address, like a phobia for instance, may be better off accessing CBT via the

NHS. It's free, and there's a good evidence base to support that way of working. Private therapy can be expensive, so if someone contacts me about starting therapy, I'll often suggest other ways of getting support which are lower cost or more effective. The CBT offered by the NHS is mostly about symptom relief and focuses less on understanding the bigger picture, but it's definitely worth considering.

How do you decide what type of therapy or mix of therapies suits a particular client?

Every client is different and every session is different. I don't start out looking for a formulation. That's the sheer joy of it, realising that you are on this journey together with some surprising twists and turns that require both of you to adjust your understanding.

It's a dance, if you like, a reciprocal movement of invitation, negotiation and clarification. That sounds as woolly as hell, doesn't it? What informs the way I work? Perhaps it's more simple than that, a questioning of 'I wonder what is going on here?' and 'I wonder what might help us both to understand this better?'

What do you enjoy most about practising therapy?

It feels very alive. Nothing is automatic, nothing is taken for granted. It's intimate and real.

I remember working with a delightful woman many, many years ago. She needed to share an untold story and yet she had no words to give in her first session. The early events of her life were unspeakable. Gradually we found a way, and she began to write single words on tissues, which she would hand to me. Then came single sentences, and later still she spoke to me. Slowly she found her voice and began to share what had previously been kept securely locked away. What a privilege to be allowed into another person's world, to be trusted with the history, the experiencing and the story of another human being.

Perhaps that's what therapists are, careful curators of other people's stories. On a good day, there's nothing like it. It's the best job in the world.

How much personal information do you disclose to clients?

I don't hide behind any mask with my clients, since what would I be modelling if I tried to keep myself away from the session? The 'who I am' and 'how I am' is there to be seen, although the everyday content of my life is not.

If you could start life over, would you still have been a therapist?

Yes, definitely. I can't think of a job that I would rather have.

What would you have done if you hadn't been a therapist?

I used to work in communications and marketing before training to be a psychotherapist. I enjoyed this work hugely, but as I began to do the therapy training I realised that working one-to-one with clients suited me much better.

A crunch point arrived when I was offered a PR job in my mid-thirties. The offer came with a swanky job title and a hefty salary, along with the proviso that I stop training and devote all my time to the new position.

Suddenly it became clear to me: my old career had to go, and I waved goodbye to the corporate world. For me, that movement from the corporate to the personal has been a liberation. I've never regretted that decision.

The client: Sachin Kumarendran

'Admitting weakness and vulnerability is never easy'

What kinds of talking treatment have you tried?

To start off with, I had the standard NHS consultations, which I didn't find helpful. I then went private and had a few time-limited sessions of CBT. It was essentially a brief attempt to alter my thought processes, particularly my tendency towards rumination and inability to break cycles of depressive thought.

The sessions weren't that ground-breaking, given such a short time period, and my memories of the techniques that I was taught are a bit hazy because one coping mechanism of mine at the time was somewhat cavalier Xanax use that blew alarming holes in my memory.

However, this treatment did at least set a precedent of me seeking help that made it easier for me to do so again subsequently; I've found that both the social stigma of seeking therapy and the initial pain of opening up and admitting weakness make this a hard thing to do.

I was also recommended the Headspace mindfulness app during this period. I've found this both helpful and extremely convenient.

After this, I was forced to move at short notice by my job, and the upheaval triggered a lot of anxiety, something I had not properly experienced before, as well as compounding my depression to a level where I was genuinely struggling to function.

I again sought help from a private therapist, who, working on a much longer time frame, was able to discuss my life and delve into the personal circumstances that had led to the depression. I've found this treatment to be immensely helpful since starting it.

My therapist is integrative, practising a mixture of psychodynamic and humanistic therapy and CBT. As my mental health has improved in recent months, we've progressed to revisiting CBT, which I have found to be more effective than when I first tried it nearly a year ago, when I was first starting treatment.

How did you go about finding your therapist?

I moved to a rural town at short notice, and in such an isolated area there weren't too many options. Looking around online, the therapist I chose seemed to be the most promising. She is a practising artist, and as someone attempting to fashion a career in the creative arts myself, I liked that this was a potential point of connection. The fact that it was integrative therapy on offer also factored in my decision, as having previously tried CBT with limited success I was keen to incorporate other approaches.

How did the first session go?

I wasn't feeling particularly great beforehand. I found at first with counselling that there was a kind of 'comfort zone barrier' in my own head, above and beyond the social stigma of therapy, that made me reluctant to open up. However, the first session was very helpful, so therapy soon became easier.

Why do you think a social stigma around therapy exists? And why do you think men can find this stigma more of a psychological barrier to accessing therapy than women?

I think that there's a wider cultural ignorance surrounding mental health generally that contributes heavily to this. It's still not uncommon for me to see depression and the like referred to as 'not proper illnesses' in the media, or the use of similar phrases to that effect, and before acquiring it, I personally never knew that depression was something you could gradually get. I only had a vague awareness that certain major events (e.g. bereavement) could trigger it.

Likewise, I had no idea anxiety disorders even existed until friends first began to become affected. I would have been around twenty years old then, so that seems relatively late in life to become aware of this. I think the ignorance surrounding these conditions contributes to the damaging perception that therapy is for 'crazy' people, rather than something that particularly helps the vulnerable but that anyone and everyone could benefit from.

Admitting weakness and vulnerability publicly is never an easy thing to do, whoever you are, and is probably harder for men due to cultural and gender stereotypes contributing to the backwards notion that men should 'man up' rather than seeking help.

This is especially true in the modern era, with social media and the like painting such idealised pictures of life that people are perhaps led to the idea that they are the only ones whose lives aren't going as they would like them to be. Vicariously, we see the highlight reels of other people's lives, and perhaps feel worse about our own.

David Baddiel on Men and Therapy

'I was in the therapy room like a shot'

I've had various forms of therapy: cognitive, and counselling, and EMDR (see page 231), and then for about a year a Freudian analyst – I was on a couch and everything. When I left him, Susie Orbach, who I knew, suggested my next therapist. I thought I wanted a female therapist, and she suggested a woman who was a relational therapist. I was with her for about eight years. I went back briefly for a few sessions later after my mum died.

Relational therapy basically means the therapist puts his or her feelings into the room. They can say, 'What you've said has made me feel angry', or sad or whatever. I liked that – I felt an emotional transaction needed to go on for me. I found the blankness of Freudian therapy difficult. My relational therapist was intellectual, very acute and insightful, but also emotionally generous.

I would add that I think CBT can be incredibly useful, and if I need therapy again I might go for that, rather than the psychodynamic stuff.

I think therapy has enhanced my life. Hard to tell. I was always keen on talking about my emotions anyway. I had specific issues which have got better, but I sometimes wonder if they would have anyway, with time and acceptance. Acceptance seems to me to be the key.

You ask why men find it so difficult to seek help, and how we can remedy this. I was patron of CALM, which is the primary charity that attempts to help male depression, and specifically, prevent young men from killing themselves, for many years. And my sense is it's not men, exactly, the gender; it's a specific *type* of man, usually young, from an impoverished background, with family issues. As a Jewish man, I was not like this. As soon as I felt the claw of clinical depression I was in the therapy room like a shot.

I think that men, some men, have a heroic narrative about themselves in their psyche, to which their life often doesn't match up, and this makes them feel like a failure. Men sometimes seem to need, more than women, significance, destiny, meaning (women need meaning too of course, but it seems to be less *inflated*).

I think this is why some men become terrorists, which of course is also a way of killing yourself: as a way of becoming the hero of your own life, which might otherwise have seemed so small and insignificant. But the thing that is difficult to construct is a narrative about yourself where significance and destiny and meaning come from what they actually come from, which *is* small things, domestic things, from the bits and pieces and randomness of your existence.

And a lot of men can't piece this together, and so become depressed. What is needed is a way of talking about it, and a way of talking about it that speaks to the kind of young men who don't want to talk about it. This is hard, although it is the template CALM works with.

Existential Therapy

What's this one – therapy for people who exist? Sorry Mr Ghost, you're not welcome!

The roots of this one date back a long time, to nineteenth-century philosophy. Existential therapy uses philosophical methods rather than specific techniques, which is an unusual approach in therapy. The idea is that inner conflict can occur within individuals because of the inevitable challenges of existence.

A noted psychotherapist called Irvin Yalom made a list of these challenges, which he called 'givens'.

Can you 'give' specifics?

There are four main givens. The first is freedom and responsibility. This refers to that fact that people can crave freedom in their lives, but might not want the responsibility that goes with it.

What? Surely freedom is when you don't have responsibility.

In existential therapy, they're inextricably linked. It's easier for people to fall into line with expectations than it is to do something different.

Think about it: if you decided that you didn't want to live by society's rules anymore and went to live in a hole in the ground instead, you'd suddenly have a lot more responsibilities because you wouldn't have the support of established systems.

You'd have to solve a lot more problems for yourself. It has been shown that people relinquish freedom and avoid responsibility for that very reason – it's easier. In existential therapy, that's regarded as a conflict.

Well I'm not about to start living in a hole, I'll grant you that. I'm not Saddam Hussein. What's the second 'given'?

This one's more obvious – the finite nature of life and inevitability of death.

You're a bundle of joy, aren't you?

Well, that's the point. We're all going to die – it's just something we need to get used to. It's always there hanging over us. For some, it's more pressing than it is for others, and it applies to all our family and loved ones too.

Which brings more conflict?

Right. The third one is isolation and connectedness. This is the idea that we're all ultimately alone in life, and have a strong desire to make connections with others. This desire brings conflict when those connections are either not possible or not as strong as we would like.

And the fourth?

Meaning and meaninglessness, which is the conflict between our desire to find meaning in life and our lack of certainty about what it is.

So all these things cause us anguish, and only existential therapy can save us?

The therapy doesn't assume that there is a correct response to all the givens, and your therapist isn't going to pull you to one side and fill you in on the meaning of life, but they would argue that these matters are at the heart of many of our daily anxieties.

The aim of the therapy is to help people face these issues and take control of their lives.

Well, it makes a change from Freud.

It couldn't be more different from psychoanalysis. The method doesn't assume that you are shaped by past events or that your future will depend on them. Instead, you have freedom to make what you want of your life.

Freedom? But doesn't that lead to existential crisis?

I'm not sure you're taking this seriously.

Well, all I'm hearing is that life is tough and some people feel a bit bad about it.

It can be more specific than that. If you had a terminal illness, for example, or knew someone who did, then these issues would be very pertinent to you.

I didn't think of that. I feel a bit bad now.

Maybe you could use some existential therapy?

I'll give you that one.

The therapist: Claire Arnold-Baker

'It is good to think deeply about our lives'

How would you describe existential therapy?

Existential therapy focuses on the client's lived experience, which means clients' issues are not viewed from a medical or psychological perspective; instead, they are viewed as problems in living.

The approach looks at the person as a whole, understanding that as individuals we are never in isolation, and that we are part of a larger world. Therefore, as human beings, we are always connected to other people and the situation we find ourselves in.

The existential therapist understands that clients' difficulties can also not be examined in isolation, and that we need to take the client's personal context into consideration. Therefore, clients are encouraged to explore their relationship to the environment they live in, their culture and society and their personal relationships. They will also explore their relationship with themselves.

Through examining the client's thoughts and feelings, their values and beliefs will be uncovered, which will highlight what is important to the client, but also where they find difficulties and challenges.

The existential approach assumes that it is good to think deeply about our lives. We need to become aware of the way in which we make assumptions and judgements about ourselves, others and the way we live. Through becoming more aware of the choices we make and our responses to life, we will be able to make more active choices, rather than living by default, in a passive way.

A central concept of the existential approach is the notion of freedom, and the belief that we have free will to choose the life we lead. However, with freedom comes choice and responsibility.

Realising that we are responsible for our lives may seem like a burden at times. However, it is also empowering when clients realise that they can be the author of their lives, and that nothing is set in stone. This is also linked to the existential view of self: that we are not a fixed entity, a solid self that can be defined.

Rather, we are a process of becoming, that we can create and recreate ourselves, and that we do so through our life experiences and interactions with others. Realising that we are essentially free can cause us to feel anxiety, or angst.

The existential therapist will not try to get rid of this anxiety, but instead will help the client to understand what it's related to and what it says about how they are living, how they see themselves and how they can make choices for themselves for the future.

The aim of existential therapy is to help clients live in a better way, to enable them to look realistically at their lives, both in terms of what is possible but also the limitations that they face.

Existential therapy helps to reconnect clients with what is important to them, so that they can live more meaningful lives.

What does a therapy session entail?

As the existential approach is client-centred, it means that the client determines the focus of the sessions, bringing their concerns or experiences that they need to understand in a different way.

The existential therapist will engage in a dialogue with the client, helping them to clarify their worldview and gain a new understanding of their concerns. This will inevitably lead to a more in-depth exploration of their life and way of living.

The therapy tends to focus on the here and now, with clients reflecting on what is happening to them currently, although past experiences and memories are often brought in when they have a direct bearing on what the client is talking about. The client will also think about their future in the sessions and how they envision a new way of living.

Initially, the sessions will focus on taking stock of the client's current life and where they experience difficulties or challenges. Clients need to understand their current experience before they can look at what they may want to achieve, or how they might go about achieving it.

Existential therapists employ a phenomenological approach to their work, which means they will ask clients to describe their experience in detail. Therapists will take a questioning but open approach to what the client brings so that they exhibit a sense of curiosity and naïvety.

They will ask clarifying questions and check the understanding of the meanings of the words clients use, asking for specific examples to help gain a deeper sense of the world the client inhabits.

However, the therapy sessions do not stay at the level of description, and existential therapists will challenge clients to think deeply about their own particular point of view and beliefs, and to face up to the responsibility of their existence. The therapist will help clients to explore different perspectives and new ways of being, so that they become aware of alternative possibilities in their lives.

What do you enjoy most about practising therapy?

I love the variety of the work that therapy offers. No two clients are the same. You never know who is going to walk in through the door, what their struggles might be and what they will need to do, or achieve, to live in a better way.

Being part of that process and seeing the changes that people make in their lives is a deeply rewarding experience. I find it satisfying to be able to help and support clients in their difficult times and be with them as they find new ways of being or relating.

Therapy involves a journey that the client and therapist embark upon together. How that journey evolves will be determined by what is created within the therapeutic relationship. I like to build good connections with my clients, really trying to understand them and their struggles – trying to step into their shoes and get an idea of what living is like for them.

Of course, there is always an unknown element to any therapeutic alliance as to how the relationship will unfurl and how the client will experience the process. I work hard to develop that relationship so that it provides a space for the client to feel safe enough to explore the aspects of themselves and their lives that they need to.

The therapeutic process is co-created by the relationship between the client and therapist. Each therapeutic alliance is unique to those two people, and because it is a co-creation, inevitably we are both changed in the process.

I will often think, when working with my clients, 'What does this client have to teach me?' – personally about my life, or professionally about the way I practise, or in terms of how I can understand human existence better? Each client will broaden my horizons, expand my knowledge and present me with a new perspective.

How much personal information do you disclose to clients?

On the whole, I tend to keep the amount of personal information I disclose to clients quite minimal, although the existential approach doesn't particularly demand this in the way that some theoretical approaches require the therapist to be a blank screen to their clients. But I also want to relate to the client in a real way – as two human beings in dialogue.

I will, therefore, answer personal questions which are related to creating a good relationship with clients. For example, if I cancel a session because I'm going on holiday and my client asks me where I'm going, I would tell them, because to do otherwise would seem churlish. However, I would not go into great detail about it.

I will provide basic information about my life to clients if it seems relevant to our connection, or their understanding of me as a person. There will be times when the client will explicitly ask for personal information and at those times I will consider the impact my answer will have on the client and our relationship when deciding how best to respond.

If a client seems to be asking a number of questions about my life then I might ask them about this. I would ask them to reflect on what it is like for them not to know much about me and what that means to them.

There will be other times when I might feel tempted to disclose something of my own experience because I feel it is relevant to what the client is experiencing. In all those situations, my overriding question to myself is, 'Will it be helpful to the client?' In the majority of these occasions, the answer to this question is 'No'.

Clients are mostly not interested in what their therapist does, or what experiences they have had, as their focus is on understanding themselves. It might be tempting to share what we would do in that situation, but the client needs to find their own particular way of dealing with the situations that they find themselves in, which will be unique to themselves.

The therapeutic relationship is very different to most other social relationships in that it is intimate, but also one-sided. The focus needs to be on the client, and so any self-disclosure has to be in the client's best interests.

What can a client do to help themselves during therapy?

Therapy starts a process of reflection for the client. Clients will inevitably begin to think deeply about their lives when they start therapy: how they live them, how they relate to other people and how they think about themselves. This reflection doesn't stop when the session is over, and those clients who continue to reflect on themselves between sessions often make the most progress in therapy.

The client can help themselves by starting to notice themselves in the midst of the difficulties that they experience in everyday living. If the client has a difficult relationship with someone, for example, it would be helpful for them to notice what happens when they are with that person. How does that person make the client feel? How does the client respond to the other person?

To start with, the client will follow their original pattern of relating to the other person. They might say, 'The same thing happened again. I was left feeling unheard and not able to get my point across.'

However, as the client discusses this relationship with their thera-pist and becomes more aware of themselves, they will begin to notice what happens when they relate to that person. They will come to a point where they might say, 'I realised what was happening this time, when X started getting angry with me. Although I ended up feeling the same, I noticed what was happening.'

Over time, that awareness will create a gap for the client, so that they are not just reacting to the other person but have created some space for themselves to think about how they will respond. Therefore, the client is helped to see how they have a choice and how they can respond differently. If they're able to break a pattern of relating, then they can make a change in their relationships.

The more clients are able to think about those issues that bring them to therapy and to begin to become more aware of themselves as they go about their everyday lives, the better the therapy will be. The client needs to become self-observant.

What qualities should a client look for in a therapist?

The success of therapy is often down to the relationship that is developed between the client and the therapist. Of course, the most important thing is for a client to find a therapist who is appropriately qualified, and who has been accredited by a professional body, such as UKCP or BACP (see page 309).

Clients might also seek out therapists who specialise in the area that they need to work on, which will help to narrow the choice down. After that, the choice of therapist will be an individual one. Clients need to find someone with whom they feel comfortable and to whom they will be able to open up.

It is important that clients are able to trust their therapists. The more the client can trust their therapist and the therapeutic process, the more open and honest they will be. Trust is something that will develop over time as the relationship between client and therapist grows. However, clients will probably have an initial sense on meeting their therapist for the first time whether they will be able to enter into a trusting relationship.

Some clients may feel it is easier to talk to a therapist with the same gender as themselves, and this may influence the client's choice. The therapist's way of working may also be important. Clients should think about the type of therapy that would suit them. Some therapeutic approaches are more directional and therapist-led, whereas others are client-led – and each will have an impact on how the session is conducted.

At the end of the day it is about whether the client feels they can get on with the therapist. It is not unusual for clients to have taster sessions with therapists so that they can get a sense of what therapy will be like with that person.

Are there people for whom existential therapy isn't suitable? If so, who?

Although the existential approach focuses on understanding human existence in all its complexity, and highlights the universal aspects of existence that we all share, it is not an approach for everyone. Clients are expected to think deeply about their lives.

This involves being open to the prospect of questioning themselves, and their values and beliefs. Clients in existential therapy will also need to accept responsibility for how they live their lives and their part in the relationships that they are in.

This open and questioning approach will not suit everyone. Some clients may want their therapist to tell them what is wrong with them or what they need to do in order to reduce their symptoms. Existential therapy will not help clients in this way. Having said that, most clients are interested in engaging with their struggles in greater depth. They enjoy the prospect of thinking about their lives differently and finding new purpose and meaning.

But this often comes about by accepting that life is a struggle that involves difficulties which have to be overcome, and suffering that needs to be made sense of. Existential therapy does not provide an easy solution to our problems, but by engaging with those problems in living and facing the realities of our existence we are able to live more meaningful lives as we connect to what really matters to us.

Do you ever get frustrated with clients if they are resistant to change or keep repeating the same unhelpful patterns?

Occasionally it can be frustrating when clients seem 'stuck' for whatever reason. They may be unable, or unwilling, to explore alternative perspectives or they end up repeating unhelpful patterns.

On those occasions, I look at what is causing my frustration. Is there a disconnect between what I want for my client and what my client wants? I would try and understand what is stopping my client from responding differently.

Sometimes it may be the case that the client is just not ready at this time in their life to make the changes that they need or want to. Or it may be that the client is struggling to accept the part they play in their life, and is unable to take responsibility for themselves and the life that they lead.

In these instances, I try to gain an alternative perspective on my client's life. I will reflect on possible blocks that the clients have which stop them making other choices and will challenge them about this.

It is always useful to tune in to the feelings that get evoked by our clients, as it tells us something about how other people experience them. It also tells us where their particular difficulties in life lie.

By confronting this 'stuckness', clients can acknowledge how they are making choices, how they choose to repeat unhelpful patterns, and what stops them from making choices which might be better for them.

What would you have done if you hadn't been a therapist?

I completed a bachelor's degree in Psychology, so I had already developed an interest in working in the helping professions. Although I toyed with the idea of working in market research for a while, I realised that a commercial setting was not where my interests lay.

Before training in psychotherapy, I had also been interested in health promotion, which looks at how psychology can increase awareness of health and lifestyle choices, and it was an area that I was considering specialising in.

However, I feel that I have found my perfect vocation. As a child, I was preoccupied by questions about our existence, about death and the universe. So to find a way of combining philosophy with helping people feels like a dream job!

If you could start life over, would you still have been a therapist?

This is a really tricky question to answer. The path we take in life is largely dictated by our experiences. If I had had less of an emphasis on academia growing up, then my more creative side might have been developed more. I have always had a fantasy of being a textile designer.

Having said that, I think I would have still chosen work as a therapist. I have a strong desire to help people and am passionate about social issues. The thing that I like about being a therapist is the flexibility that it gives you. You can develop a portfolio career, combining private practice, for example, with other types of work. Who knows, I might even fulfil my textile designing dream one day!

The client: Anonymous

'A good therapist trusts you as a fellow adult'

I think that for a lot of people, the shock of going to a good therapist is finding out how quiet they are. That they ask you questions rather than going, 'Right, this is what you're going to do.' I really like how gentle and non-judgemental good therapists can be. One of the hardest things about having experienced sexual abuse as a child is telling people about it in real life, because you have to deal with their reaction. They're horrified for you and they don't know what to say, and it makes you feel a bit of a freak.

To see a therapist who specialised in sexual abuse meant that what I was saying was something she'd heard a million times before. To someone who hasn't suffered abuse, that might sound awful, but you just want to be able to sort out your daily life. You want to be able to get up in the morning and have breakfast, and you don't want to walk around feeling like a freak, because that's the reason why you're having mental health problems in the first place.

The first time I had therapy, it was run by a charity and only lasted six weeks. When I look back and think of the huge amount of work my therapist achieved in just six weeks, I'm actually quite amazed. There was a lot of homework, nightly homework, which involved writing down my memories of the abuse. I was very little, and one of the difficulties with that is that you are never 100 per cent sure whether your memories are real or not, as a lot of people will say to you, 'Well you were obviously too young to remember it.' Then you'll say, 'Well, I do remember it.' And they say 'How?' And you say, 'I don't know.' So you're constantly second-guessing yourself.

My therapist very much encouraged me to stop doing that, to just write down everything I remembered. She'd say, 'If you're not sure if it's true or not, it doesn't matter.' To people on the outside, that might sound frightening, because you hear a lot of reports of people having false memories, maybe accusing people of false things . . . I've never seen it like that, maybe because I'm a responsible person or because she did it in a responsible way. It was more like detoxing, like vomiting out all of my fears about what might have happened to me.

Through having several different therapists, I know they all have a 'modality' and a thing they do, but I've always seen them as individuals, and all that matters is whether they're doing something to which I'm reacting well or badly – regardless of what they've studied. Looking back, my first therapist was so different to anyone else I've ever seen, I actually wonder whether she made her type of therapy up! She was quite political as well. Halfway through the therapy, she gave me this folder full of articles about sexual abuse – about the history of it, about how it fits into society, about stories that are in the news . . . She encouraged me to be active and see myself as part of a community.

She said that whatever it is I think of, write it down and get it out. I've taken what I call a 'buffalo' approach to my problems in that I've always had them all spread out in front of me, and I've picked through every tiny little aspect. I think that came from her. I feel like other people keep their problems in a backpack behind them until one of them reaches over and grabs them. Mine are like a big dead buffalo in front of me – one of them might start oozing, but I can see it and point at it and know that it needs to be dealt with.

After seeing my first therapist, I can remember short bursts of seeing bad therapists, and the reason that I never lost faith in it as a practice is because my first therapist had been so good. I knew that somewhere out there, there was another therapist like her.

A good therapist has an absolute lack of judgement and a calmness, and trusts you as a fellow adult. There's a natural hierarchy in that you are the insane person going to see the sane person, so the hierarchy doesn't need to be imposed by the therapist. Some therapists will put themselves above you – 'You are the client, I am the therapist, you are small and I am big and wise' – but actually, that can feel very oppressive.

For instance, one of my therapists didn't like me making jokes, because she said that was covering up emotions, but I'm old enough to know when a joke is covering my emotions and when it's helping my emotions. My current therapist will happily laugh at my jokes, and happily listen to my stories about my career, because she trusts me not to cover up my feelings for her, because we're in a working relationship.

The biggest negative of my current therapist is that it takes me an hour and a half on the train to get to her. I always arrive very calm and very sane because I've sat on a train doing admin or working for ninety minutes, so she never sees me at my most panicky or first thing in the morning when I wake up worrying about the world, or last thing at night when I'm like, 'Where is everybody, I need to talk', so I'm always worried that she doesn't have an accurate view of just how screwed-up I am!

It is also annoying how far away she is – yesterday the train was late and I missed fifteen minutes of my session – but she's great.

Therapists offer a service, and you have to understand when you go in for therapy that there are good therapists and bad therapists, just as there's good and bad in all professions. So if you're in therapy and it's really not working, then maybe that person isn't right for you.

I've had group therapy, couples therapy, hypnotherapy and a little bit of CBT (which I didn't like). My ex-therapist, who I left, was doing a different kind of therapy; my current therapist is officially an existentialist. The only difference that I've noticed between them is that my last therapist would use societal morality, judging whether what I was doing was good or bad according to societal norms, whereas my current therapist judges whether what I'm doing is good or bad depending on whether it's working for me.

So if I'm doing something that society would think is horrific, but it's not affecting my mental health or my ability to look after my children, she doesn't guide me away from it. Any therapist who sticks to their modality slavishly is not going to be a very good therapist, because people aren't robots and we don't fit into categories.

I sometimes worry that I like my therapist too much, and that I'll never leave. One benefit is that we both work weird hours, so there might be a three-week gap, or a four-week gap, but she accommodates that.

I see her kind of like a friend, but she's more stately and serious. There's something about her that says authority, even when she's not being authoritative; for example, even when we're sat on the sofa laughing about anal sex, there's still an authority about her. I take great enjoyment in saying things in a very blunt way, and I do sometimes say things that make her roll her eyes a bit, but then we have had very nourishing conversations. And there are moments I've had with her that have been life-changing.

In sunny weather, the sun shines directly on the chair where she usually sits opposite me, so she's started sitting next to me on the sofa. We have much better therapy sessions when she's sitting next to me. Sometimes we sit with both of our feet tucked up, facing each other. I said that I worry that in some ways it's too relaxed, but I feel a lot more open and I say things a lot more openly.

There is a tradition of a hierarchical thing, a man in a suit wearing glasses looking at you with a clipboard saying 'Hmmm' while you lie in a submissive posture. I much prefer it to be more equal, and as I said it's giving you back your ownership of working out your problems. It's not a teacher–pupil relationship, it's somebody facilitating an adult with pursuing their adult life.

I hope to stop seeing my therapist eventually. It will be me who ends it – I can't imagine her saying, 'You're all better.' I have had therapists tell me that they feel I'm ready to leave, but she doesn't see it in that way.

The difference once I started paying for therapy was that it makes me turn up. I have to give forty-eight hours' notice if I need to cancel. We had a Skype session which I paid for and if I'm having a panic attack I might text her saying, 'I'm really sorry but I don't know what else to do.' But the awareness that that conversation costs me money sometimes makes me stop and consider whether I *really* need to talk to her, or whether I can sort it out myself.

But then on the other side of it, a family member who is in a desperately bad situation has no money, and because his therapy is free it means he has to conform to being there at a certain time and only going for a number of weeks. He really needs intensive therapy and he needs to be able to get something that fits in with his lifestyle. What happened to him is not going to be cleared up in six weeks. I see it a lot in the mental health community I'm in, where women feel that they've only just cracked their problem at the point where the six weeks end.

The money aspect means that there is a line, that she's not my friend, we're not just having a chat. My therapist has never asked me how much my husband and I earn but she's quite frank about her money. She told me that she earns a very good living. One day we were chatting and I'd forgotten to pay her. I told her that I liked her and she said she liked me too, but could I pay her now? But that's part of her character and authority; she's quite deadpan.

I don't know what any of her hang-ups are. I think that's a good thing.

There was one day where I could tell that she was really tired and was zoning out a bit, but now that we sit on the sofa together our connection with each other has improved. She was only two yards away before, but it still makes a difference. I watched her with the sunlight on her face, melting away, and said, 'Do you want to come and sit over here?'

I talked once about what a shame it would be when we stop working together. She said it would be, but she's busy. She agreed with me though, she said she'd always be curious as to what I'm doing.

One big issue I brought into therapy was when we got a letter from the school saying that they would be doing sex education, and I thought I would be fine but I cried for three days. The thought of my innocent little girl even having the conversation felt like abuse. And there were no books – one of the projects that I want to do one day is to write a book for parents who were sexually abused as children, or even rape victims as adults, about how to talk to their children about sex, because there aren't any. I don't feel that I'm the most qualified, but maybe that's one thing my therapist and I could do together when I leave therapy.

As part of my buffalo approach, I sit down and think through what I want for my daughter, what I want my daughter to learn from how screwed-up my attitude to sex is and has been. What do I want her to take from this? She's known from quite a young age, because of the prosecution mainly, that a man hurt mummy when she was very little, and she learned that a man hurt mummy's vagina. It was at an age where she didn't associate that with anything other than violence, which is how society should regard it.

There are side issues that come up with sexuality but at the end of the day you're a child who's having part of their body attacked. There's this odd feeling that you're somehow complicit in this sexual act. It wasn't until a few months ago when the NSPCC came to do a talk at my daughter's school about sexual abuse and guarding yourself against it that she came home and was talking to me about it. I could feel myself getting emotional and I had this urge to say to her, 'Did it make you worry about me at all?' but she hadn't put two and two together.

Watching her make that connection was both painful and uplifting. She did it in a gradual way, and then her first response – bless her – was to laugh at the oddness of what she'd just worked out. She just looked at me and asked, 'Why would any adult want to do that?' That was such a wonderful question. Maybe I couldn't have had those discussions without having had therapy, because you've got to know where you are and what you think about what happened to you before you can talk to somebody else about it.

Other Humanistic Therapies

So these are therapies that aren't important enough to have their own section?

Let's just say they're less commonly used, so we're going to summarise a few of them together. Shall we start with transpersonal therapy?

Which must be for trans people?

It doesn't exclude them, but no. The term means 'beyond the personal', and the therapy aims to give clients a better understanding of themselves outside their own 'bubble'. The therapist will try to help you to see a broader picture of your existence by looking at several different aspects of it.

And what might those be?

There are many sides to our personalities. These might be intellectual, emotional, social, physical and spiritual. Instead of focusing on one of these at a time, the therapy looks to enhance the client's appreciation of all of these aspects at once.

I get confused if I think of more than one thing at once.

The therapist will help you with that. In transpersonal therapy the client is viewed as an equal, so the therapist will try to deeply connect with them to gain insight into their life. The goal is for the client to recognise their worth, harness their inner resources and channel them in the right way to achieve lasting benefits.

Lasting benefits sound good. How is it done?

The therapist will use a number of methods depending on their own judgement. These may include breathing exercises, journal writing, meditation and visualisation of life goals.

The emphasis is on positive experiences rather than looking at problems, and would be the most helpful to those who are finding it hard to appreciate life – namely those with anxiety, depression or addiction problems.

All right. What's next?

Next we have body therapy.

Do dead people need therapy, strictly speaking?

Ha ha. Body therapy's central belief is that the body and mind are interconnected, so any repressed feelings are reflected by tension in the body. Looking after the body can therefore bring improved mental wellbeing.

What, so the therapist just tells you to go for a jog? Doesn't sound much like therapy to me.

It's not quite that simple. You might be asked to look at your posture, movement and breathing as part of reaching an awareness of how your body works. There won't necessarily be any physical contact from the therapist – it's more about getting the client to understand their body's processes and its energy flow.

That sounds a bit sketchy. Are you sure this is proper therapy?

It's perhaps more accepted than it once was, but body therapy is still considered to be somewhat controversial. Some people will buy into it, others won't.

What else do we have?

Next we have transactional analysis.

Counselling for when you see your girlfriend's credit card bill, no doubt.

Very droll. It's based on the idea that we have three ego states – child, adult and parent. The child ego state is when we defer to what we learned as children in terms of thoughts, feelings and behaviour; the adult state is the more rational responses that aren't informed by the past, and the parent state is what we were taught by our parents and other influential characters. 'Transactions' refer to the interactions that occur between these ego states when we communicate with others.

You've lost me already. Can I have an example?

Well, you might automatically behave in a certain way because of things you were taught as a child, consciously or otherwise. This might be having an adverse effect on your current relationships. Transactional analysis looks at recognising these automatic responses and retraining the brain to think differently.

Sounds like CBT.

There are certainly similarities, but transactional analysis is more focused on communication and has its roots in psychoanalysis. It aims to promote greater use of the rational adult ego state and recon-struction of the child ego state in those who feel their progress is being hampered by elements from their past.

Can we have an easier one next?

166

Fine. How about solution-focused brief therapy?

Is it solution-focused and brief?

Yes. This one can last for as few as five sessions, so it's well named. Instead of spending lots of time delving into the past or planning gradual changes, this therapy looks at what you can do straight away with the resources that you already have.

So it's like seeing what you can buy at the cake shop with the change in your pocket rather than having to save up?

Yes, if you like. The first session will be an assessment of where you are and what you want to achieve, then your therapist will try to come up with a plan.

The other day I fancied an éclair but only had enough for an iced bun.

In that scenario, your therapist would help you to accept that the éclair was out of your reach and focus instead on getting the bun and enjoying it as much as you possibly could. Perhaps you used to have a lot more money and would buy three éclairs every day, but it would be important to not look back with regrets and make the best of the way things are now.

But what if you only had enough for a bag of crumbs? No one's going to be happy with that.

I think we're stretching the analogy a little now. But it's important for the client to accept their limitations in order for the therapy to work. That doesn't mean being pessimistic, just realistic enough not to expect results that are out of their short-term reach.

So this one isn't for people with major problems then. I mean, bigger problems than not having an éclair.

No, and your therapist would be able to tell you straight away if you weren't a suitable candidate for brief therapy. But if your problem is less serious, and time and money are an issue, it might be worth exploring.

I'm hungry now. What's next?

Psychodrama.

I think my ex does that.

Very funny. This one uses drama in a group setting to resolve problems.

Does it have to be in a group setting? I don't like other people.

Sorry – psychodrama is always done in a group. It examines life situations from the perspective of the past, present or future.

'Life situations'?

If you were involved, you would act out hypothetical situations based on the lives of the people in the group. Every week you would take the story of one of the members and dramatise it with the aim of resolving the issues for that person.

So if you're chosen first, why would you bother turning up for the other sessions?

Just because you might be acting out someone else's situation doesn't mean you won't learn anything – especially if the group members have similar problems to you. It would be hoped that everyone involved would form a supportive network where they could share the benefits of their own experience and offer new insights.

It sounds more like a theatre group than therapy.

It's not all acting – there will be an acting phase and a sharing phase. In the latter, the members of the group will reflect with the therapist on what happened during the session. This element will feel more like normal group therapy.

Fair enough. Are we done now?

No, there's one more in this section – personal construct theory.

Ooh. That sounds complicated.

It was developed by a man called George Kelly in the 1950s. He suggested that we all have beliefs and expectations about situations that we find ourselves in, based on past experience and intuition. He referred to these beliefs as constructs.

So one person's construct might be totally different from another person's?

Exactly. Two people can experience the same event in very different ways, or have differing opinions on, say, a piece of music.

That's obvious enough. How does it relate to therapy?

Kelly believed that all of our constructs had opposite extremes, and that we rate everything we do along a sliding scale between those points. He thought that we did this at a very low level of consciousness, but used a system called a repertory grid to analyse these responses in a therapeutic setting.

What's a repertory grid?

The grid has four parts. The first is the main topic – the thing that's being analysed. Then there will be elements of that topic, which is just a breakdown of its different parts. Next you would list the constructs – the beliefs that are held about the topic, each with its own opposite extremes. Finally there will be a space to rate each construct along its scale from one to five.

Like a customer satisfaction survey?

If you like. The therapist will then analyse the grid and look for patterns that might need to be addressed.

So if this chat was a construct, and I had to rate it somewhere between 'amazing' and 'terrible' . . .

I'd rather not know the answer to that.

The client: Jean Hannah Edelstein

'I felt as if I'd been wearing a hat made of cement, and taken it off'

What first prompted you to seek therapy?

I was first diagnosed with severe clinical depression aged fourteen and had some limited therapy – about six months of it – which was then followed by many years on antidepressants. The therapy I had then didn't do much for me – I found it boring, and I think the therapist found me a bit inscrutable. I recall making up a story about how I didn't get along with my brother, which wasn't really true, because it seemed like the kind of material that the therapist wanted from me.

I started therapy as an adult when I was nearing twenty-eight. My first book had been published and I was astonished by how unhappy I was – real joylessness about something that had been a long-term dream. The real trigger – the final straw, so to speak – was a very brief relationship, wherein I woke up one morning and realised that the situation I was in really bore no resemblance to the kind of relationship that I wanted.

A close friend who I loved and trusted spoke in very positive terms about the therapist she was seeing, and so I made an appointment. I was sceptical, but also anxious to investigate what was causing my prolonged unhappiness and difficulty in relationships – I suspected that I had locked a lot of things up over the years which were now interfering with my happiness.

I felt empowered to have made the decision to go. (Sorry, now that I live in America I use words like 'empowered' without irony, very embarrassing.)

You joke, but also make an interesting point about the differences between the UK and US: therapy seems to be more accepted and accept- able in America, and there seems to be less of a stigma surrounding it. Do you feel comfortable saying to friends that you're off to see your therapist?

Therapy is less stigmatised in the US than in the UK, but it's still pretty heavily stigmatised. Stigma is very much affected by class and race, too – for instance, white middle-class New Yorkers are pretty relaxed about talking about how they're in therapy, but in my experi- ence, people outside that group are often less so.

As far as I know, for example, no one in my immediate family has ever had any kind of long-term therapy, and when I've suggested it to them, especially after my father died and we were all understand- ably distraught, they were resistant or dismissive that it would help them. They're happy that I find it useful but don't seem to believe it could help them, too (one therapist told me that this is a case of me being the 'identified patient' in the family).

I'm comfortable to talk about it with friends, but in general I wouldn't tell colleagues who I don't consider friends about being in therapy (I'm not in therapy at the moment, by the way). I'm conscious of the risk of discrimination if people perceive me to have mental health issues. I don't feel that it's necessary for me to do the emotional labour at work to persuade people of the value of therapy, but among my friends I am very open about it and have referred many of them to my original therapist in London.

At our last appointment, as I was leaving, my therapist said, 'A few people have mentioned your name to me, thank you,' and I said,

'Do I get a discount?' He said 'No,' which made me very happy – so ethical of him!

He sounds awesome (though I'm sorry about the lack of discount!) Other than being ethical, what else did you like about his approach to therapy that led you to recommend him?

The main thing that I liked about him is that he was a total blank slate – he never showed any judgement of or emotional reaction to anything that I said, which gave me the freedom to discuss issues that I had never articulated before, because I was too concerned about how friends or family would react.

I'm hyper-sensitive to other people's feelings – I call it extreme empathy, and it can be very destructive, as it makes me feel responsible for everyone's emotions. So talking to someone who showed no emotion was perfect for me.

This, coupled with his incisive and thoughtful questions, made it possible for me to address and release some issues that I'd carried for years.

I used to describe the way I felt when leaving therapy: as if I'd been wearing a hat made of cement, and taken it off.

In contrast, I was seeing a therapist in New York for a bit last year, but had to quit after he told me that it was very important to him that I liked him. I found that unacceptably needy of him!

I love that analogy about the hat of cement. And it's interesting that his lack of reaction was what made it so easy to talk to him. When researching this book, I asked friends for questions I could answer about therapy, and the journalist Kate Copstick replied, 'What is the fucking point? Why not just find a friend and talk?'

Perhaps part of the reason is that friends can react so emotionally to things – and they can judge you and jump into your thinking space with their suggestions for what you should do (and refuse to accept your way of doing things). Also, they often tell other people all your stuff! Whereas therapy is, or should be, the opposite of that – a private, confidential time and space for you to think and reflect and find your own answers, without the complications of judgement or emotion.

Would you say these are the main differences between friendship and therapy (other than, hopefully, that you don't have to pay your friends)?

Yes – as I said before, I tend to get overwhelmed by a sense of responsibility for other people's feelings, so it was really never possible for me to talk about my darkest thoughts with friends, for fear that it would be too upsetting for them to hear. In particular, some of the more existential anxieties that I was dealing with were not things that a friend could assist with – for example, if I expressed concern that I would never find a partner, a friend would say, 'Oh, you're great! You'll be fine', whereas my therapist would say: 'Why do you feel that way?' which was actually much more productive.

Privacy was important, too – in therapy I was never concerned that my therapist would use anything I said against me, whereas with family and friends there's always a risk that they'll gossip to other people or cite something that you've said in confidence when you're in a conflict about something else.

Lastly, how would you say therapy has changed you?

I think this is an important distinction and one that people who are therapy-averse might find useful, as I think that folks who fear it often do so in part because they have a belief that it will brainwash them in some way (the other reason I think that people fear it is that they will actually confront their feelings, which is not an unfounded fear, but one that's best gotten over).

I guess you could say that I've always had quite a high level of emotional intelligence about other people but therapy was a tool that has helped me to dramatically increase my emotional intelligence about myself. This, in turn, has helped me move through life with greater ease – in particular through being able to identify and quell negative thought patterns.

Thanks to the empowerment of therapy, I came off medication for the first time in fifteen years. To be clear, I have used antidepressants again since then – I am not anti-medication by any means, but now use it on a more short-term basis, rather than as a permanent treatment. When I was a teenager, a psychiatrist shrugged and said, 'Well, you'll just have to be on this for the rest of your life,' and for a long time that opinion was why I didn't investigate therapy. So, I'm glad that I did and I'm glad that I now feel I use medication thoughtfully rather than as a default.

Family/Systemic Therapy

So which is it? Family or systemic?

Family therapy might be the more familiar name for it, but it's also known as systemic therapy – so-called because it was adapted from systems theory, which looks at how things work together in nature and society. In the therapeutic sense, it looks at family relationships and how they can be improved.

Right. I'd better take notes for this one.

How we relate to our family members is regarded as an important part of our mental wellbeing. Since we can't choose who we're related to, tensions are common and often complicated.

I know. I don't communicate very well with my brother.

Perhaps you could persuade him to try therapy with you?

I doubt it. I haven't spoken to him for three years.

Well, of course, all the affected parties have to agree to the therapy. Forcing someone to be there isn't likely to produce good results.

Are the sessions just for two people?

Not necessarily. The therapist will have their own guidelines for how many people they're willing to see, but it's possible that they could use a co-worker if there are several people involved in the session. This colleague might have an active role, or just quietly monitor how it's going and contribute as necessary.

Would fourteen family members be too many? I'm . . . asking for a mate of mine.

Yes, that's probably too many even for two therapists to handle. Perhaps you could break it down into smaller groups. I mean, your friend could.

Right. Too many fights to split up. Are the sessions the same length as for individual therapy?

Sessions can be as short as fifty minutes or as long as ninety, depending on your therapist and the nature of the help required. As ever, these details will be agreed at the start.

Does it take long? My uncle's court case is up in a few weeks and we're not sure how it's going to go.

Family therapy is geared towards fast results, so there could be as few as six sessions. It's recognised that people are unlikely to maintain family therapy for months on end.

It could end up causing more arguments than it solves.

Family therapy isn't just about resolving arguments. It might be that factors such as illness, divorce or addiction are causing stress and affecting communication. The therapist is an impartial mediator who will establish how things can be improved and how the family works.

My mum keeps telling me I should work.

I'm sure she wants the best for you.

The therapist: Rachel Lewis

'Be prepared to leave your comfort zone'

How would you describe family therapy to someone who has never had it?

Family therapy is an opportunity for individuals or families to address issues that are important to their family. Through family therapy each person finds new ways to express themselves. They can come to new understandings about their relationships with each other.

They can learn what matters most to each member of the family and can develop shared goals or values. This can help them gain the energy, commitment and team spirit to tackle problems head-on and to find new solutions.

What does a typical family therapy session entail?

There is no such thing as a typical family therapy session. Just as family members can be different from one another, so family therapy can vary quite a lot too. Some family therapy approaches like to talk about the 'problem', while some only like to talk about solutions.

Some approaches use non-verbal forms of expression such as role play or art. Others use lots of talk and family discussion. However, whatever the approach of the therapist, there are certain ways of recognising that you are in family therapy. You will notice, for example, that every family member is being invited to contribute.

Everyone's input is valued, especially those who don't tend to voice themselves much in the family. The therapist works to make sure that no one feels blamed. As a result, each person comes away with a greater sense of togetherness, and a greater sense that all are sharing in either the understanding of the problem or the development of a solution.

What can a client do to help themselves during family therapy?

It helps to keep an open mind and to be prepared to leave your comfort zone. Family therapy offers new ways for families to engage with each other and to communicate. This may feel a little odd at first, as you try out new ways of saying, doing or listening.

However, never be afraid to ask questions about what is going on. Family therapists tend to be open and transparent. They like to make sure that everyone is on board and that no one is feeling at a loss or left out.

What should a client consider before having family therapy?

Think about what each family member might gain if things changed for the better in your family. Ask yourself who in your family might be most reluctant to attend therapy and try to figure out what their concerns might be. With the therapist, you may be able to come up with ways of talking about the therapy so that everyone feels welcome and hopeful about attending.

Are there people for whom family therapy isn't suitable? If so, who?

Family therapy is not a good idea while there is domestic abuse going on in a family. If you are at the receiving end of abuse then you need time away from the abuse to process what is happening, and support in ensuring safety for yourself and your loved ones.

If you are perpetrating abuse then you need individual support in understanding your actions and their consequences. You need help in finding other ways of responding to difficulties in your life.

How do you ensure that all participants in family therapy are heard equally?

I am always curious to get to know everyone and to understand their perceptions. I use techniques that are aimed at engaging all family members and I adapt my approach to make sure that everyone has an opportunity to express themselves. If there are young children this can mean including play therapy techniques with little miniature figures, puppets or pen and paper.

Generally, once individuals settle into family therapy, they tend to notice a new energy in approaching family communication and can feel emboldened to express themselves in ways they have not done before.

What do you enjoy most about practising therapy?

Family therapy can surprise and energise me and it can often be very moving. Time and again, new families will come into my office, locked into patterns of communication that have served them for years. Through ingrained patterns of interaction, they have become used to only showing certain sides of themselves.

As things start to change, I begin to see each family member in a new way. It feels empowering, hopeful and like an incredible privilege to be invited to bear witness to such change.

How much personal information do you disclose to clients?

It's impossible not to disclose. Every smile, gesture or turn of phrase gives something of myself away. I don't tend to go to any lengths to hide aspects of myself. In fact, I try to be open and honest because I think that it helps clients feel more at ease.

I do think, however, that I'm there to hear about them and their lives. If I spent the hour talking about my own personal experiences, I would worry that I was wasting their time and money.

If you could start life over, would you still have been a therapist?

I have tried my hand at teaching. I have also engaged in psychological research. However, nothing gives me the same feeling that family therapy does. It has taught me about human resilience and about the power of relationships to support positive change.

What would you have done if you hadn't been a therapist?

I enjoy research and hope to continue my work in exploring how couples manage closeness on the autism spectrum.

The client: Francesca Baker

'My family felt that they were being blamed at times'

I had family therapy in hospital, while being treated for anorexia. I was used to therapy, having had various kinds for ten years, so found the process of discussing ideas and questioning things perfectly normal, but I know my family found it hard and felt that they were being blamed at times.

I think, in this kind of situation, parents worry that they should or could be able to help more – all parents want their child to be well – and so it was a natural feeling that was compounded by their experience. My younger brother wouldn't come, and my younger sister came once, but felt uncomfortable.

Despite this, I would say that family therapy was helpful, as it made all of my family engage in dialogue about 'bigger' things than we may have done previously. For me, it was never about finding a cause or root of my anorexia; instead, it was about empowering us as a family to fight a terrifying and malicious disease.

Group Therapy

Is this for when there aren't enough therapists to go around?

Group therapy is for small groups of people with similar problems who can support and learn from one another. It was developed in the USA in the early 1900s by Joseph Pratt, Trigant Burrow and Paul Schilder.

How many people are in these groups?

Typically between eight and twelve, with one therapist overseeing everything.

Why would anyone want that? Surely the more people there are, the less attention each one is going to get.

The idea is to create a trusting and supportive environment with people who can relate to your situation. It's true that you won't always be talking, and there may be sessions where you don't talk at all, but for many people it's beneficial just to know that they're not alone. Hearing others' stories and how they have dealt with their challenges can be therapeutic in itself.

I've seen on telly where someone stands up and introduces themselves and everyone else claps.

That's usually for addiction groups, but group therapy can work for a number of different problems. The shared experience between group members is the important thing. Hearing something from a therapist may be helpful, but hearing it from someone who has lived through the same experience as you might have more impact.

The flipside of that is that they may be less tactful when responding to you, so you might want to be prepared for that if you're sensitive.

Is it difficult to get into group therapy?

Groups can be open or closed, but because it's an intimate environment where trust is crucial, members may be asked to commit to a certain number of sessions. If people could come and go as they pleased, that sense of community would be lost.

It's not always possible to keep the same people, of course, but any changes are likely to be gradual rather than turning up and finding a totally new set of members. That would be somewhat disconcerting and against the spirit of group therapy.

I'm just thinking that if someone quiet and shy like me turns up, they might get dominated by the others.

The therapist will try to ensure that everybody gets a chance to speak, if indeed they would like to. Any group will have natural leaders and it may take a while for some to feel comfortable enough to contribute, but it's up to the individual. The therapist may encourage bonding by using group exercises.

Running on the spot?

No, I mean trust exercises.

Oh, I did one of those at college once – the other person had to fall backwards and I was asked to catch them.

That's the kind of thing, yes. How did it work out for you?

I was replying to a text and they cracked their head on the floor.

Well when trust exercises are done properly, they can be a good ice-breaker.

Rather than a skull-breaker?

Yes. They work, as it's much easier to open up to others if you feel a sense of camaraderie with them, although no one will be forced to take part in the trust exercises if they don't want to.

What if I wanted to do both group therapy and individual therapy? Is that allowed?

Of course. Some people might start off in one-to-one therapy and move on to a group, or vice versa. Your therapist may be able to help you find something suitable. If you decide that you find both valuable, you can absolutely do that. The only limits are your time and finances.

Isn't group therapy much cheaper though? Don't you divvy the fee up between the members?

There are no set rates, but it may be less expensive than individual therapy. Everyone still has to pay in full. The sessions are likely to be longer though – some can be up to two hours.

So do people end up making friends and going on holiday together?

You may find that members are discouraged from socialising outside the group. It's a bit like the relationship you have with your therapist – it works better if it's professional and you don't know too many details about their life. If people become friends, it's more difficult to be honest with them.

Maybe that's why I feel I can be honest with you.

Erm, thanks.

The therapist: Liz McLure

'Curiosity is encouraged'

How would you describe group therapy to someone who has never had it?

There are several different models of group therapy, group analysis being one of them. Group therapy is based on the view that deep and lasting change can occur within a carefully constituted group whose combined membership reflects wider society.

The more difference the group can tolerate, the better the experience. The group provides a supportive and challenging opportunity for individuals to explore past and present difficulties, and to understand themselves and their relationships more deeply in order to change unfulfilling aspects of their lives.

The group may be 'slow open', where new members join when someone leaves, or 'closed', where members meet for a specified period of time.

What does a typical group therapy session entail?

The group meets for ninety minutes at the same time and place on a regular basis. Up to eight members sit facing each other in a circle. There is no set agenda – it is up to group members to bring things in.

A primary goal of the group is to work towards increasingly open, frank and meaningful communication. Given time and the development of mutual trust, most members will find that it is possible to share intimate matters with the group which they may have previously withheld for reasons of embarrassment or fear.

The therapist is called a conductor. They will only intervene to pass on important information or to offer an interpretation to facilitate the therapeutic process.

What can a client do to help themselves during group therapy?

Be as open and honest about your personal experience as you can be in the group. Be prepared to listen and to share. Curiosity is encouraged. Try to be tolerant of others until you know why whatever they do that bugs you gets under your skin.

You don't have to constantly be active. Much of what you learn in a group is vicarious. Endeavour to attend all groups on time – absence and lateness are disruptive to the group and the reasons for this will be explored. If you know you are going to be absent, discuss it in the group, and if you can't be there at short notice, let the conductor know.

What should a client consider before joining a therapy group?

There will be a comprehensive assessment with the conductor and perhaps some preparatory sessions. Remember: this is your opportunity to assess the conductor to decide if this is right for you. You will be asked to give a commitment to stay in the group for at least three months. You can stay for as long as you need to be there.

When you leave, you must give notice to allow you and the group to work through the ending. Group members do not meet up outside the group, as this interferes with the course of therapy. Chance meetings are brought to the group for discussion.

The group is of course confidential to those within it. Therapy can change your life and the way you view all relationships. If possible, it is useful to have support from friends and family to allow you to change and grow.

Are there people for whom group therapy isn't suitable? If so, who?

Groups can be daunting for some, often those who would benefit from them! If, however, you are prone to psychosis or are in crisis and perhaps self-harming, or if you have uncontrolled substance misuse, then a slow open group may not be right for you at this time.

Some individual work or medical intervention to control substance misuse may need to come first. There are other types of groups specifically focused and tailored to meet your requirements, and your therapist can advise you on this.

People who can't cope with the intimacy of one-to-one therapy often do well in groups, especially if there are others 'like them' in the group.

How do you ensure that all participants in the group are heard equally?

If a member of the group is silent most of the time, the conductor will judge whether to 'bring them in' and invite them to speak. Often other group members will notice and do this too. When there is conflict, all parties are invited to present their point of view without attributing blame or stating who is wrong or right.

Often, others say the thing that is on your mind and you don't feel the need to speak. Sometimes someone will try to dominate the group, and they and the group will be encouraged to think what this may be an expression of and help the person to moderate their input.

What do you enjoy most about practising therapy?

I like people. It's an honour to be part of someone's therapeutic journey. People become more beautiful when they can have a good enough relationship with themselves – this in turn makes for better relationships with others.

It takes the whole group to help to make this journey. I also work with individuals, and employ a group perspective in exploring their lives.

How much personal information do you disclose to clients?

A lot of information is 'out there' and visible to all. They observe me in action in the group, therefore I am already 'known' at some level. What is going on in my life, I keep private if possible.

If I need to be absent, I occasionally say why, but this depends on the circumstance and the group. I consider whether this will get in the way of the therapy, or if it will be too anxiety-provoking to leave the group fantasising about it.

I do sometimes share my feelings, especially if they have been elicited by something going on in the group that is being ignored.

If you could start life over, would you still have been a therapist?

This is a difficult question, as I was in teaching and nursing before becoming a therapist. I was the 'listener and carer' in my family, so was already pre-destined to continue in this vein.

Becoming a therapist allowed me to use all the skills and knowledge that I accrued over the years. It just seemed like a natural progression. I also benefited greatly from the six years of personal group analysis during the course of my training.

What would you have done if you hadn't been a therapist?

At sixteen I had notions of becoming a motor mechanic, but my dad wouldn't let me leave school. I was in a phase of following on with the things that I enjoyed doing with Dad (that didn't take much analysing in therapy).

I have a tendency to be promoted into teaching or management roles, so I suspect I would still have been in charge of something! I am currently self-employed.

The client: John Crace

'There were questions like "Have you felt like killing yourself today?"'

What kinds of therapy have you tried?

I started off exploring all the therapy options – I tried just about everything. Psychoanalysis, CBT, couples therapy . . . I'm currently doing group therapy once a week. There are people there with addiction problems and people who just can't cope.

I've been in this group for about fifteen years now, though of course various people have come and gone. There are times when you go along each week and think, 'Why am I here?', because life's ticking along quite nicely, but invariably something comes along to kick you in the teeth and you remember exactly why you're there.

You have all these support mechanisms, a series of safety nets, to try to mitigate the emotional and mental collapse.

How did you get on with CBT?

It didn't work for me, partly because my therapist seemed more anxious than I was! They kept having these mood scores for how you're feeling each day, and I can remember there were questions like 'Have you felt like killing yourself today?', and to me that was a frequent thought. I can't imagine not having it. It's not frightening, but it's there as a thought, a suggestion, a possibility throughout.

Despite that, I never felt that suicide was a serious option; in a way, that made my depression worse. I felt that other people had options whereas I knew I was going to have to see it through. I'd had serious drug problems long before the depression came in, and when I cleaned up there was a moment of realisation that I wanted to live more than I wanted to die.

I don't think I've ever lost that sense of wanting to live. I have two grown-up kids and I don't feel that I could do that to them. I just can't go there.

You told me that therapy can be hit-and-miss. Can you describe a bad experience you've had in therapy?

The worst one was when I was in psychoanalysis, and that's what put me in a mental hospital the first time. I was seeing the therapist three times a week, lying on the couch, and she just didn't seem to get that I was in absolute crisis. Her only view was that I should perhaps come four times a week, and that all of my feelings were about some kind of suppressed anger or love for her. It was like the whole therapy was about her rather than me.

And your best therapeutic experience?

I think with my present therapist, the group therapist, which is one of the reasons I've been there for so long. She's very empathetic but she also has a great sense of humour. I did see her one-on-one about thirty years ago but then went back to see her for group therapy on the back of my bad psychoanalysis experience.

By then I'd come out of the mental hospital and turned my back on CBT. I feel that she knows me, when to press and niggle at something, or when to back off and leave it a week or two.

What happens in group therapy?
The sessions are an hour and twenty minutes long because there are eight of us. People just talk about whatever they want to. What I like about it is that it's quite demanding. Firstly, it's not just about me – there are seven other people's lives that you're remembering and being involved in.

Also, I think that you can get very locked in and used to a way of relating to a therapist, so some things can get hidden at times, whereas in group therapy you've got these other people coming at you with thoughts and ideas, so everyone will react to what you say in a different way.

You can end up with six pieces of bland feedback but then there's one comment that's absolutely spot-on. It can be quite painful, because people are very honest. It's not like a tea support group.

If you're being annoying to people and they notice that you've got a way of relating that's unpleasant, they react to it. It's useful because if there's something at work that you need to get done, you might realise that you're going about it the wrong way.

Did you find it more constructive to have group therapy than one-on-one?

Not initially. I now feel that when you first go into therapy you have a lot of childhood stuff to go through, things about your parents, but I don't feel as though there are any big surprises about my life that I've yet to uncover. It's all an open book. So in a way, therapy is more about an ongoing dialysis if you like, processing things and making sure that my childhood stuff doesn't have an adverse effect on the present.

Some people take the view that if you get to the end you can heal yourself, make yourself whole again and there will be no more need for therapy. I don't take that view. I look on my psychiatric condition as an ongoing problem. I'm not suddenly going to become a different person who's better adjusted just because I understood that my mother was a hopeless case at times.

In terms of how the group therapy is structured, does everybody get an equal amount of time or is there more time for those who need it?

It's entirely self-regulating. There are times when the therapist may move the process along, as though we've gone far enough with something, and occasionally she'll try to bring someone in because they're being quiet. You never know if someone is being quiet because they've got nothing to say, or if they have so much to say that they don't quite know how to articulate it. So she'll try to make the space for them.

Do you ever go along thinking that you've got nothing to say this week, so you'll just listen to other people?

Yes; sometimes that's correct, but sometimes I'd find that I had lots to say but just needed the right catalyst. You have to trust the people, which is partly down to the skill of the therapist in putting together a group that will work and not just thinking that she's got eight patients who could use some group therapy and throwing them all together.

I think she thinks quite hard, when someone leaves the group, about whether to replace them and with whom. It's not just a case of the next person on the waiting list – it's carefully curated.

What is the mix of people like?

We're all over forty. It's 50:50 male to female, there are various ethnicities, but in terms of age and experience I don't think it would work if there were members in their twenties. She's also chosen people who've been in therapy for a while. By dint of your age, if you're in your early twenties then you won't have been in therapy for very long.

Do people break down and ask for help, or is everyone relatively stable on the outside?

I don't think we've got anyone in major crisis at the moment. There have been times when people have been through divorce, or serious illness, and they might break down and cry but it's not seen as a particularly big deal. It's fine. If the therapist is aware of someone in crisis mode, she offers them a chance to see her one-to-one, so it's not a sink-or-swim scenario.

Do you ever socialise outside the group?

No, that's part of the understanding, although you kind of know these people in a way that you don't know others; I probably know more about them than some of their partners do. But conversely I also know next to nothing about them – that's the deal. At times it feels constricting because you might think, 'I really like this person, it would be nice to spend some time with them.'

There are moments where I've invited them to a book launch, or attended a funeral with them, so it's not like you have to avoid them at all costs, but what group therapy has to avoid is the members having special relationships. If there were two or three people who suddenly became best mates it would just be weird, especially if they developed allegiances.

You have therapy before you go to work on Wednesdays. Do you feel better on those days?

It depends on how the group has been – sometimes it feels like everyone has just skimmed over the surface, but other times it feels really intense and you feel bonded afterwards. At other times, I'm distracted because I know I've got a big work day ahead, and I haven't been able to engage in the group quite as much as I would have liked to. Life can get in the way.

Are there ever times when you skip it?

Yes. I have to skip it during party conferences, and I had to miss it for seven weeks during the election campaign. Luckily our therapist is quite flexible. I've heard of groups where not turning up is considered to be a crime! There are some groups where I think I'd have been asked to leave because I wasn't there enough. Thankfully that doesn't apply to my group.

You must have to get up very early to make the sessions before work.

6 a.m. I drive there, because I think that getting public transport there would mean getting up at 5.30 a.m. and it would be very difficult. I get up at 7 a.m. the rest of the week. It does take a special effort, but I see it as an investment in my own psyche.

The sessions are £30 each, which sounds reasonable, but as it's group therapy she makes £240 from everyone for an hour and twenty minutes. I must have spent tens of thousands of pounds on therapy over the past thirty years, but it's a wider investment than just being able to cope and form relationships with people.

I feel that it informs my writing as well; it gives me insights. As a political sketch writer, much of my job is observing. I'm not there to report the news, I'm there to think about the subtext of what politicians are saying and the way they're saying it – the dynamics of government. Those insights give my writing an immediacy, so hopefully people read it and find it real.

Relationship Therapy

I don't need to guess what relationship therapy is about, do I?

I hope not. As you'd expect, it's therapy for people who are having relationship problems.

My girlfriend keeps suggesting that we try it. She doesn't like it when I talk to other women.

Well, a relationship therapist would give you both a chance to air your views, and try to improve communication between you. Jealousy is a common problem, so the therapist would try to establish why your girlfriend feels that way and give you a chance to respond.

Oh, I know why she doesn't like it. It's because the other women are in strip clubs.

I'll leave that one with you, shall I? The therapist is there to offer a neutral viewpoint, which is very important. When couples are having difficulties they often seek advice from friends and family, but they're rarely impartial and so it's not very helpful. Relationship therapy is about seeing things from the other person's perspective and talking about things before arguments can develop.

But what if my girlfriend kicks me in the balls during a session? Will the therapist wrestle her to the ground?

That's not really in their remit. They're far more likely to try to defuse the situation and encourage more productive expressions of dissatisfaction. The goal is to make both parties more empathetic of their partner's feelings and needs so that flashpoints are less likely to arise.

Sometimes I quite enjoy a good row.

It's normal to have disagreements in relationships, and they don't necessarily indicate that you need therapy, but if they're making one or both parties miserable it can be a good option – even if the problems are long-standing.

What if you haven't been together very long? Are you still allowed in?

There are no criteria – it's for anyone who thinks they could benefit from it. Relationship therapy is often thought of as a last resort, but it can be preventative too. Some people might do it even if their problems aren't too serious just to keep on the right track.

Does it cost double as there are two of you to sort out?

The cost will vary, as with other therapies. You might pay a little more, but the sessions are also likely to be a little longer to give you both a chance to express your views.

How long does it take to fix a relationship?

Sorry to be vague, but it depends on the problems and the attitude of those involved. If one partner is a reluctant participant, progress might be slower. There's no time limit though, and your therapist will encourage you to assess your progress at regular intervals.

I think I might just find a new girlfriend. Seems easier.

She might like that solution.

Anything else?

I just wanted to run through another related treatment called EFT, which stands for emotionally focused therapy, and also looks to improve relationships.

Does it use a different approach?

It's similar, but as you might expect, there's more emphasis on each partner's emotional response. It was created in the 1980s by a Canadian psychologist called Sue Johnson, who wanted to help people resolve their relationship issues by encouraging them to connect on an emotional level.

She based it on something called attachment theory, which states that people rely on emotional contact with others and are healthier when they have it.

When you say emotional contact, do you just mean crying in front of each other and stuff?

As ever, it's not quite that simple. One of the key concepts is that relationship difficulties are caused by insecurities; one or both partners might be uncertain about how the other feels. The therapy seeks to address this in order to promote stronger bonds. It's more than just listening to each other, it's about understanding and appreciating each other's emotional needs.

I cry quite a lot, but only because my football team isn't very good. So how does the therapist go about all this change?

To begin with, they would sit down with both parties and try to identify the issues that are causing concern. These are likely to be things that crop up again and again rather than one-off flashpoints. There would then be a three-stage approach to resolving the problem.

What's first?

The first stage is called de-escalation. This is to identify problems and stop them from growing by reducing unhelpful interactions between the couple. The therapist will try to establish whether there are emotional requirements and attachments that are causing the conflict.

Then what?

Stage two would allow each party to voice their emotional needs and acknowledge those of their partner. Each would get equal time to talk about this in a trusting environment.

And stage three would fix it all?

The therapist would teach the couple new skills to help them communicate better and suggest solutions that they might try. The couple would aim to use what they'd learned so that they have a firm basis from which to work after the therapy has ended.

Sounds straightforward enough.

Actually, there is some potential for confusion where EFT is concerned.
    There is another therapy with a very similar name, but which is quite different. It's called emotion-focused therapy, and is also shortened to EFT.

You're right, I'm confused. How can it be different?

Emotion-focused therapy tends to deal with individuals rather than couples. It was developed by another Canadian psychologist called Leslie Greenberg.

Are Canadian women just particularly emotional?

No, because Leslie Greenberg is a man. He had the belief that emotions are a key part of our identity as individuals and have a large impact on our decision-making processes. His version of EFT aims to help people understand and control their emotions, which doesn't specifically address relationships but could help an individual to improve theirs by making them more reflective and empathetic.

I don't know how I'm going to remember the difference between EFT and . . . EFT.

I wouldn't worry yourself too much. Just remember that there are two and that you should check which one you're being offered before you start.

Thanks for that. It's been emotional.

The therapist: Kate Moyle

'Sadly, some couples do leave it too late'

What happens in a relationship therapy session?

The content of sessions is completely couple-dependent, as the goal of therapy is to create change, and the form of this depends on the needs of the couple. Relationship therapy offers a space for couples to feel that they can discuss important topics that are impacting their lives and relationship.

However, it is more balanced, and with a therapist there, a couple can be helped to see beyond situations that are too difficult to discuss with just the two of them, or that often end in conflict. As strange as it sounds, couples often find it difficult to discuss sensitive topics in private, so having someone else there can help to defuse that.

The timing of when couples attend is also important. It may be after an event or trigger, or period of change or transition, or one of them may have decided that they are not satisfied with something in the relationship. A large part of the therapy is about changing patterns for the couple and allowing them to understand both each other and themselves differently.

Patterns can become entrenched, and it can be difficult to even know how to start getting out of them. Reflections and interventions from someone trained to help you do so, such as a couples therapist, can be a good catalyst for that change.

Often sessions will entail communication exercises, understanding each other's wants and needs, as well as practising listening skills, and acknowledging past hurts. There may also be more practical exercises to be carried out by the couples (touch-based exercises outside sessions) which are about managing their lives in a different way, or taking on new responsibilities, or managing finances differently.

In terms of sexuality and intimacy, a couple may also be given exercises to help them gently integrate intimacy, sensuality and touch back into their life together.

How do you mediate between couples who are engaged in unhelpful behaviours, like criticising or insulting each other in the therapy room?

Couples are often stuck in negative patterns when they present for therapy, so getting them to stop and actually listen instead of making assumptions about what they think the other will say is an important start.

Often, our behaviours are based on emotions and feelings that we are having, so criticism or conflict can actually be about how the individual is feeling, and the fact that they are trying to communicate that hurt or disappointment to their partner.

Getting to the bottom of how both partners are actually feeling and how that resonates for each of them can create an important shift in how they relate to each other.

And are there ever couples where you think they've come to the end of the line and should split up?

Sadly, some couples do leave it too late before coming to therapy, and by the time they try and work through things there is already too much hurt or damage done.

It is not a relationship therapist's job to keep couples together at all costs – more to help them better understand themselves and each other, how they are relating to one another and how they can then move forward.

Obviously couples come to therapy for all sorts of reasons. Some seek help to get through a life stage or decision-making process; others need assistance because of broken trust or lack of intimacy. There can be different emotions associated with each individual set of difficulties.

What would you advise clients to look for in a therapist?

The most important factor in any therapeutic relationship is the relationship between therapist and client; that the clients feel that they are able to trust the therapist, and establish a temporary secure base and relationship with them.

A therapeutic relationship is an intimate one in many ways, and clients may share things with a therapist that they have never shared outside that room. This is facilitated by the relationship, assured confidentiality and the boundaried nature of that relationship.

Understanding what training a therapist has undertaken is also important. There are many routes to becoming a therapist and lots of different trainings, but finding out if a therapist has a speciality and approach that is right for you is important.

For example, you may be looking for a psychosexual therapist for dealing with a sexual difficulty or problem, or a therapist who has done more in-depth training than just a weekend course in working with couples when seeing people as a couple.

It is also important to bear in mind that some therapies might have more of a focus; for example, psychodynamic therapy will focus more on how the past has impacted the present.

How much do you disclose about yourself to clients?

You are obviously physically presenting yourself in front of clients as you are in the room with them, so the way you dress, your gender and factors like age are visible to clients, but the focus should be on them and not on the therapist.

It is also about working with a client and responding to their experiences from the position of a therapist, not as an individual, but of course the way that you work and your style and approach are also shaped by how you are as a person.

A family therapist named Peter Rober talked a lot about 'the self of the therapist' and the idea that therapists are responsible for managing those boundaries around the personal and professional, but also that an impossible part of being human is that we are always shaped by our personal experiences, and that there is no such thing as completely neutral. This is why therapists have such rigorous training to understand themselves.

The position of the therapist not oversharing their personal experiences is also a valuable one. When we discuss things with friends and colleagues, they will often recount a similar situation they have had or try to help you by relating to how that went for them or what they did. The fact that a therapist doesn't do that is what makes the therapeutic relationship different.

What do you enjoy most about practising therapy?

To practise as a therapist is such a privileged position. People allow you into their lives, trust you to be able to help them and – importantly – trust you with their confidential, personal and vulnerable information. The fact that you can make a difference in people's lives, however small or potentially invisible to others, is the most rewarding part of the role and the job. Another enjoyable part is building relationships with people.

Ultimately, people come to therapy to seek change in some shape or form, and to help people achieve that, give them more confidence and help them move forward in a slightly different direction is what it's all about.

As a psychosexual therapist, I realise that the problem a client may be experiencing can be invisible to others but having a huge impact on how they feel and see themselves. Creating change in their sex lives, sexuality or sexual functioning can be quite transformative, and it's so exciting to see where that may take people.

Do you ever get frustrated with clients if they are resistant to change or keep repeating the same unhelpful patterns?

Getting frustrated isn't helpful, and even if that feeling comes up it is likely that's based on how the client is feeling. It's always important to take a step back and think about what it is that is keeping them stuck or resistant. Perhaps, for the client, changing things is scarier than things staying the same, even if what they are currently doing isn't working.

It is rarely deliberate resistance on the part of the client, and so understanding why it's happening is the most important factor. It's about looking at the dynamics of what is going on rather than the results.

What would you have done if you hadn't been a therapist?

I would have wanted to be something creative like a jewellery designer or artist. I have always loved creativity and making things, and fashion. I also love to see how art, design and jewellery are put together in parts to create a complete whole, and I am a real magpie – never to be seen without big earrings!

I suspect a lot of that curiosity ties into my understanding of how people work. When working out and understanding psychosexual problems in therapy, you also need to look at the full picture and context to create a full idea of what is going on.

If you could start life over, would you still become a therapist?

Absolutely. To be a psychosexual therapist genuinely was my dream job since studying psychology and sexuality, and I feel so lucky to be able to work in a role that I love. It's a role that offers different challenges and variation on a daily basis, and lets me work with people on a personal level, which I have always wanted to do.

Yes, of course there are hard days and moments where you feel stuck. Sometimes you need to think differently or take an alternative approach, but these are huge learning experiences and only help you to understand how you can work better with someone else in future.

Every session and client teaches you something. Ultimately, in a world that is based around people, I believe that it is human relationships that transect it all.

The client: Anonymous

'Relationship therapy saved our marriage'

I called Relate in distress after a big bust-up made me think my marriage (and so family) was coming to an end, and they set up an assessment session within a couple of weeks. Which sounds like a long time, but actually just knowing it was booked helped both me and my wife.

Relate was the first and only organisation we tried; we felt our assessment counsellor was very understanding and saw through our immediate problem to deduce what sort of help we really needed, and assigned us a counsellor based on that.

My big fear was that the therapist would say, 'Good grief! There's no hope! Get a divorce!', and so I liked that the first thing she did was to describe the process we would be going through, so I understood that it would certainly not end in her giving us advice one way or the other.

We stuck with her because every single session left us feeling like we'd moved forward, and because – it sounds weird – but she made the counselling fun! Not always, of course; you address some very emotive and contentious issues, but honestly, we both looked forward to those Thursday afternoons.

What I would advise other people to look for is something our counsellor had in spades – safety. You will be talking about things that hurt. A lot. The only way it works is if the counselling room is a completely safe place to address these things that you simply cannot address at home without making everything far worse.

I always felt as though our therapist was absolutely impartial. I think both me and my wife feared that we'd be seen as the one in the wrong! But our counsellor never gave the slightest hint of taking sides, which provided a large part of feeling safe. In fact, one of the key things I got from counselling is that I needed to throw away the idea that there were opposing sides to be on at all.

Having therapy saved our relationship. Or to be more accurate, it took us to a place where we could save it ourselves. When we started, I said that I didn't want our relationship repaired, I wanted it built again but better, and I really feel that happened. It got us both out of destructive habits, and helped us both to spot new ones forming.

It helped me see that there can be deeper reasons behind arguments – I'd always prided myself on being able to see other people's point of view, and it made me realise that I wasn't really doing that with my own wife – it is hard when it's so close to home! I guess one way I'd put it is that we'd kind of ended up being together ten years without our relationship really keeping up, and therapy helped us to make that happen.

The client: Hayley Webster

'Marriage counselling only really works if you are both invested in it'

When our marriage ran into difficulties and we decided to seek help, our friends were all seemingly happy couples, so we figured none of them would have any ideas as to how to find a relationship therapist.

Incidentally, I now know that at least two of these other couples had serious relationship issues. I feel that if we had talked about it more, maybe we could have helped each other.

In our case, we literally googled 'marriage counsellor' and picked a therapist based halfway between his workplace and the train stop I got off at after I finished work. Funnily enough, choosing a therapist was one of the first things we had compromised on in about a year.

Our therapist was great straight off the bat, so we didn't really see the need to shop around.

He wasn't 'fluffy'. He didn't spout clichés, he simply got us to talk and listen to each other. That was half the trouble – we hadn't really talked in years. My husband was career-driven and threw himself headlong into his dream job. I didn't feel I could tell him how unhappy I was that we had left our lives and our families to move to another country, so we could follow his dreams.

I think we stuck with our therapist because he inspired change in us. He almost became like this wise father-figure, and I for one didn't want to let him down, though that sounds kind of weird and creepy when I think about it. I'm sure Freud would have had a field day on my daddy issues!

I'd advise other couples to go with what works for them. Don't let other people tell you what you need, because what works for them might not work for you. While I like a logical reasonable therapist, a friend of mine might need someone more 'fluffy'.

When I refer to someone as fluffy, I mean they are more idealistic and maybe more romantic. Sure, love is wonderful, but relationships are more likely to work if you have the tools to make them work – you can't keep a relationship alive on fairy tales and wishes.

I always felt as though our therapist was completely impartial. He stated clearly that he wasn't there to fix everything – he was there to talk us through the tools we needed to make a relationship work.

He never made either of us feel like one or the other was to blame, and he set 'homework' for both of us to do together. Things like taking a walk together, and having a meal with no screen or distractions – something that is very hard to do in the age of smartphones.

One issue that came up in therapy was that neither of us wanted to be the one to say sorry. I think it was because we were both raised in environments where apologising was an admission you were wrong.

One of the biggest lessons I took away was that an apology wasn't a sign of weakness; it is an expression that you didn't want to hurt the other person and you are remorseful for any hurt you did cause.

Both of us worked really hard during therapy to make the relationship work. I think the problems started again when we were advised we didn't need any more sessions.

After the sessions ended, we didn't have that routine to follow, someone giving us homework and checking in regularly. So naturally, we slipped back into old habits of working hard at our jobs and not talking for days on end.

Therapy outlined for us what was wrong with our relationship, that we didn't have the necessary skills to work on it. Part of that was because we were both very young when we got married (I was twenty-one, he was twenty-four), so we hadn't the maturity or experience to cope with the conflict we had. I think we both tended to be very self-centred at times, which didn't help.

Ultimately, our relationship broke down, and after all the hurt we had inflicted on one another we couldn't even salvage a friendship from the wreckage, so we broke all contact. He moved to Australia, and then moved to London. I decided to come back to New Zealand and start again in a new city.

When the paperwork came through for the divorce, I was really thankful – he had done all the hard work and made that happen. Some people might not see it like that, but I think what he did was kind, and I am truly thankful that he tried to make it quick and clean.

We still have mutual friends, and I hear snippets of what he is doing through them. Perhaps he has heard snippets about me too. I have heard he is engaged and honestly, I am happy for him. He and his new partner are making things work, and perhaps they are better at it because of what we both learned.

I think one of the things I took away from therapy is how to recognise things that therapy can't fix. I have walked away from a few relationships since where I recognised there were fundamental problems that no amount of therapy would ever mend.

Going back to a therapist would depend on why I was going, and to an extent, who I was going to therapy with, and what attitude they had towards it. Marriage counselling only really works if you are both invested in it.

If one or both of you have 'checked out' of your relationship, no therapy will fix it. You might as well throw money down a wishing well and hope everything will work out.

Rosie Wilby on Choosing an LGBT Therapist

'The most valuable part of therapy for me? Just having a space to be seen and heard'

I had a big and traumatic breakup at the beginning of 2011. My girlfriend was not out to her parents, so the relationship had been kept secret for five years.

I've always lived fairly openly as a gay woman, so this sense of shame about our relationship was something new to me, and was hard to understand or process. I just didn't get why people were homophobic and why the woman I loved had had to absorb and internalise this prejudice.

It felt particularly painful at a time when many of my friends were starting to be able to have civil partnerships and be more accepted. So there was definitely a huge amount of baggage from that relationship.

I went to therapy to sort this and other things out. It was important to me to find a therapist who identified as LGBT, as so many of my struggles are tied up in a feeling of invisibility due to being in that secret relationship. And I felt that only someone LGBT would really have lived that invisibility and know and understand it.

The therapist was someone I'd heard about a couple of years earlier through the LGBT grapevine. I'd previously had some sessions via PACE, a charity that sadly lost its funding and closed down. I spoke to my therapist on the phone prior to beginning sessions and, for me, it was really all about being 'seen'. She just sounded right.

She is a clinical associate of Pink Therapy, who work with gender and sexual diversity clients, and is also a member of London Sex and

Relationships Therapy group practice. So I guess those things stuck out to me: that she was in the LGBT world and experienced in sex and relationships work.

We talked a lot about consent and explored the possibility that some of my sexual encounters had been less consensual than maybe I recognised at the time. So when I began a new relationship during the period in which I was having therapy, I was very careful to get all those discussions about boundaries and consent right. Having someone to talk that through with was really valuable.

We often had a particular issue we were going to discuss in each session. My therapist did 'double sessions' every fortnight of an hour and forty minutes in total, which felt pretty intense. I would talk, and she would generally get me to slow down and unpack things a bit more rather than rushing and babbling. The life of a comedian is particularly frenetic at times, so we do often talk and think at breakneck speed.

My therapist got me to think about what was actually happening in more detail in the experiences, relationships and conversations I was describing. When I first arrived at her therapy room, I was suffering a little with anxiety and my normally pretty good sleep patterns were very disrupted.

So we were able to just calm things down a lot by doing some visualisations and just being that bit slower in thinking things through.

We had the obligatory childhood session, and looked back at possible early origins of my sense of invisibility. I was an only child whose parents both lectured at the same higher education college. So they often talked about work while I was in the back of the car on my own, making up stories in my head.

That's not to say I had a terrible childhood. But it was lonely, and instilled in me a sense of having to be fairly self-sufficient, which made it difficult to be truly intimate when it came to adult relationships.

We also talked a bit about my therapist's work with lesbian couples, and she said that she saw many who would make brilliant friends but who perhaps shouldn't be romantic partners. She felt that in heterosexual relationships, there was more language around 'friend zoning'.

Harsh as it is, it's probably better than feeling obligated to get into a relationship because a woman seems nice and relatively sane – something it's tempting to do if you're gay, because it's just so rare that you meet other people who are gay, particularly now there's no real gay 'scene' any more. So when you find someone who seems OK and is available, then you go for it!

So we talked a bit about how there are just fewer narratives and role models to follow as a gay person, and the particular challenges of that.

The most valuable part of therapy for me was just having a space to be seen and heard. It's certainly helped me articulate boundaries and desires with my new partner.

Funnily enough, she'd also been thinking about having therapy. When I mentioned it had been helpful for me, she also started seeing someone (not the same therapist, of course!).

Art/Drama/Music Therapy

This looks like Thursday on my old school timetable. I used to hate Thursdays.

They're not all bundled into one – it's three separate therapies which all aim to help people to express themselves. Shall we run through them?

Go on then. What's art therapy?

It's where art is used to help people convey how they are feeling. It's a good option for those who find it difficult to express themselves verbally, or who have other communication difficulties.

I'm no good at drawing. Besides, it's quicker to take a photo.

No one is going to judge your artistic skills. It's just about trying to show your feelings through the medium of art. And it's not necessarily just painting and drawing – photography could well be used if that's what you feel comfortable with.

So I'd just take a selfie of my frowning face and tell the therapist I'm depressed?

That's not what I meant. Whichever medium you choose, the therapist will talk to you about what you were feeling at the time and how your piece captures that.

I still think the selfie does that pretty well. Anyway, what about drama therapy?

It's stylised as Dramatherapy in the UK. The therapy is along similar lines to art therapy, but uses scripts and improvisation to help people act out the way they're feeling. For some people, it might be easier to talk about things if they are playing a character different from themselves.

They put me in the school play once. I was a tree.

Then you might know that being part of a play, or just a few scenes, can help develop social skills and teamwork. Many people who have tried Dramatherapy report increased self-confidence as a result.

And then there's music therapy. Is that listening or playing?

It can be either, or both. And before you ask, it doesn't matter if you can't play an instrument.

I can, as a matter of fact. I used to play triangle in the school orchestra.

Music can be good therapy because most people have songs or pieces that they can relate to or that make them feel a certain way. If you can't play an instrument, you might just use percussion or perhaps try singing. Music has always been used as a means of expressing a wide range of emotions.

I take it all these therapies are done in groups then.

Usually, but not always. Some therapists will work with individuals and get good results by using these methods, but working in groups can be more fulfilling and help those with low self-esteem. The therapist can also conduct the sessions in a variety of locations, such as schools, care homes and prisons.

That would cover most of my family and friends. But you could do all of these things yourself, so why pay for the therapy version?

Because you'll be getting specialist guidance and help along the way. And while we can all listen to music by ourselves, for example, we don't often get the chance to share that experience with like-minded others. The therapeutic model offers a focused and methodical approach.

It might make you think of things in a way you hadn't considered before. Also, the creative therapies can be used to help those with learning difficulties, physical disabilities or those with dementia.

Fair enough. I was just wondering, though, what happens to the stuff you make in art therapy? Is it sent off to be analysed for hidden meanings?

Nothing like that. You could keep it, or your therapist may even ask if it can be included in an exhibition. You're free to refuse, of course, but having artwork displayed in public can promote a feeling of acceptance – especially if it represents something that you're sensitive about.

'Accept me, accept my painting' you mean.

Yes, although it might be a drawing or a sculpture.

Right, I'm off to sculpt a face out of cheese to see if it makes me feel better.

I hope it works for you.

Well if not, I'll just eat it. That'll definitely make me feel better.

The Dramatherapist: Christina Anderson

'I could have become a statistic, either in prison or dead'

How would you describe Dramatherapy to someone who's never had it?

Dramatherapy is a form of psychotherapy that uses a broad range of creative stimuli. Clients who find it difficult to verbalise are able to communicate whilst expressing themselves through alternative means. Various art forms such as story, role play, metaphor, instruments, sounds, games, objects, play and movement enable clients to gain personal development through self-awareness and interaction with others, as well as self-exploration.

Drama and movement therapy is non-judgemental and non-confrontational. The intervention is client-led, and employs the language of symbol and metaphor through play. Clients engage in the experience of exploring the possibility of change. As drama and movement therapy is created through self-exploration it is difficult to explain in a linear way, as each participant's personal experience would vary.

As a person who had never experienced Dramatherapy prior to my training at The Royal Central School of Speech and Drama, I think the only way to describe the process is through the art form itself and through symbolism and metaphor. Therefore, symbolically I would describe Dramatherapy as a tool, a compass that points you in the direction needed to embark on your journey of 'self'.

An individual may seek therapy for anything. Frequent examples include life changes, bereavement, relationship difficulties, depression and anxiety, work-related issues, sexuality issues, eating disorders, divorce/separation, processing trauma, communication difficulties, adolescence and self-harming. Words can sometimes disconnect us from what we feel, so Dramatherapy can help to remove this language barrier and stop unnecessary intellectualising of what to say.

This can allow access, despite a client's protective layers, to a deeper inner core which may have become disconnected. I believe that harnessing the client's playfulness can allow deeper exploration of their emotions and intuition, which in turn makes it possible to help them return to their inner self.

What does a typical drama therapy session involve?

There are a range of different Dramatherapy trainings in the UK, each with a slightly different theoretical model. My training was at The Royal Central School of Speech and Drama, and was called Drama and Movement Therapy (Sesame).

A Dramatherapy session can be facilitated on a group or one-to-one basis. Generally, a session lasts between forty-five and sixty minutes depending on the organisation and/or the needs of the individual. In the first session, a working contract is introduced; this is an alliance between the organisation and/or individual and Dramatherapist. This is an extremely important part of the process as the agreement establishes a therapeutic relationship between individual and therapist. It offers containment for the 'journey' that the client is about to embark upon.

This boundary aims to help build trust in the therapeutic relationship. The Sesame approach to Dramatherapy is facilitated obliquely. The session starts with a 'focus', where you are invited to do a form of check-in, done symbolically through gesture and sound. This allows the individual to arrive and prepares their mind and body to connect and communicate with their unconscious using the art form.

The 'warm-up' allows the client to get into the different parts of their body and helps them to adjust to their new environment; it is done through voice, gestures and/or imagination. This is also an opportunity to warm up the mind, the body and the soul. This is followed by the 'bridge-in' which is exactly what it sounds like: a bridge into the unconscious, where you are guided by the therapist crossing over into a world of possibilities and taken on a 'treasure hunt'. The client can experience a knowledge that the tools they seek are within.

While the client begins to explore, they are unaware of what they might find. The 'main event' is similar to being taken to a location where the client searches for the 'sunken hidden treasures' which may have become lost.

Next we have the 'bridge-out'. Here, the client conducts a personal inventory, deciding what to take or leave from the experience. Once the bridge-out has been realised, what remains of the Dramatherapy process is the 'grounding'. The grounding brings you back to consciousness, to the here and now. This prepares the client for the end of the session, so that the client is ready to leave the therapeutic space and enter reality, as the cycle is complete.

What can a client do to help themselves during Dramatherapy?

They should always aim to be true to themselves. They should also do whatever it is they need to do while in the space, so that all feelings have the opportunity to be expressed. The journey is the client's, and this is paramount to full realisation of the journey.

The responsibility of the therapist is to ensure that the space is safe and contained, while providing a platform suitable for the client to be able to explore what they need. It is important that the client remains in the therapeutic space, which can sometimes be challenging.

What should a client look for in a Dramatherapist?

Once again, it is about being true to themselves and trusting their intuition. Trust the same instinct that has led them to Dramatherapy. The first lesson I learned while training was that you cannot become a therapist unless you have had therapy yourself. This first-hand experience helps the therapist gain an in-depth understanding of themselves as an individual/therapist as well as of the process that the client is going through.

The sympathy and care that might be felt can develop into an empathic sharing of emotions and understanding in a professional manner. As drama and movement therapy is heavily based on using other forms of communication, you need someone who you believe truly sees you and not the mask you have created. Therefore, it's really about the connection you feel with the therapist.

Are there people for whom Dramatherapy isn't suitable? If so, who?

Dramatherapy can be suitable for everyone and for all age groups, as it is versatile and adaptable. People often wonder how a Dramatherapist can work with someone with no language, or profound disabilities. The approach is based on theories of Peter Slade's work in children's play, Rudolph Laban's Art of Movement, Carl Jung's psychology of the unconscious and Sesame's very own founder Marian Lindkvist's non-verbal language of Movement-with-Touch-and-Sound.

A man once asked me, 'How would Dramatherapy help my dying father who is in a home and disconnected from society?' I explained that it could be a bridge into his isolation and help him make sense of what is happening to him, and perhaps explore what legacy he would be leaving behind.

Do you need any acting abilities to get something out of Dramatherapy?

No, the client will not need any acting abilities to benefit from Dramatherapy, because the method meets the individual wherever they are. In addition, our everyday experience involves a level of performance, and we are constantly adapting ourselves depending on our environment. We may 'be' one person when around our loved ones but someone very different when we are not feeling safe.

When babies come out of the womb and enter the world, their first form of communication is sound (the cry), to let air into the lungs. As we develop, we begin to explore our surroundings through play (building bricks, drawing, playing with instruments, dancing, mirroring facial expressions).

Later, children might be introduced to music, dance, singing and maybe even drama classes. We all learn through play from child-hood; this is our first form of communication. Nevertheless, as we get older, we forget this natural function as we get caught up in the reality of the everyday, and as a result we lose the purest form of communication.

Dramatherapy allows us to connect to that lost language, allowing the client to reach into the true wisdom of their own self and integrate it into everyday life, thereby making healthy new life choices.

Unconsciously, we already have all the abilities we will ever need in therapy.

What do you most enjoy about practising Dramatherapy?

I enjoy being with and working alongside the clients, witnessing their discovery. I enjoy the moment when clients first allow themselves to make steps to change their present circumstance and begin to develop a form of resilience and a greater understanding of who they are or who they might become.

How much personal information do you disclose to clients?

On the one hand through the art form I am disclosing a lot of personal information, as I am authentic in the exploration – that's the power of Dramatherapy. I am modelling to my clients through our interaction.

However, at the same time I would not usually disclose personal information. It would depend on the question asked by the client: I would want to understand why I was being asked, and what was really being communicated.

If you could start life over, would you still have been a therapist?

Yes, I believe my life journey has led me on this path: Dramatherapy chose me. For as long as I can remember, my life has been immersed within the creative arts. I have taken part in theatre productions and documentaries.

However, I have always felt there was more to acting than taking on a character; I realised that, for me, acting became a tool for self-expression within the containment of the role. Dramatherapy saved my life; I could have become a statistic, either in prison or dead, as I was considered a delinquent adolescent at high risk.

What would you have done if you hadn't been a drama therapist?

I would have been an actor and comedian. I would have used comedy to mask my pain, while helping another to laugh.

The art therapist: Jo Ray

'Artistic skill can be a challenge to overcome'

How would you describe art therapy to someone who has never had it?

Integrative art psychotherapy can help with problems that may be difficult to verbalise. Many psychological issues are multi-layered, and we often learn to skilfully avoid core feelings. The arts can help us identify, connect to and experience emotions on a deep non-verbal level.

Psychological healing and growth is similar to embarking on a journey. There can be challenges and obstacles along the way. An integrative theoretical approach provides flexibility to adapt the therapeutic work as the journey unfolds, working together to find the right way forward for you.

What does a typical art therapy session entail?

This is a difficult question to answer because it is so different with each client. However, I would say it often starts with talking and re-establishing the therapeutic connection. At some point, there may be something that comes up, or a regular theme, that warrants deeper exploration.

It is often at this point that I offer an art form as a suggestion of how the client might use the arts to explore this further (they are always free to say no and we may explore why if relevant). Some clients come straight in and have their own ideas about how to put across what they want to explore or communicate. There is often a personal pattern that becomes established with each client as the therapeutic relationship grows.

There can be practical aspects of the art making at times, such as cleaning brushes and palettes or finding appropriate ways to store a clay model that needs to dry; or if someone wants to do something like splat paint, we might need to put up protective sheeting or take into consideration how we can facilitate what they wish to do.

It is often quiet during the art making, but again, this varies according to the situation. Often there is a moment which seems right to begin to explore the client's meaning of the image (including the process of creation) and maybe reflect back to other images from earlier sessions, if relevant. Sometimes, in a single session, a client might move from one art form to another in the process of exploration.

What can a client do to help themselves during art therapy?

I would say they are already doing it by seeking therapeutic support. They can help themselves by being as authentic as possible and bringing their thoughts and feelings, whatever they are, into the therapy (assuming it feels safe enough to do so).

How would you reassure a client who worries they have no artistic talent, or that they are not a creative person?

I state in my information: 'No artistic skill is required. In fact, artistic skill can be a challenge to overcome when using the arts on a psychotherapeutic journey. It is not important what the "image" looks like, but what it represents to you, how you felt while you were making it and the links we make together, over time, between the images.

'Maybe it is a scribble on a scrap of paper; a scrunched-up bit of tissue paper; a lump of clay thrown down on the table, "thunk"; a particular puppet that always seems to draw your attention; a song that holds specific meaning to you; a poem; stories; films; music; the noise of a creaking door in the hall; a leaf you picked up; a postcard . . .

'I will offer the arts in a supportive way, always working with you to find non-verbal expression you feel contained and supported by and, above all, safe.'

Are there people for whom art therapy isn't suitable? If so, who?

Mostly I would say it is a personal choice of the client. Some clients I see choose not to use the arts. I am not sure that I would state that art psychotherapy was not suitable for a specific client group. Instead I think about it this way: 'Does the art provide a means of exploration leading to deeper understanding that talking has, so far, not provided?'

I see the arts as an additional way to communicate, not an alternative way.

What happens to the artworks after they have been created?

While a client and I are working together, all artwork produced in the session is kept confidential and securely stored. However, there can be times when artwork is treated differently for some reason, which would always be decided in discussion with the client.

At times, some clients bring images or art of some kind into the session and they often keep this themselves, but occasionally have asked to store them with their artwork.

At the end of the therapy it is usually part of the ending process to reflect back over the art made, and discuss what the client wishes to do with it: take it with them at the end of the last session; dispose of it by some means in the sessions (put it in the bin, shred it, tear it up, put on an exhibition and invite a significant person to come and view it – the options are varied and personal); leave it with me or ask me to dispose of it in specific way (burn it, bury it, plant it, store it for a specified amount of time in case they change their mind).

What do you enjoy most about practising therapy?

The clients. They are brilliant, and I learn so much from them.

How much personal information do you disclose to clients?

It depends on the client and the reason for the disclosure. When I do disclose personal information, I usually explain to the client why I am choosing to do so. It can be a very meaningful aspect of exploring the therapeutic relationship.

When I consider disclosing, and choose not to do so, it is usually because I feel it is not in the client's interest. It can be a compelling idea to put something of yourself in the therapy room at times, but whose need is it fulfilling?

It is one of the important aspects of the personal work psychotherapists undergo in their training, and an ongoing part of supervision and personal and professional development.

What would you have done if you hadn't been a therapist?

Being a psychotherapist is my second career; I was a graphic designer previously and ran my own company designing drink brands, although I originally went to art college to study photography. If I were starting over now, I might choose carpentry or model making. I love building things.

The client: Francesca Baker

'It helped me articulate ideas that were sometimes difficult to bring up'

I was an inpatient at a north London hospital for fifteen months, being treated for anorexia. I had art therapy for the majority of my time there.

There were four people in my group. A typical session would involve a check-in to see what was happening that week and how we were feeling, followed by half an hour of art making, and then a discussion about our work and what it might have brought up for us.

We used everything from pencil, paint and chalks to clay and collage. I remember one day I decided to do feet painting, dipping my feet in paint and walking across a big roll of paper.

I often drew abstract pieces, just to get my mind in the flow of creating, or images of a place I wanted to be, like a calm environment. Often people cut out words from magazines that might have articulated things they felt or wanted to say but couldn't.

221

The work was interpreted by us, the individual, but the therapist provided a safe space for us to do so and to bring up ideas and thoughts. I don't believe that the artwork ever revealed anything we didn't know already, but it was another way to express ideas and feelings we may have been struggling with.

It was my favourite part of the week, but I wouldn't say it was fun . . . I often felt drained afterwards. But good drained, like I'd processed something.

It helped me articulate ideas that were sometimes difficult to bring up. It also offered a safe space to be creative. I really liked my therapist as she was gentle and held space well, but was also strong and confident. I felt I could be vulnerable with her.

The art was kept and given to me on discharge, although there was so much that I threw it away. Perhaps this was a shame. I think I've always thought of myself as creative and knew that art therapy wasn't about producing great works but the process.

On occasion, I dabble in art again. I wish I did more. I'd love to find an art therapist again, but they're not very available on the NHS for outpatients.

If there was more opportunity to do this kind of thing as an outpatient it would be hugely beneficial for many people, I think, as a preventative measure.

Mindfulness-Based
Cognitive Therapy (MBCT)

More mindfulness? I thought we were done with that.

I'm afraid not. It's pretty important for this one.

Go on then, give me the history. I know you want to.

In 1979, a fellow called Jon Kabat-Zinn developed a programme that he called Mindfulness-Based Stress Reduction, or MBSR. It was an eight-week programme to help people with both physical pain and psychological problems.

Hang on, you said it was MBCT . . .

I'm getting to that. Three people called Zindel Segal, Mark Williams and John Teasdale then adapted the programme to help people suffering from repeated bouts of depression. They called it Mindfulness-Based Cognitive Therapy.

How did it differ from the stress reduction thingy?

They focused on major depression for a start. Then they applied the mindfulness to existing CBT methods to see if it would reduce occurrences of relapse.

I suppose it must have worked, or it wouldn't be a 'thing'.

It has been shown to be effective, yes. It aims to break the downward mood spirals that people can find themselves in.

What's a downward mood spiral?

When depression starts, it can be easy to start thinking negatively and stop noticing the good things in our lives. It can remind people of bad experiences from their past and make them worry more.

If they think of their emotional state as being a problem that they need to solve, it can be frustrating if the solution isn't obvious. They can start over-thinking and fixating on those feelings.

Which just makes things worse.

Indeed, especially if someone has had depression before, because they fear its return. They might even try to suppress their thoughts, which doesn't tend to work.

The mindfulness element of MBCT is about allowing these thoughts and feelings to pass through – acknowledged, but not given undue prominence. By not resisting these emotions they can be 'held in awareness' – existing without causing damage, as if placed in quarantine.

So how long does the therapy last?

It's an eight-week programme, just as the MBSR was, and takes place in a group setting. There's something I haven't mentioned yet, though – you're also asked to take part in guided meditations.

Whoa, whoa. Meditations? You mean sitting with forefingers and thumbs pressed together going 'ommmm'?

There are different meditations that you do at various stages of the therapy. One focuses on different parts of the body, there's stretching and breathing exercises, yoga, sitting in silence . . .

Sitting in silence? Are you sure this isn't a scam?

It's obviously not for everybody, but it's worth being open-minded about these things. The meditations are structured and timed, but of course you can continue doing them as often as you feel is helpful.

Do you need to grow a beard and become a hipster?

You can if you like. There are no rules.

I think it'd be too itchy. But seriously: what if you fancy giving the mindfulness a go but think the meditation stuff is a bit too hippy-like? Can you give that a miss?

Not really, it's part of the deal. If you're not willing to explore that side of things you might want to try something different – but if you've got serious depression, you may be willing to give almost anything a chance.

The therapist: Ruth Baer

'Thoughts are just mental events that come and go'

How would you describe MBCT and MBSR to someone who has never had them?

MBSR is an eight-week mindfulness class that meets weekly for group sessions of two to two-and-a-half hours. It uses a variety of meditation practices and other exercises to teach skills for being mindfully aware of whatever is happening in the present moment.

For most people, this increases awareness and enjoyment of pleasant moments as well as the ability to respond constructively to stress and difficult emotions. MBSR asks you to do a fair amount of mindfulness meditation at home between sessions. It can be difficult to find the time, but mindfulness isn't something you can learn just by hearing or reading about it. You have to practise it yourself to benefit from it.

MBCT is an adaptation of MBSR for people with a history of depression. It uses many of the same meditation practices and exercises as in MBSR, along with a few different ones. MBCT has been adapted for other problems and is sometimes offered for general stress reduction. Many people could benefit from either one.

What do typical MBCT and MBSR sessions involve?

After everyone comes in and says hello and gets settled, the session usually starts with a meditation practice, for about thirty to forty minutes. It might be a body scan, some gentle mindful yoga, or sitting meditation. This is followed by a form of discussion called 'inquiry'.

Group members have the opportunity to describe what they noticed during the practice, and there will be some dialogue with the teacher that brings out lessons that can be learned from the practice and how mindfulness can be helpful in daily life. Speaking up during inquiry is not required, but it can be very helpful.

Next is discussion of the home practices during the week. Group members can share what came up for them while practising at home (or not practising, if they've had difficulty finding the time) and the teacher will use this dialogue to explore what they noticed and what can be learned from it.

The rest of the session could include introduction of new practices or exercises, some educational material about stress, depression or another relevant topic, and assigning of home practices for the coming week. The session usually ends with a short mindfulness practice.

What are the similarities and differences between MBCT and CBT?

One of the main differences is that MBCT is based primarily on mindfulness meditation. CBT generally doesn't include meditation. In addition, MBCT focuses on learning to see what's happening in each moment (thoughts, bodily sensations, emotions, urges) without necessarily trying to change these experiences. CBT is more focused on change.

In CBT, for example, participants learn to recognise when their thoughts are distorted and to answer them back and come up with new thoughts that are more realistic and balanced. MBCT puts more emphasis on recognising that thoughts are just mental events that come and go and we don't have to be controlled by them. We also don't have to change them. There is a fair amount of common ground but I think they feel distinctly different.

What can a client do to help themselves during MBCT and MBSR?

One way to help yourself is to let go of expectations, keep an open mind, and do the course as best you can. This means showing up for every session and doing the home practices as much as possible. More practice seems to be related to more benefit.

At the same time, it's important not to be critical and judgemental about what you can do. If you can't practise every day, don't beat yourself up about it, just do what you can. It's also important not to expect a quick fix. Sometimes it takes a while before you can tell if it's making any difference.

It's probably best to give it the whole eight weeks before trying to come to any conclusion about this. I like the term 'gentle persistence' as a way of summarising a helpful attitude. It's important to be gently persistent and persistently gentle about doing what the course is inviting you to do.

What should a client consider when searching for an MBCT or MBSR therapist?

It's important to know what training and background the teacher has. Depending on what you're looking for, a strong background in mental health, wellness, or stress reduction is probably important. The teacher should also have a lot of experience with mindfulness and meditation.

Are there people for whom MBCT and MBSR aren't suitable? If so, who?

It's important to be able to commit the time and energy to do the practices. If you're severely depressed, you might be very low on energy and motivation, and that might make it hard to do the practices. It might make sense to do a form of therapy that's effective for severe depression first, before participating in MBCT or MBSR.

People with a traumatic background who suffer from post-traumatic stress may find the meditation practices difficult, especially if they cause traumatic memories to come up. On the other hand, a skilled teacher may be able to guide you through the practices in a way that's very beneficial. It's probably wise to discuss your personal situation with the group leader before making a decision about whether to participate.

What do you enjoy most about practising therapy?

I enjoy seeing people come to a clear personal understanding of what mindfulness is and how it can help them.

How much personal information do you disclose to clients?

It's understandable for clients to be curious about their therapist or mindfulness teacher. I often answer basic questions that are based on normal curiosity. I also consider what's behind the question – does the person have a concern that I could address?

If you could start life over, would you still have been a therapist?

I'm a professor, though I teach CBT and mindfulness-based therapies to doctoral students. There's a good chance I would do this again if I were starting over.

What would you have done if you hadn't been a therapist?

I might have been a science journalist, writing about new research for the general public.

The client: Kieran Walsh

'The sessions really helped me, and I still use the techniques I learned now'

I did a series of mindfulness sessions during a stay at the Priory rehab centre. They were group sessions, and usually featured two therapists giving instructions. The therapists would encourage us to find a comfortable place lying on the floor, and would then talk us through the process.

Each session we were told to try to remain in the moment, and if we found our minds wandering, then to try and return our thoughts back to our breathing. We were encouraged to 'take long breaths in through your nose and out through your mouth'.

The sessions would often consist of a therapist reading out a story or a poem, and we would be encouraged to concentrate on this. We would then be asked how it made us feel afterwards. There was one session where we were given an object and asked to think about its texture, smell, feel and taste. Thankfully it was a raisin, so it was OK!

The sessions really helped me, and I still use the techniques I learned now. If I am sunbathing, for example, I like to feel the grass or sand that I am lying on, so if my brain wanders and I start thinking of other things as opposed to just enjoying myself, I will just return my thoughts to the feel of the grass.

Mindfulness was probably the best form of therapy I had. It meant that I stopped catastrophising. Because of my depression, my brain takes a negative thought and over-thinks it until it turns it into the most paranoid and destructive thought possible. By being mindful of my thoughts, using the techniques I learned, I can almost stop myself from getting to the 'destructive thoughts' stage.

Mindfulness also helps me when I am out with my kids or my friends. If I find myself thinking negatively about things, I take a moment to concentrate on my breathing, which brings me back to the present and parks those thoughts.

It's made me happier, and a nicer person to be around.

Eye Movement
Desensitisation and Reprocessing (EMDR)

Therapy for people with sensitive eyes? That's pretty specialist.

That's not what it is at all, though it is very unusual. EMDR uses techniques such as side-to-side eye movement to reduce stress from past traumatic events.

Ha ha, nice one! What's it really about?

No, it's true. It was developed by an American psychologist called Francine Shapiro in the late 1980s. She was out on a walk one day and noticed that certain eye movements made her feel calmer about thoughts of her own traumatic past. She did some experiments with volunteers and found that others with similar trauma also felt relief from using the technique.

Why would moving your eyes around make you feel better? It would probably make me dizzy.

The idea is that when we experience trauma, our usual coping strategies can be overwhelmed and our brains can't process the information properly.

As a result, the memory isn't stored in the same place as our other memories and becomes a kind of sticking point – because it's not connected to other neural processes, we get trapped there. The eye movement, when associated with the traumatic memory, can act as a route back to calmer thought patterns.

I worry about people not looking where they're going. I fell down a manhole once.

You're likely to do EMDR when sitting still in a chair. There are also other techniques that are used in EMDR treatment, such as hand tapping and listening to certain audio tones.

This Shapiro lady does some weird stuff when she's out for a walk.

The other two were probably discovered later. Anyway, all three techniques are used in a series of thirty-second bursts while the client recalls a traumatic memory. The eye movement is done by asking the client to follow the therapist's finger with their eyes. After each burst, the client will be asked to think about the memory again to see if their stress levels are reduced.

And this actually works?

Do you remember NICE (see page 46)? Well, they recommend EMDR as a treatment for post-traumatic stress disorder, so they obviously think it has merit.

Is it just for people who have suffered traumatic events?

Not necessarily. It could be used on people prone to panic attacks, those fearful of certain situations, or even people with eating disorders. An assessment would be carried out first to determine whether you would be a good candidate for the treatment.

How do the sessions work? Do you just sit down while the therapist waves their finger around?

A session would typically start with some relaxation exercises to create a calm atmosphere. This might be through meditation or breathing techniques. The treatment would then take place before further relaxation exercises at the end.

Can the client later use these methods on their own?

The long-term aim is for the client's brain to be 'reprogrammed' so that they feel a greater level of control when they experience stressful memories. The fear of having panic attacks when out in public places can be very debilitating, so successful treatment can give people a lot more self-confidence.

Will they ever be cured completely?

The bad memories won't go away, but with time clients might find that they have less impact, even without having to use the EMDR techniques.

Reprogramming brains sounds a bit scary.

Then think of it as reprocessing a traumatic experience – as the name suggests.

Oh, I forgot what the name was as soon as you said it. I'll just call it the movey-eye thing.

Francine Shapiro would be so proud.

The therapist: Oliver Wright

'Clients are often surprised at how quick and effective it can be'

Tell me a bit about EMDR.

The experience of having EMDR therapy can be emotionally intense but clients are often surprised at how quick and effective it can be, especially for one-off adult traumas. But it would be a mistake to see it as a 'quick fix' session or two. The therapist needs to conduct a careful assessment to understand the client's symptoms in the context of their history and family relationships.

This helps to identify not only other earlier traumatic memories that may feed into the current experience, but also the client's own resources (whether they felt safe, loved and valued as a child and if these feelings are present as an adult).

Clients who can recover from a trauma quickly and easily are using their own internal resources to do so, and those who struggle to feel safe or lovable or valued after a distressing incident often did not feel these things as children. The number of sessions needed and the complexity of the work very much depends on these considerations.

Clients often ask me how EMDR works. In order to understand the therapy, we must first understand a bit about traumatic memory. When we are in a high-stress traumatic situation like a car crash or a near-death experience, our stress hormones are so high that they affect the hippocampus – the part of the brain that normally records the date and time and the context of a memory.

This means that the memory is dysfunctionally stored in the brain with all the emotional and physical information, but not the wider context. The classic example is a war veteran who jumps for cover when he hears a car backfire. His brain is telling him he's still in danger even many years after the war has ended.

So how does EMDR help? The truth is that although we have research to show that it is effective, there is still debate about what is happening in our brains during EMDR therapy. Some specialists say that it is a similar phenomenon to REM (rapid eye movement) sleep, where the brain is sorting out and resolving the difficult stuff of our daily lives. Others say that by taxing our working memory, we ensure that we are reliving these disturbing memories in a less intense way.

My own experience is that the first effect of bilateral brain stimulation is to connect up our rational thoughts (left brain) with our emotional and physical memory networks (right brain). This is like bypassing our normal defences and tapping into our emotional memories. We might feel more upset, more angry or more scared, as if we were reliving the memory again. This is particularly the case for clients with severe PTSD who feel like they are reliving memories on a daily basis.

The next thing we notice is that as we keep going with short sets of say twenty left–right eye movements or hand taps, the client reports that they are experiencing less intense feelings and that the memory is becoming less disturbing.

At this stage, the memory is becoming a more normal memory. It is no longer just emotional and physical memory stored in the right brain, but it is becoming connected up with our rational and contextual brain. Crucially, the client begins to *feel* that they are safe rather than just thinking this is true.

What does a typical EMDR session entail?

Early in treatment, the therapist will aim to explore and build the client's inner resources. These might include a calm place or a very positive memory that felt good. The therapist needs to know that the clients can calm and soothe themselves before starting work on traumatic memories with EMDR. For some clients, it can take months before they feel safe and resourced to start work, but for others it can be just a few sessions.

The therapist will usually work with the client to build a list of traumatic memories that will be ranked in terms of how disturbing they are and by theme, according to the negative belief that the client has about themselves that relates to the memory. Often they will start work on the first or the worst memory.

The therapist asks a series of questions, for instance: 'What is the negative thought that you have about yourself when you think of that memory? What is the positive thought you would prefer to have? What emotion do you feel? Where do you feel it in your body? How disturbing is the memory, from 0 to 10?'

Then the therapist might say, 'Think of the image of the worst moment, the negative thought, and notice where you feel that in your body.' At this point the therapist will start moving their hand from left to right in front of the client's eyes and asking them to follow with eye movements while noticing any sensations in the body.

After twenty to thirty eye movements the therapist will pause and ask the client what they notice. Often the client will say something like, 'I have a really bad feeling in my stomach' or 'I feel the fear in my chest'. Then the therapist will say, 'Notice that' or 'Go with that', and continue with another set of eye movements.

The emotion will often feel stronger when the eye movements start, but as connections are made and the brain's own healing process kicks in, the memory will start to become less disturbing. These sets of eye movements will continue until the memory is no longer disturbing.

Finally, the therapist and the client will look to pair a more positive belief with the memory, for instance, 'I'm stronger now' or 'I got through it', and work with eye movements until this positive statement feels totally true.

The session will often end by going back to a 'calm place' in the client's mind so that they can leave feeling relaxed.

What can a client do to help themselves during therapy?

It helps if the client comes prepared to engage emotionally with the process. If they are not prepared to connect emotionally, then the process will often be much slower.

Another important predictor for good outcomes in therapy is the work that the clients have done on themselves to build their own resources. This might include mindfulness meditation, yoga, breathing exercises or other self-soothing resources.

What qualities should a client look for in an EMDR therapist?

An EMDR therapist should have completed a level III training with an approved training provider, and be a member of EMDR UK (or a similar international EMDR body). More experienced EMDR therapists will be accredited EMDR practitioners or EMDR consultants.

Are there people for whom EMDR isn't suitable? If so, who?

Most people are able to benefit from EMDR. However, if a client has very complex problems or early childhood trauma then it is important to be cautious about starting EMDR processing. Some therapists will spend an extended period of time preparing the client, so that they are able to tolerate strong emotion without dissociating (feeling or thinking in the way that they did at the time of the trauma or losing contact with their adult sense of self). Other therapists will prefer to use another approach with these clients, for example Trauma-Focused CBT.

What would you say to people who are sceptical about EMDR?

EMDR is an evidence-based treatment. It has been shown to be equally as effective as Trauma-Focused CBT. It may sound like a strange thing to do in therapy, but most clients are very positive about their experience of EMDR. Having worked in many different ways therapeutically, I have found EMDR to be by far the most effective. I now use this approach with nearly all my clients.

What do you enjoy most about practising therapy?

Being a therapist gives me the freedom to work in a profession where I am continually learning and experiencing new things. My private practice gives me freedom to work around my life rather than the other way around.

But I am also lucky to be working in a specialist trauma team in the NHS, where I have colleagues who share the same passion that I have for the work and for constantly finding new ways to help patients.

How much personal information do you disclose to clients?

I generally tell my clients very little about my own life, as it should always be about them. But I do sometimes share something – for instance, my dyslexia – if I think it will make them feel more comfortable in sharing their own issues.

If you could start life over, would you still have been a therapist?

Yes definitely. I have had many other jobs before I became a full-time psychotherapist, but I always had a feeling that this would be right for me.

What would you have done if you hadn't been a therapist?

When I left university, I thought about becoming a teacher or a youth worker. I guess these professions are not so different in many ways. I might still do some teaching in the future if the right opportunity comes along.

The client: Anonymous

'I was a mental and emotional mess'

My first pregnancy's due date came and went, and a whole two weeks later I had a chemical induction. It did not go well. I won't go into detail as it might trigger me, but about halfway through the labour I nearly died. Once I was stabilised, I was able to continue with the 'natural' birth, but it turned out my baby had a bigger than average head.

She got stuck, so the doctor took a scalpel and sorted that little problem out. Unfortunately, he also took a nice chunk out of one of my large veins without realising. The result was a massive haemorrhage, one passed-out momma, and four blood transfusions over the next five days in hospital.

This brought with it further issues. Having lost my beautiful uncle when he was only twenty-seven to the HIV virus, I was terrified of blood products but I wasn't given a choice, the same way no one spoke to me about choices during the birth. I felt violated and invalidated. I was so ill, I was unable to breastfeed, so I also felt like a complete failure. I had failed to birth my baby, I had failed to breast-feed and now I was going to catch AIDS and die.

I also didn't sleep: as my brother had died at just eight weeks old, I knew that Sudden Infant Death Syndrome could strike at any time, so I needed to stay awake for eight weeks at least. I was a mental and emotional mess.

It turns out that this kind of traumatic birth can lead to PTSD: post-traumatic stress disorder. Feel free to scoff; I know I did. I hadn't been in a war or witnessed a horrific terror attack, I had just done what thousands of women do every day. Not everyone who experiences a traumatic event develops PTSD – a lot depends upon your life experiences up to the point of the traumatic event, and in my case there were a few factors that came into play.

I wasn't diagnosed immediately. I barely left the house in six months and the health visitor, who could see my child was thriving but that I was a mess, decided to refer me to the perinatal mental health team. They diagnosed me with PTSD, and I went to weekly group therapy sessions with some amazing mums until my baby was one. At that point, the service had to end due to lack of funding, and I was discharged. I was dosed up to the eyeballs with anti-anxiety meds, and back to work I went.

Things got progressively worse. I would break into a cold sweat if someone mentioned pregnancy, birth or hospitals. I continued with medication and had CBT. My poor husband must have thought many times of leaving: I was so unpredictable, the night-mares were unbearable and I wanted to die but I did not want to leave my baby, so I medicated with food and alcohol. I gained six stone.

I should probably also mention that I continued to work full-time, so in effect I remained fully functioning. But one day I found myself sobbing to the nurse at the GP practice that I couldn't have a smear test because of the violation. She brought the doctor in, and they considered admitting me to a mental health unit but agreed that I could be treated at home with regular visits from a community psychiatric nurse. She was wonderful.

Visits started immediately, and after a few weeks the nurse told me about this new technique called EMDR (eye movement desensi-tisation and reprocessing) being used on veterans with PTSD. Wondering if I might be suitable for it, she sent an exploratory email to a clinical psychologist in the health board.

The psychologist was fascinated by my story and agreed to see me. My baby was already four years old, and I had struggled constantly in that time. I was so desperate for help I was willing to try anything, but I was also very cynical.

At my first meeting with the psychologist, she told me two things: firstly, that she didn't know how EMDR worked, and secondly, that it might not work for me. I nearly didn't go back, but I so desperately wanted to get better. I have an amazing bond with my daughter and I didn't want her to grow up with this mother who was emotionally numbed by medication or off-the-wall insane.

In order for EMDR to work, you have to think in great detail about the trauma you are trying to fix but first you have to deal with all the shit that came before it. This involves picking apart virtually every distressing event you've ever experienced. Sounds fun, right? Wrong!

I should probably explain that the hardest part of the PTSD was the nightmares. 'Graphic' isn't a strong enough description – the images in my dreams were horrendous, with things I've never witnessed conjured up in minute detail. The same images would spring into my mind at any time in the day, and I rarely went two or three hours in a working day without some kind of PTSD attack.

These would usually end with me sitting in the disabled loo (more private), crying and shaking. Basically, PTSD fucking sucks and EMDR means facing every horrible experience face-on, visualising every image, while an incredibly well-educated lady waves a pen in your face.

There is some theory behind it: apparently the images are linked to thought processes which are knotted in your brain, and the eye movements force you to engage both sides of your brain and this smooths out the knots. That's how it was explained to me, anyway.

It took over a year of weekly, two-hour visits before it hit me that my dreams had stopped. I'm not even exactly sure when they stopped, I just realised one day that it'd been days since I'd had one. We kept going for a bit longer to make sure it wasn't a fluke, I came off my medication, and so far, over a year later, I haven't needed it again. Neither have I had one of those dreams since.

I don't know if the PTSD will come back, but I really hope not. I still have other issues: I haven't managed to get my weight back under control but I've kind of put that in the fuck-it bucket, because I'm more like a human being again and that's more important than being slim.

I'm still a little crazy, but I think I always was! I'm still married – my husband is something of a saint, and my kid is surprisingly well balanced, so I think I managed to hide the worst bits from her.

The combination of PTSD and medical issues means I am too scared to have another child. I've come to terms with that, and luckily the one I have is amazing. I can't pretend it doesn't make me a bit sad sometimes, but at least now the words 'pregnancy' and 'birth' don't result in me having a PTSD meltdown like they used to.

Who knows, maybe one day I'll be able to watch *Call the Midwife* and find out what all the fuss is about.

Interpersonal Psychotherapy (IPT)

This one's about people, isn't it?

Well deduced. Specifically, it's about resolving problems with relationships, how people interact with others, and the effect it has on their life. It aims to alleviate depression.

Don't other therapies deal with those things?

They do, but this one specialises in it. It identifies the issues that the client is having with relationships in their life and focuses on them within a set number of sessions.

How many?

Usually between twelve and sixteen. Because of this time limit, the main issues are identified in the early sessions and targets are set. These targets are discussed and agreed with the client.

So is it like relationship therapy?

No, it's for individuals. It's not just for romantic relationships either – the idea is that problems such as anxiety and depression are caused by difficulties in dealing with others.

It might be specific people in your life, or it might be something like extreme shyness that affects your dealings with everyone. It could be friends, family or a partner. The scope is quite large, but results tend to be best for those with clearly defined problems.

Interpersonal Psychotherapy (IPT)

What if the person's problem was a fear of therapists?

OK, I'll humour you. If that was the case, the therapist would recognise and acknowledge that fear and try to establish a trusting atmosphere. The early sessions would be about developing that trust, and the therapist wouldn't push things too far at first.

Results tend to come later in the process, when the client feels more comfortable – that's all allowed for in the time frame.

What if the person had no friends at all? That's kind of a people problem.

Of course it is. IPT would certainly cover that, as not having anyone close to talk to can lead to stress and depression.

I wasn't talking about myself, by the way. I have lots of friends. They're just . . . away at the moment. But isn't there a danger that a lonely person could become attached to the therapist? If it's short-term, they might get upset when it came to an end.

Again, that would be covered in the sessions. As the end approaches, the client would be invited to explain how they felt about it and discuss any worries they might have. The hope, of course, is that what they have learned during the process will give them the tools they need to deal with it.

What else does the therapy cover?

There's something that's known as an interpersonal deficit – this is when someone isn't getting what they need out of their personal relationships. It might be that they have a friend that they can't trust, or that their partner isn't giving them the attention they would like, or that someone they like isn't returning their affection. All these things can have a big impact on somebody's mental wellbeing.

Seems pretty comprehensive.

Changes in a person's circumstances can also lead to feelings of loss. Moving to a different part of the country or changing job can be difficult adjustments to make. All of this would be covered by the therapy.

OK, I'd better be off now. I need to call . . . one of my many friends.

Naturally.

The therapist: Bob Pritchard

'It's a good idea to set small and achievable goals'

What is interpersonal psychotherapy?

Interpersonal psychotherapy, or IPT for short, is a type of therapy which helps many people recover from depression. It does this by working to improve the relationships in the person's life, and by reducing their symptoms of depression. They and the therapist will also work out how these two things are linked.

Say, for instance, there's someone who's having ongoing arguments and fights with her partner. These might make her feel really bad and bring her mood down. She might also spend more time in her room on her own, avoid eating with her family, or her sleep might suffer. Imagine how much worse another argument with her partner might be if she's low, tired and hungry.

In this way, this pattern of arguing with her partner keeps her stuck in depression.

IPT was initially developed in the late 1960s for the treatment of adults with depression. Since then, there have been loads of exciting developments and changes, which mean there's evidence that IPT can help more people, including young people and their families, people experiencing trauma, and a briefer intervention called Interpersonal Counselling for those who are struggling but don't have a diagnosis of depression.

Interpersonal Psychotherapy (IPT)

What happens in a typical therapy session?

IPT is a brief type of therapy lasting between twelve and sixteen sessions. It's split into three phases over these sessions, which broadly cover: working together to find out what's wrong and agreeing what will help it to get better; working on the problem in sessions with the therapist and practising with the help of the people in your life; and carefully planning for ending, thinking about keeping getting better and staying well once therapy ends.

With the example of the person with depression arguing with her partner, we'll start a typical session carefully looking into how her symptoms have been over the past week. If, for instance, her sleep has been bad, we could think about ways to make it better.

One of these might be, for example, don't use your phone just before going to sleep.

We'll then make links to things that might have happened with other people to have made symptoms worse, such as arguing with her partner. If that's the case, it's often really helpful to reconstruct in detail what happened in that argument, thinking about things such as intention, tone, volume, and maybe if doors were slammed!

We may have figured out in previous sessions that some of the problems with these arguments are that she thinks her partner never listens, or that she can pick quite bad times to talk to him, for instance if he's just come in from work. We might look for some of these patterns in the example from the week, and then crucially plan and practise together how to do things differently.

It's also a good idea to set small and achievable goals for the week. In this case, it might be to not ask her partner for something as soon as he's stepped in the door, but wait until he's had his dinner first.

IPT isn't a solo therapy either, so if it's appropriate, we'd plan to invite an important person or people from the person's life in. This way, we could work together to help the person recover.

What can a client do to help themselves during therapy?

IPT uses a social model, and also a medical model which doctors use, seeing conditions like depression as an illness which can be treated. So in this model, it's important to remember that depression is not the person's fault, that it's treatable, and that loads of people recover from it.

Also, the person can work their happiness muscle. They might not be feeling like they used to when they do things they used to enjoy, or they may have stopped doing those things altogether.

You wouldn't wait in the middle of a field for a bus to come; you'd wait at a bus stop. In the same way, the *happiness* bus stop may be seeing friends, playing tennis or doing yoga. Continue going to the bus stop until the bus shows up again.

There may be things the person in therapy has to consider taking their foot off the pedal with until they feel better again, as it's too much when you're feeling ill. Basically, go easy on yourself. If you're a runner, maybe don't run that marathon, but think about the half instead.

There are other things that'll help too. If your doctor has prescribed medication, then take it as required. It might seem obvious, but trying to keep to a regular sleep pattern and eating healthily can make a big difference. Drinking too much alcohol or using street drugs like cannabis and cocaine definitely won't help things either.

IPT is all about working with the people in the person's life. It's important they don't keep how they're feeling to themselves, but instead, plan with their therapist, who might be able to support them. Working with their therapist will definitely help them to get the most out of therapy. This includes letting the therapist know if something isn't working.

What qualities should a client look for in a therapist?

An IPT therapist needs to be registered with IPT-UK, and this can be checked easily on our website (see page 312). They can be registered as either a student or a practitioner in order to practise. Training is very thorough and comprehensive, and standards of skill and competence must be met before a student qualifies. If your therapist is registered here, then you can be assured that they can work with you using IPT to help you get better.

Clients should look for a therapist who makes them feel respected and comfortable, and who makes them feel like they can be trusted. The therapist should show them that they understand that starting therapy can be difficult, and that the person might be apprehensive and nervous.

The therapist should be dependable, and treat information as confidential. The therapist should be interested in the person and their story, be active in helping them, and work with them to help them get better.

Are there people for whom IPT isn't suitable? If so, who?

IPT has proven to be hugely adaptable, largely because so many mental health problems which people experience happen within an interpersonal context. Initially developed for the treatment of adults with depression, adaptions were made to treat older people, adolescents and pre-adolescents; it covers a very broad range of ages in a person's life.

There are some areas where we know that IPT works less well. For example, IPT has some known effect on anxiety where depression is being treated primarily, but has no known positive effect on anxiety alone. There is also no evidence that IPT works with substance use, OCD, or schizophrenia and other psychotic disorders.

Do you ever get frustrated with clients if they are resistant to change or keep repeating the same unhelpful patterns?

Often that well-trodden path is the easiest one to follow, and it can seem genuinely scary to try a different way, even if the path you know makes you feel rubbish. I think this happens to all of us to some extent. Not wanting to change, or not feeling able to, are actually important steps in the change process. Working through these with your therapist can lead to change.

But do I ever feel frustrated? Of course! That's good though, as that's something we can work with. As IPT is all about relationships, then the relationship the person has with their therapist can be an excellent practice ground. Sensitively letting the person know that an aspect of their communication can feel frustrating can be important to hear.

Imagine if a person didn't know that they had a tendency to interrupt others, but they wondered why people became irritated and distanced themselves from them. It can be a delicate but essential thing for a therapist to address in a session.

What do you enjoy most about practising therapy?

I do love that sense of flow that can happen in sessions. It feels like a wonderful balance of creativity and collaboration that can come from two people who are working together to figure something out. Also, the clients often make huge leaps between sessions. The session after this happens can feel really joyous.

How much personal information do you disclose to clients?

Not much at all; I'm also pretty difficult to find online. I've found disclosing too much might detract from the person's problems. However, I am human, and I seem like one too! In our building there's a walk up a couple of flights of stairs to the therapy rooms, and we have a chat about general things on the way up.

During these conversations I might cover general things; I ride a bike, I've just been on holiday and it was nice thanks, and yes I have just had my hair cut!

If you could start life over, would you still have been a therapist?

And would I even still be me at all? I'd like to think I'd still be doing what I'm doing. Having a childhood experience of both parents being in caring professions, and then being involved in youth work in my late teens and early twenties put me on this path.

To be honest, I don't really consider myself a therapist; I'm a social worker who has trained in this particular type of therapy. Something called The Children and Young People's Improving Access to Psychological Therapies programme (CYP-IAPT) was a game changer for me.

It helped me to develop my therapeutic skills no end, and helped the service I work in become accessible, participatory, and the best as possible at delivering the therapy which the evidence shows works.

What would you have done if you hadn't been a therapist?

I always wanted to be a *Blue Peter* presenter!

The client: Meryl O'Rourke

'Therapy was a really nice, safe and nourishing space'

Recently, I wrote a sitcom based on my experiences of post-natal depression, so I went into therapy at the same time. Working through the sitcom with my therapist was a really nice, safe and nourishing space to be able to talk about my genuine feelings about my post-natal depression, while also putting them into a context of what I was going to do with those feelings artistically.

I never had therapy for post-natal depression at the time, just one meeting with a psychiatrist who seemed very out of his depth – he just told me to sleep more. But as I left he commented that I'd been rocking my baby during the appointment and that, though I was clearly very ill, he didn't see that often and felt I'd be all right. I held onto that.

Because of this I think it's key that the baby is present for all post-natal appointments. I used to say that if I had an hour away from my baby to talk to somebody, I wouldn't have post-natal depression anyway . . . Seeing how you're behaving with that baby and seeing if there is a feeling between you puts everything into context. People say it's important to give mothers a break, but I needed to spend time with my baby, and have somebody talk to me about how to just 'be' with her.

There's a scene I've worked on where the lead woman tries to kill her baby, because I thought that writing about post-natal depression without mentioning thoughts of infanticide would be the elephant in the room. There are few women with post-natal depression who don't have that thought. I workshopped this with my (now eleven-year-old) daughter. It was important to me that she knew how I was treating the worst year of her life, that she was able to clear it.

It's also been comforting to actors and producers that she approves. I've been open with her about my PND since she was six, in case I got it again with her little brother. I didn't want her to blame him. It's much easier to talk to her about it through comedy.

I also ran through this scene with my therapist. If you mention any thoughts of harm to children, therapists have to report you. My therapist didn't because it was very much in the past and was a passing thought that wasn't acted on in any way. She knows I'm not going to smother my eleven-year-old! But it's probably one of the reasons that people with post-natal depression still don't talk about it.

When I was interviewed for the sitcom programme, one of the best questions I was asked by the head of production was, 'Are you just going to hand me a list of your problems and pretend it's a script?' I thought that was a very wise question because I'd written a version for a different company and did fall to pieces.

I was able to say to him, 'No, I have a therapist, that's what my therapist is for and I will be keeping her on board for the entirety of the programme. If I have a wobble and a worry and some regressive memories that make me hate where I was when I had post-natal depression, she'll be getting that and I won't be telling you.' And I stuck to that.

Hypnotherapy/Hypnoanalysis

I didn't realise hippos had psychological issues.

Very amusing.

But seriously, we can skip hypnotherapy. I already know all about it.

Really? Enlighten me.

The therapist swings a pocket watch on a chain, tells the client they're feeling very sleepy, then makes them dance around the room pretending to be a chicken. Not sure how it helps, but that's what they do.

Do you ever think you should watch less television? To be fair to you, there is a widely held perception that when you hypnotise someone you can control what they do – but that's not actually the case.

Eh? What about the chicken dancing?

That's stage hypnotism. Those people are carefully chosen to be compliant and exhibitionist, and of course it's purely for entertainment. Hypnotism in a therapeutic sense is very different.

Spoilsport. Go on then, what happens?

The therapist will use relaxation exercises to put you in an altered state of consciousness. People have described this as being like a daydream where they are completely focused on what the therapist is saying, but still aware of everything around them.

The important thing to remember is that you're not in a zombie-like trance and can't be forced to do or say anything against your will when in this state. In fact, you can't be hypnotised at all unless you're willing to be.

If it's all about relaxation, is it just for treating anxiety?

The relaxed state is key to the therapy, but it's not treatment in itself – although it might be a pleasurable feeling. The idea is that when you are in the altered state of consciousness, your mind is more open to change. When the therapist makes suggestions for behavioural changes, they are more likely to take root because they aren't being automatically rejected by the conscious mind.

This can help with social phobias and self-esteem issues, as well as habitual problems such as smoking or weight control. It's basically for anything that you're struggling to achieve by normal thought processes.

So it actually works?

Hypnotherapy is a controversial field. There is limited evidence for its efficacy, and even those who think it works might disagree about how it works. Since you need to be compliant in order to be hypnotised in the first place, the anecdotal evidence is a bit self-selecting.

Assuming it did work, couldn't the therapist just look around in your head for weird stuff instead of making suggestions?

Well that brings us to our final therapy: hypnoanalysis.

Oh, so they do rummage around?

That's probably not how they'd put it. Hypnoanalysis has its roots in Freudian psychoanalysis, perhaps understandably – the notion that subconscious thoughts hold great power is pure Freud. So yes, the essential difference from hypnotherapy is that it looks at causes rather than symptoms.

Would they use the same techniques to hypnotise the client?

Yes, and everything I said before about not being forced into anything still applies. Once in the altered state, however, the therapist would be looking for the root causes of problems that the client is perhaps not consciously aware of.

Sounds a bit heavier than the other one.

It tends to deal with larger issues, yes. While hypnotherapy attempts to address something you are already aware of, hypnoanalysis might uncover things you weren't expecting. You need to be prepared for this and ask yourself if you're willing to act upon the information you receive.

Like kicking footballs at a hornets' nest. My mum warned me about that when I was a kid.

Did it end badly?

Nah, my aim wasn't good enough. So how does the therapist extract this information? Do they make you think about horrible things from the past?

As I said, you remain in control and don't have to do anything that you don't want to. Assuming that you agree though, the therapist might use techniques such as free association and direct regression. Free association is also used in psychoanalysis, if you recall, and involves the client saying whatever words come into their heads without attempting to make sense of them. The therapist will then try to interpret the results.

And 'direct regression'?

That's where the therapist will actively try to find the root cause of a problem. They will guide you towards it by asking you to talk about a situation where you felt the symptoms.

How long would it take to find the cause? And when they do, is that it?

It really depends on how complicated the problem is. There might be more than one incident that has contributed to it, and the revelation might require further examination of where you are in your life. It's not regarded as a short-term therapy, though, so don't expect to get everything resolved in your first session or you could be disappointed.

I'm definitely disappointed about the chicken dancing.

With the clients' best interests at heart, I'm sure.

The therapist: Tom Fortes Mayer

'Hypnotherapy is the art and science of having a good day'

How would you describe hypnotherapy to someone who has never had it?

It is the art and science of having a good day. I would also explain that hypnosis is a natural state that we go in and out of many times a day. When we are middle distancing, lost in vacant thought, driving on autopilot or just groggy in the morning, these are natural hypnotic states. When hypnotised, you don't lose control, you are fully conscious and in many ways, actually more present.

What does a typical hypnotherapy session entail?

First, a meet and greet which includes an overview of how the process works. This is about rapport building and putting the client's mind at rest.

Second, analysis of the 'problem' and/or development of therapeutic goals.

Third, a description of the hypnosis process and further explanation to the client, and gaining consent.

Fourth, induction of hypnosis relaxation.

Fifth, deepening into a more profound state of hypnosis.

Sixth, the therapeutic application. This is the use of any number of different therapeutic hypnosis techniques to create change. This can be visualisation to enhance performance; visualisation to aid mediation and forgiveness; regression therapy to find and release repressed emotion; entry into a discussion with aspects of the client's psychology to negotiate a change in feelings, thoughts, beliefs or behaviour.

Many therapists will also use metaphors or storytelling to create change on the unconscious level. I personally use powerful, emotionally evocative film music to inspire my clients to change. Music can also be used to heal old wounds and release limiting thoughts, feelings, beliefs, behaviour and even out-of-date identities that may be holding them back.

What can a client do to help themselves during hypnotherapy?

The best approach to experiencing hypnosis is to be curious, open-minded and collaborative with the process, and not to be attached to having a specific experience or outcome. Hypnosis is a simple state and sometimes people are disappointed because they are hoping for an intense magical experience or they expect to be essentially asleep while the hypnotherapist does all the work.

A good hypnotherapist will manage their client's expectations and get them on board with the co-creation of the experience.

What qualities should a client look for in a hypnotherapist?

Speak to them on the phone before you select them. They should be excellent communicators, clear, charismatic, capable and ideally with many years of experience, with hypnosis being their main job.

If they can't build rapport with you over the phone, then keep looking for someone else. Check out their website for (ideally video) testimonials.

Are there people for whom hypnotherapy isn't suitable?

Yes, hypnotherapy is contraindicated for people with psychosis, schizophrenia, multiple personality disorders and dissociative personality disorders.

What do you think of the stereotype that a hypnotherapist will make you do crazy things?

This is created by the nonsense of stage hypnosis which makes it look like the hypnotist has all the power. It makes it look like the people are under their spell. This is a total misrepresentation of hypnosis and it exploits a certain kind of individual who enjoys being given permission to goof around and entertain people.

In those settings, the hypnosis removes their inhibitions and rewards them with applause for being crazy. Unfortunately it makes most normal people really afraid of being hypnotised.

What do you enjoy most about practising hypnotherapy?

I love that sometimes in one session you can empower someone to think completely differently about themselves and life. Sometimes it can still take time to help people change, but sometimes a lifelong anxiety, depression, phobia or addiction (and many other things) can be resolved in one session. When that happens it is the best feeling in the world.

How much personal information do you disclose to clients?

I think that the relationship between therapist and client is a huge part of the healing process. I therefore choose to be an authentic person. I share information freely about my own life.

First, I have learned lots of valuable lessons and telling my story has a lot to teach people. Second, the more open I am about my own process, the more open the client is with me and the less likely they are to idealise me as a perfect person (the risk in therapy). I prefer to show my vulnerability so that I can show them that success in life is not about being perfect. It is more about loving the entirety of our being including all our personal challenges and limitations.

If you could start life over, would you still have been a hypnotherapist?

I now train people to be hypnotherapists, and there is nothing (professionally) that brings me more joy. I also use hypnosis in my drug- and alcohol-free raves that I run. Helping people unlock their potential and understand the extraordinary power of the human mind is an incredible pleasure and privilege. If I won the lottery and never needed to work again, I would still do hypnotherapy and teach people hypnotherapy.

What would you have done if you hadn't been a hypnotherapist?

First and foremost, I am a writer. Even with my love of hypnother-apy, sitting down at a desk and pouring my thoughts and feelings into words on paper is my greatest vocation. I have been published twice now, but I have ambitions for much more success in that area. That is my present reality and also my parallel life fantasy. I hope, in time, both will converge.

The client: Charlie Brooker

'I went along, thinking: "This probably isn't going to work"'

Before trying hypnotherapy to quit smoking, I think I'd tried most things. I'd tried going cold turkey, and I was rubbish at that, because within about twenty-four hours I'd find myself walking to a night garage in tears to buy some cigarettes. Whenever I'd try and quit, I'd become obsessed with the notion of having a cigarette, and it was unbearable, like a voice constantly tormenting me.

I tried nicotine gum, which it turned out I didn't know how to use properly! I hadn't read the instructions, because why would you read the instructions for chewing gum? I didn't know you were only meant to chew it once every ten minutes, otherwise it releases so much nicotine that you faint. So that was horrible.

Then I tried nicotine patches, which worked, and I quit for five years – then started smoking again. The next time I tried patches, they didn't work for me. I'd put the patches on during the day and then peel them off and smoke in the evening.

So I literally turned to hypnotherapy out of desperation. Smoking affects your self-esteem, as it's so self-destructive and pointless. People can drink and argue that it's making them relaxed, but the only thing that smoking alleviates is the tension of not having a cigarette – so it's completely self-cancelling.

Someone suggested googling 'quit anti-smoking hypnotism' so I did, and found this guy in Tooting. I went along, thinking: 'This probably isn't going to work.'

The therapist worked out of his home. There was a pile of lighters there – the whole house was a fire hazard. He asked me to hand over my lighter and any cigarettes I had, and he just started talking.

I don't even remember what he said, but I quickly started feeling a bit weird. You know that feeling when you're trying to stay awake in the cinema or a lecture hall, and you can't quite manage it? It was like a twilight zone between being awake and being asleep.

He asked me several questions: 'When did you first start smoking?', etc. Then his questions became increasingly abstract: 'If you could give that feeling a colour, what colour would it be?' I went into a trance and lost track of time. I think some people are susceptible to hypnotism and some aren't, but it turned out that I was.

An hour later, the therapist said: 'You're back in the room and you're now a non-smoker.' I remember sort of nodding and saying 'Yes' and thinking 'Bullshit'. I left and had to wait for a bus, and there was a newsagent's nearby. Normally I'd go in and buy some cigarettes, but I didn't.

When I got off the bus, there was another newsagent's, but I didn't buy cigarettes there either. I thought: 'No, I won't, because I've done this thing that tells me I won't smoke any more.' I went into my flat and the familiar craving began.

To start with, it's a slowly rising tension, a bit like hunger, but it doesn't feel like hunger in your belly – it's like a strange itching need for something. Then you're irritated, like you would be if you were very hungry, thirsty or tired. Beyond that, you start getting symptoms a bit like a cold, which is your system clearing itself out.

Normally this would have had me running to a shop to buy cigarettes, but as I was feeling the tension and annoyance and anxiety and anger from non-smoking, I kept thinking: 'This is annoying that I'm having all these symptoms, because I don't smoke now.' Rather than thinking: 'Oh, I feel shit, I'll go and buy some cigarettes and smoke them,' I thought: 'Oh, I feel shit because I don't smoke any more.'

It's like having a cold virus and it being annoying. That was how I was seeing these symptoms, like, 'This is an irritating thing but it will go away.' I kept drinking water, because I'd read somewhere that every time you want to smoke you need to drink or eat. So crucially, what had happened is that the therapist had managed to reframe my perception of smoking, and I now considered myself a non-smoker.

Now, I don't believe that a hypnotist could do this if you didn't want it to happen. You speak to people who ask: 'Weren't you worried he'd turn you into an assassin, or make you jump out of a window?' and I'm like, 'He couldn't – not unless I actually wanted to do those things.'

It's not like the hypnotism in *Get Out*, though in *Get Out* the depiction of him sinking into the sunken place is similar to the feeling you get when in a trance, but more in a warm drowsy way. It's quite pleasant, a bit like on a sunny afternoon where you start to drift off on a sofa.

The first hypnotherapy session worked without me needing to have any more, but it takes about three months for you to become a non-smoker. Seventy-two hours is the point of the drug leaving your system. There is a point around then where you reach your lowest ebb, and I remember being furious at the sky! Because the sky was annoying me, for some reason.

And that starts to go away, and then psychologically you're getting over the habit. I kept feeling as though I'd forgotten something, and I was like, 'Oh, it's because I don't smoke any more.'

Then nine months later, someone lit up a cigarette in a pub, and I had one and thought, 'Where's the harm, 'cause I don't smoke any more?' and that broke the spell. A few days later I had another one, and another one, and then a week later I bought a pack of cigarettes.

Eventually, I had myself hypnotised again by the same guy, who didn't charge me this time – that was part of the deal. Then I failed again after two years. I went four times in total, the last two times to different hypnotists.

The last one I saw was ridiculous and really expensive. He'd literally drawn an eye on the palm of his hand, which was just silly! I'm not sure that time whether I quit out of bloody-mindedness, because it was just so much money.

I also paid for the director on the show I was working on to get hypnotised, because I thought that if he was smoking around me it would set me off. It didn't work at all for him – he thought it was nonsense.

But it worked for me, without a shadow of a doubt.

Hypnotism recordings zonk me out. I can't be that person who listens to them while driving. I'm particularly susceptible.

Hypnotherapy took something I felt helpless to control and reframed it, so that my viewpoint and relationship to the symptoms I experienced shifted, so I didn't see them as signs I had to go and smoke a cigarette. It reframed my perception of who I was.

I was tempted to have more hypnotherapy for arachnophobia, and maybe for insomnia and fear of flying, but I didn't.

Although, weirdly, I have listened to fear-of-flying hypnotherapy recordings, and I've got a lot better at flying recently. It might just be due to having to fly more, but I can now get on a plane without having to drink beforehand or take Valium. I can be completely stone-cold sober.

260

These days, I've completely kicked smoking. It's such an insidious drug. I haven't even been tempted to have an e-cigarette. I have no desire to find out what that's like, otherwise I'd end up buying those liquid capsules.

Looking at the therapy afterwards, I realised that it was useful not to try and shove all thoughts of smoking out of my head. Whereas I think that's what I used to do. I would still occasionally crave cigarettes or see someone smoking and think: 'I could do that.'

I gave in once and knew that was a mistake, because I spent the next week thinking about cigarettes, so I realised I couldn't have even one. But it was useful to not deny the fact that I wanted one.

Every so often I would see someone smoking and I would just say: 'God, I wish I could have one of those.' It's odd, but it sort of loses its power to control you. Whereas if you think: 'God, I mustn't think that I want that,' you sort of end up craving it more.

I realised a couple of years ago that I hadn't wanted a cigarette for years. And it wouldn't occur to me for a second to have one now when I see someone doing it. It would be like me looking at someone shooting a squirrel with a bow and arrow. I wouldn't think: 'I want to have a go at that!'

Computerised CBT

I knew this day would come. They're replacing therapists with robots, aren't they?

Relax, that hasn't happened yet. Computerised CBT is a service to bring assistance to a wider range of people with mild to moderate symptoms.

So all you need is a computer?

A computer and an internet connection, although it will also work on a tablet or smartphone.

Great! What's the website address?

Slow down. There isn't a single source for this type of treatment, and you'll need an assessment first.

But I know how to use a computer.

They're not assessing you for that. You might be referred for CCBT by your GP, but to gauge the sort of help you need, you'll be assessed first by an expert. This will probably happen over the phone.

So they tailor the test to you?

It's not a test! The programme is something you'll do weekly for a certain period of time, but it's not conventional therapy as it's all automated. It's designed to help with things like your thinking patterns, behaviours and sleep routines. As you might have guessed, it uses CBT methods to foster a healthier state of mind.

Is it free?

It's free on the NHS, and available at reduced waiting times compared to conventional CBT treatment. If you wanted to pay, you could also seek private assistance.

Is it as good as normal therapy? Aren't therapists unhappy about losing business?

Therapists aren't necessarily unhappy about it, especially if it reduces their workload, but they would point out that for serious problems it would be better to speak to somebody face-to-face. CCBT isn't seen as a suitable solution for people with severe depression or anxiety, for example, but for those with less serious conditions it might be all you need.

Is it mainly for depression and anxiety then?

No, it can also be useful for conditions like agoraphobia, because obviously the sufferer wouldn't be comfortable leaving their home. Mobility or other travel problems might also lead your GP to recommend CCBT as a first step.

I guess it can't be too bad if doctors are suggesting it.

It's actually a recommended intervention by NICE.

That's . . . nice. Are there any other benefits?

It might be a good option for people who worry about the stigma of seeking help for mental health issues, or those who find it difficult to get time off work. Convenience is a big deal these days.

And you absolutely promise there are no robot therapists yet?

No, you can relax. For now.

The client: Ariane Sherine

'I knew it was just a stop-gap'

I was referred for computerised CBT at a local library when I was experiencing extreme claustrophobia, before I started cognitive analytic therapy. I knew it was just a stop-gap until I could be seen by a 'real' therapist, but was slightly disappointed by how simplistic it was. The questions the programme asked me to answer seemed to be tailored to somebody much younger – I guess the programmer had to cater for all abilities, but I saw it as dumbing down, and it didn't fill me with confidence.

In retrospect, I should have been more open to CCBT, but I think that given the horror I'd been through that resulted in the claustrophobia, I needed the compassion and understanding of a human being rather than a screen. I stopped the CCBT after a couple of sessions.

It would take another three years of struggling before I would get back on the Tube regularly, and I'm still not comfortable in lifts. This wasn't the fault of CCBT – as with all therapy, the client needs to engage fully with the process, and confronting my fears just wasn't something I was willing to do at that stage. I imagine CCBT would work for someone with a milder phobia, or milder anxiety or depression. I don't think it's suitable for people who have undergone serious trauma.

James Brown on Therapy for Addiction

'One of my therapists helped me to save my life'

You wrote a big piece for the Telegraph magazine about having therapy. How did that come about?

They called and said that they needed someone to write honestly about therapy. I said I could write about the therapy that helped me to stop using drugs and drinking, because it could be of use to someone else. I didn't want to write about subsequent therapy that was more to do with my childhood, or relationships, because it involved other people. I didn't think those people would like to read about themselves.

There are lots of people who struggle with addiction, in whatever form it takes, and so far my recovery has been a success – so I thought other people may get something out of it because they're either struggling themselves or know someone who is. When I was drinking a lot and using drugs, there were very few voices around me that were contrary to the way I was behaving.

Only a couple of people had a word with me. I remember them clearly standing out – one of them was the fashion designer Sir Paul Smith. Sometimes it can just take a caring sentence to jog someone in a different direction. I hoped my article might show people in the thick of it that there is another way if you can get there.

There's so little honest discussion about therapy, the nuts and bolts of it.

For a lot of men, I think the most common access they may have had to someone taking part in therapy would be from *The Sopranos*.

There was *Analyse This* as well which was the same premise, and a very funny sitcom with Paul Whitehouse called *Help*.

There's also a show called Gypsy *on Netflix, starring Naomi Watts. She's a bad therapist who has sex with her client's ex-girlfriend. Have you ever thought of any of your therapists in that way?*

I've never wanted to have sex with any of my therapists. That's a cliché isn't it – that people will fall in love with their therapist? – but I go there to be selfish and talk about me. I don't care what they're thinking about. They say things that help but I'm not there to fall in love. It's a strange theory because there's nothing there for me – it would be like falling in love with my fridge.

I go into that room to get away from the concept of falling in love, or to get some feedback on it, but not to add to it! I did once meet a therapist when I was making a documentary and I thought she was nice, but that was a one-off meeting rather than a regular professional relationship.

Your article declared that therapy saved your life. Is that true?

I think my rehab therapist, Clive Meindl, helped me to save my life. I said that to the lady who commissioned the article and she interpreted it as him stopping me from killing myself, but it wasn't that at all. He saved me in the sense of helping me find a different way of life, a life without dependency on drugs and drink. I was using and drinking most days for an intense period of five or six years. So he helped save me from a life that, internally, I didn't like.

Externally, my life looked very attractive and was – I had a successful job, at the time I was considered the best at what I did in Britain, I had all the top magazine editing awards and praise, and I lived in a very exciting, glamorous world. Inside, though, I had all of this turmoil that was being accentuated by the drugs and the drink. Therapy saved me from that feeling. I've been clean longer now (twenty years) than I was drinking (seventeen). Had I continued as I was, I could have died. I have friends who did. I don't know that I will always be like this, but so long as I don't pick up and use a drug or a drink today I'm good with that.

Thinking about it now, it doesn't seem like a long time, but some people can have one bad experience and stop drinking or taking drugs, but I was having intense experiences every day. I got used to dealing with that. I knew how to deal with a hangover, but what you can't deal with is the depression that comes with it. People say they're never going to drink again after a bad night, but I never said that. I kept going, like the Circle Line. The only break would be the few hours that I was asleep.

I like the exercise you outlined in the Telegraph piece, where your therapist got you to put an imaginary alcoholic drink on a chair, then put five things in the middle that you'd like to do instead of drinking it.

I only remember one of them, and that's playing football. I think I probably said, 'Have a family,' but I don't know if I did think that at the time. I thought, 'I can't just put football.' It seemed a constructive thing to want. I imagine wearing clean clothes daily was probably another attraction. I was definitely a man who dressed from the floor or wherever my clothes had been thrown.

So you can't remember if you managed to do your list of things when you managed to give up alcohol?

I probably did because they weren't things like climbing Everest. They were pretty everyday things. The chaotic nature of having an active addiction and alcohol problem meant that there was so little organisation. Now I'm clean, my manageability isn't always the best but on a day-to-day basis I manage to do a lot more things rather than just not showing up.

Regarding the article about therapy in the *Telegraph* magazine, I thought that because I was so celebratory about drug and drink culture in *Loaded*, I ought to show that if you get into trouble that there is another way.

It provoked a positive response. I've had quite a few first-hand conversations or emails saying 'This is what my life is like', or 'I've given this to someone I know'. I mentioned my former rehab therapist in the article and he tells me that he's still getting referrals because of it. Even last week, two years on from publication, someone wrote to me requesting a copy of the article so they could give it to a relative.

There's a part of your article in which you say your therapist made an analogy of your life as a clock, with the hand at the bottom meaning you would go to prison, get raped and die. He told you that you were at twenty-five minutes past and accelerating . . . So that's what made you decide to change?

The fear that image generated in me is what made me stop. I thought, 'I don't like this! I've still got the equivalent of four minutes further to fall!'

At *Loaded*, the levels of excess were never over-exaggerated. People would ask if it was really that bad and I would reply that no, it was much worse! We had people with heroin addictions on the staff, we had people in and out of mental health hospitals, there were people running drugs on the bike service . . . It was chaos, because we were doing so well and no one was coming near us. We made the company so much money in our own building, we were left to get on and do what we wanted.

I was in São Paulo on the way to Rio with four or five of the staff. We were covering the Jordan race team at the Grand Prix, and I'd had a very, very excessive few days. There was a nice guy driving us around, a student doing a summer job. I'd given him a massive tip and had always been polite to him. When he was dropping us off at the airport he turned around to everybody in the bus, most of whom worked for me, and said – as if I wasn't there – 'I like James. He has been very kind to me. However, I must warn you: if he behaves in Rio de Janeiro the way he's behaved in São Paulo, he will be raped and then murdered.' You know, that's something you don't want to hear.

So when we got to Rio, I didn't go out on the first night. I'd been there before when I was very young, about twenty-three, and it had been rough then. So the others went out and had a really bad night, or a good night depending on how you saw it, and I stayed in the hotel pondering whether to go to *GQ*, which I'd been offered before the trip. When you're kind of powerless over that kind of behaviour, which I was, it's a terrifying thing.

My therapist had told me that if my clock hit rock bottom, I could end up dead. At that point I thought, 'God, that's what that guy in South America said!' When more than one person tells you that you might end up dead, it starts to ring bells. Big Ben-sized bells! A colleague at Loaded had gone absolutely bonkers and had been in a mental hospital for six months, so I knew that drug taking wasn't all supposed glamour.

Did you enjoy going to your therapist? Or is 'enjoy' the wrong word?

My therapist wasn't very prescriptive. I'd just sit down and offload – it would all come out like an avalanche – and I'd feel better. It was like taking off overcoats that were made of concrete. I was talking to a stranger in private about things I'd never talked about. I was telling him about what I was doing each night and how I felt each night.

I would tell my mates where I'd ended up, but talking to someone about how I felt in those circumstances was very liberating and different. I was told to go to proper residential rehab, but I didn't want to do that. My ego wouldn't let me. I thought I wouldn't be able to carry on being editor of *GQ* if I disappeared for a month. I'd only been there for eight weeks!

Do you think your addiction was a response in part to the pressures of your job?

No, I'd been drinking heavily since I was a teenager. The best definition of alcoholism I've heard is someone who drinks more than they want to. People think of alcoholics as street drinkers, but it could be perfectly successful, functioning people who come home wanting to have one glass and then find themselves opening a second bottle.

When I was at the *NME*, I threw up all over the editor's desk after a lunchtime interview on speed and vodka with a singer called Zodiac Mindwarp! I liked the pressure of the job though. I was good at editing. If there's a big challenge I can calmly work my way through it, but I get irritated by much smaller things.

So the pressure was fine. I did some work on the *New European* newspaper over the past year that used to take me five days when I was at the *NME*, but I can do it in about two hours now. If you're naturally interested and skilled at doing something, pressure can be a good thing. It's only a bad thing if you can't cope with what you're trying to do.

When firefighters attend a fire, they're obviously under an enormous amount of pressure – it's dangerous, physically uncomfortable and they have limited time – but they know what they're doing, so the pressure just adds to the focus that they need to apply.

If you're good at what you do, pressure just enhances the situation. People turn to drink to relieve daily pressure but I was drinking because I liked it, I liked the way it made me feel. Also I thought it was part of the job in a way. Music and journalism, two areas you wouldn't be bollocked for being pissed at work.

But when you're the editor, the buck stops with you.

At *Loaded*, the challenge was to keep the staff unaware of what the bosses were saying to me, and to keep the bosses away from the staff. That's a pressure that a lot of people don't see. They were working to different agendas. That's an invisible pressure when there's somebody above you and somebody below you.

You say in the Telegraph *article, 'Give an extrovert an opportunity to talk about themselves and every session will seem to end too early.' Is therapy easier for people who are natural extroverts?*

This morning on my way to therapy I was trying to prioritise what I should talk about, because I wanted to talk about bigger things and didn't want to get distracted. I would now call relationships surface stuff, so I wanted to focus on other things. I'm very aware that I can talk excessively if I'm not focused. Once I was asked to give a commentary at an away day in London for an upmarket men's fashion magazine and I spoke for three hours!

Are you more likely to listen to a therapist than a friend?

I don't go to a therapist primarily to listen, I go to talk and discuss and think. I don't want to bore my friends or feel like I'm imposing on them. I do listen to the therapist, but I do most of the talking. Needless to say, what she can feed back or move me to consider is usually more interesting than me just banging on.

I broke up with my long-term girlfriend who I have a child with this year, and at times I could have done with a bit more attention from my friends, but you end up pretending everything is fine. I think if a woman breaks up with a man, the first thing they might do is call their friends, whereas if a man breaks up with a woman the first thing they might do is turn the football on.

A man will try to cover up his feelings where a woman would open them up and seek support and reassurance. So I haven't really spoken to any of my mates about the fact that this ten-year relationship – the best I've ever had – has ended. And none of them have asked if I'm all right! I appear OK, so they assume I'm OK.

Men I've spoken to have said that they were encouraged from an early age to bottle feelings up and not talk about them. Do you think that if therapy was mandatory for men then male suicide rates would be lower?

I don't think making something mandatory helps. I think more people would benefit from doing it, and I'm not embarrassed to talk about it, but at times it's very self-indulgent. If you can afford it and you can get it then it's helpful. That's why *The Sopranos* is good, because you see Tony's awkwardness at the beginning. He's the archetypal alpha male and he says at the very beginning when he goes to see Doctor Melfi, he could get killed by his peers if they think he's discussing his world.

She has to work out what he does for a living and it takes her a while. The whole series is about this man with two families – his biological family and the Mafia – and how he seeks help from a therapist to deal with both circumstances. There's also a very good book called *The World Is (Not) a Cold Dead Place* by Nathan O'Hagan. It starts with an OCD sufferer being forced to stop therapy. If more men had easier access to and were comfortable with therapy, then less might die at their own hands.

You said that Tony Soprano was the archetypal alpha male. Do you think you're a real-life alpha male?

No. When I got clean I no longer needed to be the best at stuff. I dropped some of my ambition because I felt that it was fuelling my self-destruction.

Are you happier than before?

Yes, definitely. I have more insight into my life now, so I know that if I'm feeling down it won't last and those feelings will move on. I read a really good interview this morning with Vanessa Feltz by Simon Hattenstone. It was a great example of a good interview because you feel like you're with the person.

I have no real interest in Vanessa Feltz's career, I don't see or hear her shows, but she said something really shocking and funny when I was on a radio show with her once so I thought, 'I'll have a read of this, it might be quite interesting.' After I'd read it I felt like I'd just spent half an hour with her. I tweeted Simon, saying, 'Really good interview Simon, you are the best.' He got back to me, saying, 'Thank you James, that's made my day.' It's a tiny thing but if he was having a shit day, just getting that message has made his day better. So I know that feelings can change quickly.

When I used to use drugs, my feelings would become like an anchor. I'd take out negative feelings created by one situation on the next person I encountered, often when it was totally unwarranted. At *Loaded* I had very bad narcotic-influenced mood swings, but I don't have that any more. Sometimes I find it's a good idea to write a letter to someone who's upset you, but not send it. It gets your feelings out by articulating them in writing, but it doesn't prolong the situation.

There are things like these, that I have learned through therapy, that have improved my life.

If I get wound up by someone or something now, I try to think, 'Hang on, why am I feeling like this? What's my part in it and how am I going to deal with it?' So I'm mentally responding to my feelings rather than lashing out. I could often talk to the *Loaded* staff in a really sharp, cutting way one minute, but I would justify it to myself because the next minute I would say, 'Yes of course you can go to New York! Take the credit card, buy the tickets . . .'

So I was like a benevolent dictator, and it caused resentment. I was very young though, and professionally immature. That can happen to people who are good at what they do because they get high up very quickly and they haven't had the years to mature as they gather experience. They're just hurled up the ladder, or they run up the ladder if they can get up it themselves easily.

At IPC, they identified me as a future editor within about three months of me being at the *NME*; I was twenty-one. I didn't shave or even own a shirt with a collar. As you get older you mature and develop social skills, but back then I didn't have either.

Do you think that payment renders therapy more effective because you're more likely to take it seriously if your bank balance takes a hit?

Well, it means that I don't like cancelling sessions at short notice. I've had to do that a few times. I don't think about it much. All the stuff I did with Clive was paid for by Condé Nast's health insurance so I was lucky.

Do you think you'll ever stop having therapy, or are we all works in progress?

I don't think about stopping completely, but sometimes I wonder about who I'm doing it with and whether I'm getting too friendly, whether I'm too relaxed. There are long periods of time when I don't see a therapist.

But if you're so relaxed that you can say anything to somebody, doesn't that help?

Yes, that's true. I can certainly be myself.

You said in your piece that a therapist was holding a metaphorical mirror up. Do you think that's effective because most of us walk around not really knowing what we look like inside?

A lot of us don't really know what we look like on the outside. It's always a shock when you see what you really look like. I did have a good session with the woman that I went to after Clive where she got me to identify myself through four stages of my life; from being a little kid, my early teens, my early twenties and early thirties, which is how old I was at the time. Then she asked me to think about what I wanted to be like.

That was really good, to be able to project what you hoped you would be in your ideal self, and being able to use it in a line from the people you'd been in the past.

I spend too much time in my head, and going to therapy allows me some time to get out what's going round in there. You asked earlier why it was different from talking to a friend, but if someone is a professional, they know how to behave. A friend might not know the best way to respond to a situation.

Bibliotherapy

This is a bit controversial, isn't it? Recommending the Bible as therapy?

That's not what it means. Bibliotherapy is the use of books for therapeutic purposes.

But the Bible is a book, so . . .

I was thinking more of therapy self-help books.

You mean you don't even need a therapist for this one?

No, although you might use it together with another type of therapy. Your therapist might, for example, recommend some books for you to read.

The last book I read was Fifty Shades of Grey, *and that was embarrassing enough to take to the counter. I don't need the shame of buying self-help books too.*

You can always buy them online.

But then MI5 will be able to find out I've bought them.

Sounds like you need a copy of *Overcoming Paranoid and Suspicious Thoughts*.

Is that an actual book, or are you making fun of me?

It's an actual book in the popular 'Overcoming' series. You can also get books that will aim to help you deal with depression, anxiety, OCD, eating disorders and pretty much any condition that adversely affects your life.

So there's no structure then – you just read as many as you want?

Of course – it's entirely up to you. For many people, bibliotherapy is the best option if they're short of time or money.

Are there a lot of self-help books to choose from?

There are countless self-help books! But with such a vast selection, the quality of the content will vary wildly. Luckily there's a scheme called the Reading Well Books on Prescription scheme, which produces lists of recommended books for common mental health conditions. It also allows users access to libraries to get hold of these books.

So why even bother with therapy if people can just read books instead?

A book isn't a substitute for a trained therapist. It can't give you feedback and you shouldn't underestimate the value of having someone who will listen to you in confidence.

However, if you've already had some therapy it might be a good top-up, or if you're unsure about having therapy it could be a good introduction to what to expect. There's no limit either – you can take in as much or as little as you like.

OK. I'll have to finish Fifty Shades *first though. I spent a lot of money on cable ties, I don't want it wasted.*

Whatever.

The client: Jules Bristow

'Your readers aren't stupid. Treat them with respect'

I've been reading self-help books for the best part of a decade, to help with my depression. I found the books *Overcoming Depression* and *The Compassionate Mind* the most helpful, as they offered an explanation of the mechanism of depression and provided non-judgemental, practical, CBT-based exercises to help you work on things. I also read a number of other books.

The least helpful book I read was about depression and productivity. The message was basically just 'snap out of it and get on with it', which I wanted to do and would have done if I'd been able to, but couldn't. It left me feeling thoroughly demoralised and like I'd just been lectured for not trying hard enough.

I don't think any of the books I read helped me get rid of my depression, but all of them, with the exception of the book above, taught me strategies for being more functional while living with the illness. These included ways of redirecting negative thoughts; writing down a 'to do' list so everything was on paper rather than floating around my head and making me worry I'd forget things; and being patient with myself instead of getting angry at myself for feeling like this.

The best thing about self-help books is that you can read them at your own pace when you need them, and dip into chapters in the order that suits you best. They give you back a bit of control.

Self-help books are primarily suitable for people who learn well from written material, which I know I always have. I'd imagine that people who prefer to learn by practising things or through conversation wouldn't find them as useful.

If I had to give advice to someone thinking of buying one, I'd say to read plenty of reviews and see if it sounds like something that fits with what you find useful. I did a lot of reading about depression online and went for the ones that seemed to come highly recommended, but I realise I'm a bit of a nerdy academic type who is used to doing lots of research, so it wasn't so much of a mental effort for me. I'd imagine someone who didn't find that sort of thing easy might struggle with doing a lot of research during a mental health crisis.

If I had to give advice to someone thinking of *writing* a self-help book, I'd say: 'Your readers aren't stupid, and they are already trying their hardest. Treat them with respect.'

Medication

Medication? It's Talk Yourself Better, *not* Drug Yourself Better!

Yes, but medication is often offered to patients alongside or instead of therapy, so it makes sense to have a section of the book about it.

Still, I'm guessing you'd choose therapy over drugs? After all, this book is called—

Yes, *Talk Yourself Better*. But you're wrong in your assumption: I actually think that, for very mentally ill people like me, medication is more important than therapy.

What? So you wouldn't recommend therapy after all?

Of course I would – I wouldn't have spent six months of the only life I'll ever have writing a book about it otherwise. But whether you should try therapy, meds or both really depends on the severity of your mental health problems.

If you're as suicidal as I was, there's often no point in having therapy straight away, as it won't have any effect. You need medication to take your anxious, depressed or paranoid thoughts back to a stable level where you're able to respond to rational conversation.

Conversely, if you've got mild depression or anxiety, you're better off with therapy. Bringing out the big guns like antipsychotics is massive overkill, and might have unwanted effects.

Ah yes, I've heard about those side effects. My brother is on antidepressants and apparently he can't jizz any more.

Well, that's the sort of side effect a lot of people can put up with. When I was on 10mg a day of the antipsychotic olanzapine, I couldn't do anything but eat and sleep. It literally knocked me out for sixteen hours a day.

Wow. I bet even Floyd Mayweather couldn't knock someone out for that long.

I needed to be knocked out at the time, because I was having such extreme anxiety and suicidal thoughts that sedation was a relief, but it wasn't practical in the long term. Anyhow: I was on a hardcore med, but I was way too scared to have therapy, because I thought everything I did was being monitored.

Why? You don't seem especially interesting to me.

Thank you. I was having terrifying paranoid thoughts because I wasn't able to think rationally. Any time a doctor would see me during my breakdown, I would refuse to tell them anything, because I was so afraid.

Why, was your doctor Harold Shipman?

Thankfully not. Anyhow, eventually I got to see a brilliant psychiatrist. He took me off olanzapine and put me on a drug called pregabalin. Neither worked on its own, but there was a short crossover period when I was taking both drugs, and it was a miracle: I felt close to normal again when it came to paranoia.

Not happy, exactly – I still had terrible OCD and intrusive thoughts – but I didn't think I was being monitored by the government. The psychiatrist had hit on the right drug combination for my paranoia, but entirely by accident.

As for my OCD, I did some research online into drugs that could treat obsessions and intrusive thoughts, and stumbled across a drug called clomipramine. When I asked my doctor if I could try it, he said, 'I suppose so, though I don't think it'll be a magic bullet.' It was a magic bullet.

So what you're basically saying is, doctors and psychiatrists have no idea what they're doing, and you were just a guinea pig who happens to be good at research?

No, I'm saying I was very lucky. Psychiatrists and doctors have an incredibly difficult job: everybody's brain chemistry and mental health problems are different, and they have to judge the correct drugs and dosage for each patient. It can be a case of trial and error. I don't envy them: it's a huge responsibility. But when it works, it saves lives.

And when it doesn't work, you can't jizz?

I can't jizz anyway. I'm female.

I guess you haven't seen the same films as me. I've seen women who—

Yes, thank you. The other thing I wanted to say was that numerous studies show that a combination of medication and therapy is most effective at combatting mental illness, rather than either separately. That's what I've personally found, and I wouldn't be without either therapy or drugs now.

My mum doesn't like medication. She thinks Big Pharma are trying to poison her, so she just takes natural remedies instead.

I tried a load of alternative remedies for my illness before agreeing to take the antipsychotic. All that happened was that I continued to suffer. I'm not saying *no* natural remedies *ever* work, but when you're incredibly ill you generally need conventional medicine.

So do you think your next book will be called Drug Yourself Better?

No.

The psychiatrist: David Veale

'There is an element of trial and error'

When would you advise someone to consider taking medication?

When it is combined with therapy – ideally, in my view, CBT – if symptoms are severe or disabling, or if the person hasn't made as much progress with therapy as one would have hoped.

What are the main downsides to taking medication?

The possible side effects, and the fact that a person may need to be on meds for one to two years or longer, depending on whether their condition is recurrent.

What kind of side effects would make you advise someone to discontinue a medication?

When they are intolerable or dangerous!

How do psychiatrists decide what medication someone needs? Is there an element of trial and error?

On the basis of previous large controlled trials in particular, their condition and any side-effect profile. For example, a drug might be more sedating, but this may be helpful if the patient is having difficulty getting to sleep. There is an element of trial and error.

What would you say to people who are anti-conventional medicine and favour alternative medicine?

Do your research and make your decision.

Would you personally consider taking medication if you became anxious or depressed?

Yes, if it was combined with CBT, and if symptoms were severe or disabling – or if I had not made as much progress with CBT as I would have hoped.

The client: John Crace

'It's a bit like when there's a major fire – the first thing is to put it out. You don't just watch it and wonder how it started!'

I was amazed by the fact that many psychiatrists are anti-drugs. It was a real revelation to me, because I was invited to speak in a debate, which was that the use of medication is beneficial in treating mental illness. I'm not a psychiatrist and I don't have all the evidence, so I asked if they were sure they wanted me to speak.

They said that they'd read a lot of my stuff and they thought that my perspective would be useful, so I agreed. I thought the debate was a no-brainer – how could anyone possibly argue against the use of medication? – but there was a psychiatrist there who was absolutely adamant that all drugs were evil.

I'm not sure how self-selecting the audience was, but it was about 65–35 per cent in his favour. Most of these people were psychiatrists and psychiatry students, and I just thought it was mad that these people were going into a profession where they apparently believed that drugs were doing more harm than good.

I came out of the debate feeling rather traumatised, because some of the criticisms and levels of argument were very personal. I wrote an article about it. It still astonishes me that there is that level of hostility within the profession towards itself. It feels as though it's a profession tearing itself apart.

Most of the emails I received in response to my article were entirely supportive. I also got some lovely emails from people who attended the debate and agreed that it was a bear pit and that I was caught in the middle.

The psychiatrist who was speaking against me was perceived as a well-known controversialist, and it was suggested that the hall had been filled with some of his acolytes. I guess if you've been on medication and it hasn't worked, you have a far stronger opinion on it than if you've been on medication that has worked and you're just getting on with your life.

I don't have any major side effects to my medication. You never quite know what you'd be like if you weren't taking them. Some people on fluoxetine (Prozac) have described themselves as being remote and cut-off, but I don't feel that way – or at least, only to a very acceptable level. I need a slight detachment because in the middle of a full-blown depressive episode, you need all the help you can get. It's far preferable to not taking the medication.

I'm sixty, and I've been on antidepressants for about twenty years. In the early days, psychiatrists would say it was time to come off them, but within six months to a year I would have these crashing, depressive, anxious episodes all over again.

It also takes time for them to work, and their effects are quite subtle at times. There have been times when I wonder if it's a placebo effect, and that the act of taking the drug was reassuring. Perhaps a given episode would have only had a shelf-life of two weeks anyway, so I can't be certain, but on balance they appear to work. This is the way that I feel I function best.

Prozac was the drug I started on, and it seemed to work, so I've seen no reason to change it. I've been on it ever since.

To those who say that taking medication is just dealing with the symptoms of mental illness, I'd say that they're entitled to their opinion, but sometimes you just have to treat the symptoms.

You can spend years and years trying to find out the causes, and you may or may not get there – I'm still torn between whether depression is a physical chemical imbalance, or whether it's caused by external events.

I've had moments when it's felt like one and moments when it's felt like the other. It's a bit like when there's a major fire – the first thing is to put it out. You don't just watch it and wonder how it started!

I've always been quite lucky with my psychiatrists. I've never really stopped to think whether any of them are on medication themselves. I think perhaps I'm too self-centred to consider them as anything other than doing a job.

Mine have always been very happy to take my word for how the drugs are working rather than telling me how they ought to be working. If I was to go in and say that for some reason everything has gone wrong and I don't know why, my psychiatrist would scurry around to try to find a solution.

I do think there is an issue here of class and education in that I'm quite articulate, so I'm not intimidated by the psychiatrist/patient relationship and unable to put my views forward. I never go away feeling unheard, whereas I guess if you lacked the confidence to confront a psychiatrist, they might spend half an hour talking at you and the patient could go away thinking that they didn't listen to a word they said.

You can't blame the psychiatrist for a patient who can't express their concerns properly. They have X amount of patients to see in a day, and they can't be held responsible.

You also need to have done your research. If I see my GP for a chest infection or something like that, I'll be as compliant as the next person because I trust her judgement. I'm not going to tell her that she's prescribing me the wrong antibiotic.

It's different with a psychiatrist, because through years of therapy I've learned how to articulate my emotional and psychiatric needs. When I first went into the psychiatric hospital they put me on Prozac, and I wasn't in any condition to question anything, so I was just lucky that it worked.

If it hadn't, I don't know how long it would have taken me to ask for something else. I guess if it hadn't worked they'd have just done something else because they wouldn't have let me out of the hospital until I was better.

I think the people who are concerned about the ethics of the pharmaceutical industry are those who aren't in crisis. I'm sure if I had cancer and the doctor said, 'We're going to try this because it's the best option,' I'd just go along with it. If you google it you only get a load of information that may or may not be true.

To say I'm resigned to my medication sounds a bit passive; I'm just accepting of it. It doesn't seem like such a big deal to be on it for the rest of my life. Whenever I pack to go abroad, my drugs are the first thing I think of. I take them in hand luggage to be safe.

If I found myself abroad without them, what I would do depends on how long I was going away for. If it was for two weeks, I'd know that there was no chance. If it was a couple of days, I might try to risk it. I don't think I'd travel to somewhere remote and without access to drugs in case I had an emergency.

There was a time when we felt the Prozac wasn't working enough, so my psychiatrist doubled the dose and that sorted things out. My experience of the NHS psychiatric services is that they are over-stretched and just firefighting all the time.

They might have somebody with PTSD from Syria or something, so a bloke like me who comes along saying that his fluoxetine prescription isn't quite right probably won't feel as pressing. Everyone should be equal, but it doesn't always work that way.

Stephen Fry on Mental Health

'One wants the brightest minds of the young generation to go into psychiatry'

You were in therapy for a few months. Do you know what sort of therapy you had?

No, I don't know if there was any methodology I should have been aware of. It was the sort of therapy that you see everywhere in films and on television, and read about, which is to say that you sit there and the therapist is more or less silent but occasionally prods you, or asks questions about something you say, and you talk.

I'm sure it's very useful for certain things, but I didn't find it personally of help in terms of the illness that I had. I'm not sure it's something that can be talked away. I think, like most people, that a combination of psychiatry and psychology is better than either on their own.

So it didn't give you any life-changing insights into your condition or behaviour?

Sadly not! I don't know if that was my fault, or the fault of the therapist, or just bad luck.

The most important thing for me is to constantly remind people, because I've been out in the open about these things, that I'm not an expert. I'm not a doctor, and the first thing anyone should do with mental illness is to seek medical advice.

There are two things to remember, both of which seem

countervailing: one is that mental illness is what a doctor would call an illness with a very high morbidity rate – in other words, it's dangerous to life.

We know that suicide is the most obvious example, but also all kinds of self-harm including self-medication and the downward descent and spiral into street life, drug abuse, alcohol abuse, the loss of family and friends and so on.

It's not an uncommon thing, as we know. So people have to be warned of the real seriousness of it. On the other hand, simultaneously, you want to remind people that it's not a death sentence; that it's possible to lead a fulfilled, happy, creative life with mental illness as it is with any chronic disease, whether it be diabetes or asthma or any other form of chronic illness.

So I think there are so many tools available for people, but the most important thing is diagnosis. I'm not saying that I have absolute faith in the DSM [diagnostic and statistical manual], whichever version you look at, in terms of diagnosis, so I don't mean that you actually have to pin and name the particular disorder you have and this solves all things.

But there are unquestionably collections of symptoms that go with mental illness – say, manic depression/bipolar disorder – and it's good to speak to someone who knows about them.

And then, I suppose one is faced with the interesting challenge, if one can look at it like that, of what sort of treatment one thinks might help. There are so many different voices you hear; there are people who swear it's all to do with diet, all to do with sleep and circadian rhythms, or it's to do with exercise and fresh air, or that the way to be helped is with cognitive behavioural therapy to arm yourself with a set of tools for ways of responding to mood changes.

There are others who would recommend particular courses of pharmaceutical treatment.

I feel it's very important for me never to recommend one over the other because everybody's different. I often put it like this: we all have friends who respond to drink in different ways, and we respond to drink in different ways to our friends.

You can sit at a table with a friend and match each other for the same number of glasses of drink and your friend will turn into an arrogant, shouty, annoying arsehole and you'll feel all sleepy and cosy although you've both had the same to drink.

Alcohol is chemically a pretty simple thing, and yet its effect on different people is profound and we all recognise it. So imagine how much more complex are the effects of these psychotropic drugs and other kinds of drugs, antipsychotics and so on, that people take. It's impossible ever to say, 'This is the drug that will cure you,' because everybody is different.

We know so little about the mind. I'm very shy of ever recommending anything to anyone, except that they see a doctor and try to find out as much as they can about their condition from friends, from forums online, from books and all the sources. I'm sure your book will be a very valuable addition to that.

As someone who has been managing bipolar disorder for many years, how do you feel that public attitudes to mental health have changed during that time?

Well, it's been marvellous. That is the great story – we're not there yet, of course not, but we've taken tremendous strides in public understanding.

That's happened through governments of all political stripes who have understood the importance of addressing mental illness – both as an economic problem that affects working hours and therefore productivity and the economy, if you want to look at it in those bold terms, but also in terms of addressing stigma and giving people safe places online or elsewhere to be in touch with health professionals, or with interested people who have members of families who are affected in some way.

So the whole wealth of experience that's available online, despite all the faults of the social media that we're constantly having to think about these days, has huge advantages. It's not an absolute solution – you can be as lonely online as you can be lonely in a big city. We can't fool ourselves that it's easy for some people who find it very difficult.

The nature of a mental disorder is often that one's behaviour and one's way of addressing other people can appear needy and resentful and difficult, socially, to handle for others, and the response can alienate people. It's not easy, but it's never been a better time, put it that way. It's not the perfect time, but it's never been better.

I think the effect of the royal princes with the Heads Together campaign has been enormously helpful. They've made it so clear that they understand and they know what it's like to have a difficult time, mentally, and if *they* can from their apparent position of privilege and accessibility be open to all forms of treatment, then I think that makes others feel a little bit better about the fact that they might not be in the best mental health.

I wonder if it's also easier for young men to seek help for their problems now.

That's a really good point, because as one has had to repeat again and again, they are the most at risk from suicide, from the most extreme form of self-harm that there is.

We all know that it has been harder, traditionally, for men to speak about their emotions, feelings and relations with others. It's always been a very tricky thing for young men for all kinds of cultural reasons, and who knows what genetic reasons.

I have two reasonably public positions, one as president of Mind which is the largest of the mental health charities, and a lot of our work is to do with communication and rewarding people in the print, broadcast and online media for presenting positive images – or indeed for telling dark and terrible stories but bringing them out into the open and showing the reach and prevalence of mental health problems, and also the availability of support and help where possible.

Also, I'm an honorary fellow at the Royal College of Psychiatrists, and one of the things I'm very keen on doing is for young medical students, when they've finally learned all their anatomy, done their training and spent their hours on the wards and they're thinking about what they're going to specialise in – whether it's gynaecology, orthopaedics or whatever it might be – unfortunately psychiatry is always bottom of the list. Below gerontology, below geriatrics and all the others.

I think there are good, sound psychological reasons for that – medical students who have spent years and years studying the body have just about got to understand our physiologies, and the idea of having to spend more years trying to comprehend something as vast and unknowable as the human brain, and to deal with patients who are unstable and difficult to relate to – they think, 'Oh no, I can't do that, just give me something mechanical.'

But the really revealing thing is that when you then speak to young doctors who have been in the trade for ten or fifteen years, there's a huge number that say, 'Ah, I wish I gone for psychiatry now, but at the time it seemed like too much of an extra effort. I see now that the wealth of the mind is the most exciting field in all science, and I wish I had done that.'

They also see from their clinical work just how important it is, how urgent a crisis it is. So part of my work in the Royal College of Psychiatrists is to try to encourage medical students to think about psychiatry as an incredibly rewarding and exciting field of speciality.

I wouldn't be here if it wasn't for my psychiatrist – I'm on three drugs for the rest of my life to manage my mental illness, but that's the way it has to be, and I'm so grateful.

That's right, and one wants the brightest minds of the young genera-tion to go into that field, the brightest and most empathetic people to be psychiatrists. There are some great ones around, but it's all about getting the young, new, energetic people into the field – both clinical and of course research and academic work, because there's still so much to understand about our brains.

They say that in ten or twenty years it might be possible for them to work out exactly which chemicals you need in order to right yourself.

I'm sure you've thought of this, and I hope your book offers at least a level of optimism because of that, and because of the nature of the way that genomics and gene editing and our understanding of the brain and the endocrine system and all these different things is converging into a whole new confidence in neuroscience and brain science.

So one has reason to be optimistic, and a young person reading your book may at least have faith that in ten, fifteen or twenty years a whole new range of treatments that could transform the way that they live with their illness is likely to be available. One can't promise, but it looks that way.

Contributors

Clients

Dolly Alderton
Dolly Alderton is a journalist and writer. She co-hosts *The High Low*, a weekly pop-culture and news podcast, with Pandora Sykes. Her first book, a memoir called *Everything I Know about Love,* was published in February 2018. You can follow her on Twitter and Instagram on @dollyalderton

Polly Allen
Polly Allen is a freelance lifestyle journalist and marketer based in West Sussex. She was diagnosed with clinical depression in February 2007 and has struggled with it daily since then. In 2014, during a nervous breakdown with limited NHS crisis care, she learned that her depression was classed as treatment-resistant whilst receiving CBT. Today, she writes and campaigns to reduce the stigma surrounding mental health, as a media volunteer for Mind (including being interviewed by the BBC and Al-Jazeera) and a communications administrator for the peer support group Mental Health Mates. Find her on Twitter as @misspallen

David Baddiel
David Baddiel is a writer and comedian. He performs extensively in the UK on television, radio and stage, and has written four novels for adults and five for children. If you want to find out more about him, it's all on davidbaddiel.com

Francesca Baker
Francesca Baker is a writer, journalist and marketer committed to using words to change worlds. Passionate about good health in all facets – mental, physical, social and emotional – she runs writing for wellbeing workshops, has published a recipe book for eating disorder recovery, contributes to numerous magazines and publications, and includes therapists and wellbeing practitioners amongst her copywriting clients. You can read more at andsoshethinks.co.uk or francescabaker.com

Megan Beech
Megan Beech is a performance poet. She has performed at venues including the Royal Albert Hall, Parliament, the Southbank Centre, Glastonbury Festival and Cheltenham Literature Festival. She is the author of two poetry books, *When I Grow Up I Want to be Mary Beard* (2013) and *You Sad Feminist* (2017).

Her poetry has featured on Sky One and the BBC and has been profiled in publications including the *New Yorker*, the *Guardian* and the *Huffington Post*. She was featured in the *Guardian*'s list of Must-Read Books of the Year 2014 and *Evening Standard*'s list of Ten 21st-century Feminist Icons.

Jules Bristow
Jules Bristow was a scientist studying insect chemical ecology, which is a fancy way of saying why flies are attracted to the smell of poo, until the brain weasels got her. She has been trying to fight them off ever since and now works wrangling databases instead of flies, which are fractionally less co-operative. She lives on the south coast of Britain and her love of the wildlife of the local woods and chalk Downlands, as well as the support of her friends, have helped her through depression.

She blogs at tangledbankblog.wordpress.com and tweets at twitter.com/afewbugs

Charlie Brooker

Charlie Brooker is a satirist, broadcaster, presenter, producer and writer. He is the creator of the futuristic Netflix horror series *Black Mirror*, for which he won two Emmy awards.

As well as writing for television programmes including *Black Mirror*, *Brass Eye*, *The 11 O'Clock Show* and *Nathan Barley*, he has presented a number of television shows, including *Screenwipe*, *Gameswipe*, *Newswipe*, *Weekly Wipe*, and *10 O'Clock Live*.

He also wrote the zombie horror drama *Dead Set*. He has written numerous columns for the *Guardian* and is a creative director at television production company House of Tomorrow.

James Brown

James Brown is a writer, broadcaster and media entrepreneur. His five-a-side memoir *Above Head Height* was a number one Amazon football bestseller. He started the mass market men's sector magazine genre, creating *Loaded* magazine, and edited *GQ* and *Jack* magazines. He posts on Twitter and Instagram as @jamesjamesbrown

John Crace

John Crace is a journalist and critic. He writes the famous Digested Read column in the *Guardian*, and is also the parliamentary sketch writer for the paper. He has written several books including *I, Maybot: The Rise and Fall*; *I Never Promised You a Rose Garden: A Short Guide to Modern Politics, the Coalition and the General Election*; and *Vertigo: One Football Fan's Fear of Success*.

He supports Tottenham Hotspur, and blogs about them for ESPN FC.

Jean Hannah Edelstein

Jean Hannah Edelstein is a writer. Her memoir, *This Really Isn't About You*, is out now. Her weekly newsletter has been featured in *Vogue* and *BuzzFeed*, and it's free to subscribe: tinyletter.com/jeanhannah

Stephen Fry

Stephen Fry is an actor, screenwriter, author, playwright, journalist, poet, comedian, television presenter and film director. His acting roles include the lead in the film *Wilde*, Melchett in the BBC television series *Blackadder*, a recurring guest role as Dr Gordon Wyatt on the crime series *Bones*, Gordon Deitrich in *V for Vendetta*, Mycroft Holmes in *Sherlock Holmes: A Game of Shadows* and the Master of Laketown in Peter Jackson's *Hobbit* trilogy.

He has written and presented several documentary series, including the Emmy Award-winning *Stephen Fry: The Secret Life of the Manic Depressive*. He was also the long-time host of the BBC television quiz show *QI*.

Katy Georgiou

Katy (known professionally as Katerina) Georgiou is a qualified Gestalt counsellor and registered member of the British Association for Counselling and Psychotherapy. She sees clients in a GP surgery and in private practice and runs KG Counselling & Psychotherapy.

She is also a writer, published in the *Independent*, the *Guardian* and *The Times*, and hosts a mental health and music podcast, *Sound Affects*, after having spent many years as a music and dance writer. Prior to this, she worked for Samaritans during their Men on the Ropes research campaign into male suicide.

She was a Samaritans helpline listener for four years and a trained life coach for Mind, supporting vulnerable young adults in the care system. Visit her website at kgcounsellor.com

Sarah Graham

Sarah Graham is a freelance journalist specialising in feminism, refugee rights, mental health, wellbeing and sexual/gynaecological health. She was previously deputy editor of *Feminist Times*, and communications executive at the charity Women for Refugee Women. Sarah writes regularly for *The Debrief*, *NetDoctor*, *Broadly* and *Refinery29*, and has also been published by the *Guardian*, the *Telegraph*, the *Independent*, *i*, *New Statesman*, *Cosmopolitan*, *Grazia*, and *The Pool*. She's particularly interested in the health implications of sexism and gender inequality – covering everything from women's reproductive rights to suicide rates amongst men. Find out more at sarah-graham.co.uk and @SarahGraham7

Atalanta Kernick

Atalanta Kernick is a practising artist and librarian who lives in London. She has also owned a cafe and art space and taught Media Art and Photography at degree level. She has worked in a wide range of media, from drawing and painting to electronic art. She is interested in the uses of technology for art, particularly virtual reality. She also completed an Introduction to Counselling Course and gained valuable skills which she has put to use at Echo (LNASG) Peer Counselling Group.

Sachin Kumarendran

Having won the 2016 University of Birmingham's Got Talent performing an original stand-up comedy routine, Sachin Kumarendran has since headlined the 2016 Valefest festival and worked in a paid role as a comedy writer for the Labour Party. At the time of writing he is in the semi-final of the 2017 national stand-up competition So You Think You're Funny. Sachin has also gained a role writing, producing and presenting a four-part miniseries for the television show *The Chrissy B Show*, and had artwork exhibited for the 2017 Ashurst Emerging Artist Award.

Cosmo Landesman

Cosmo Landesman is a freelance journalist who has written for a wide range of publications. He is the author of *Starstruck: Fame, Failure, My Family and Me*.

Graham Nunn

Graham Nunn designed the adverts and posters for the Atheist Bus Campaign, which ran on eight hundred buses around the UK in January 2009. He also contributed to the bestselling book *The Atheist's Guide to Christmas*. Since then he has been working on various creative projects.

Musa Okwonga

Musa Okwonga is a poet, author, sportswriter, broadcaster, musician, public relations consultant and commentator. A former City lawyer and an award-winning writer, Musa has been commissioned to write poems for the BBC World Service, the FA and Sky Sports, has published two books on football and one collection of poetry, and has written essays for, among others, the *New York Times*, the *Economist*, ESPN and the *New Statesman*. He lives in Berlin.

Meryl O'Rourke

Meryl O'Rourke is a gigging stand-up comic and TV writer. Having worked closely with Frankie Boyle for nine years, she is a regular support act on his tour shows. She became the first recipient of the Betty & Peter Sitcom bursary where she was gifted £10,000 to write about her experience of post-natal depression. Her stand-up show *Bad Mother . . .*, about growing up with a holocaust escapee mum, earned a clutch of five-star reviews. She pops up on *Front Row* (Radio 4) usually gabbing about feminism in comedy, and empties her brain endlessly onto Twitter @MerylORourke

Rae Ritchie

Rae Ritchie worked as an academic historian for a decade before a particularly bad episode of mental health issues resulted in her taking a break from work for a few months. During her recovery, she began writing and is now making a living as a freelancer. She shares her experience of borderline personality disorder, depression, anxiety and PTSD on a number of outlets, including *Mental Health Today*, where she has a twice-monthly column. Rae also writes about fashion, beauty and lifestyle and is especially interested in eco, ethical and sustainable brands. Find her on social media at @rae_ritchie_

Kieran Walsh

Kieran Walsh is a stand-up comedian, MC, joke writer and qualified massage therapist. He is a divorced father of two wonderful little girls, Freya (aged twelve) and Isla (aged eight). They are the light of his life and help him stay grounded and focused. In his spare time, he likes to practise yoga and meditation, and also enjoys theme parks and pints with his mates.

Hayley Webster

Hayley Webster is a producer, improviser, stand-up comedian and podcaster based in New Zealand. She is one half of the podcasting duo 'Comic Service Announcement'.

Rosie Wilby

Rosie Wilby has appeared many times on BBC Radio 4 and at major festivals including Glastonbury and Latitude. She was a finalist at Funny Women 2006 and Leicester Mercury Comedian of the Year 2007, and has been touring award-winning solo shows internationally ever since. Her writing has been published in the *Sunday Times*, *New Statesman* and more. Her first book, *Is Monogamy Dead?*, follows her TEDx talk of the same name. She co-hosts *Radio Diva* every Tuesday on Resonance FM.

Find her at rosiewilby.com or @rosiewilby

Therapists

Christina Anderson

Christina Anderson was born in Kingston, Jamaica, and arrived in the UK at the age of ten. In 2012, she completed a BA (Hons) in Drama and Performance Studies at London South Bank University, followed by an MA in Drama and Movement Therapy (Sesame) at The Royal Central School of Speech and Drama (RCSSD), London. She is now a visiting lecturer at RCSSD and a consultant therapist looking at ways to explore challenges within the corporate industry, creating a unique approach using Dramatherapy. She is registered with the Health Care Professions Council (HCPC) as an arts therapist as well as with the British Association of Dramatherapists (BADth).

Learn more at facebook.com/avidyatherapy or twitter.com/Avidyatherapy

Claire Arnold-Baker

Dr Claire Arnold-Baker is an existential therapist working in private practice. She works with clients with a range of problems in living.

Claire also works as a perinatal therapist and specialises in maternal mental health. She is the programme leader for the D.C.Psych. in Counselling Psychology at NSPC – the home of existential training – which is a joint programme with Middlesex University, where she also teaches introductory workshops on existential therapy.

Claire has also co-edited *Existential Perspectives on Human Issues* with Professor Emmy van Deurzen. A co-authored book with Emmy van Deurzen entitled *Existential Therapy: Distinctive Features,* will be published in 2018.

Further details about Claire's practice can be found at clairearnoldbaker.co.uk

Ruth Baer
Ruth Baer is Professor of Psychology at the University of Kentucky and author of *The Practicing Happiness Workbook: How Mindfulness Can Free You From the Four Psychological Traps that Keep You Stressed, Anxious, and Depressed.* Her research and scholarly work focuses on assessment of mindfulness, effects of mindfulness-based interventions, mechanisms of change in mindfulness training, and professional training and ethics in the mindfulness field.

She developed two of the leading self-report questionnaires for measuring mindfulness skills, and has edited three books for professionals on mindfulness-related topics. She serves on the editorial boards of several peer-reviewed journals and gives talks and workshops about mindfulness. She also teaches and supervises several mindfulness-based treatments.

Her website is ruthbaer.com

Sandra Ballester
Sandra Ballester originally trained as an autogenic therapist in 2002 with the British Autogenic Society (BAS), London, and has been in private practice since then as a stress management therapist.

Later, she trained at the Institute of Psychosynthesis, London, becoming first a counsellor and then a psychotherapist with her MA in psychosynthesis psychotherapy.

She is a member of the UKCP, BAS, BACP and APP (Association for Psychospiritual Practitioners). Her psychotherapy practice is based in Norwich where she lives with her human family and four-legged menagerie.

More information on Sandra's work is available at sandraballester.com and stressfreenorwich.co.uk

Veena Ganapathy

Veena Ganapathy is a psychodynamic psychotherapist who trained at WPF Therapy. She has a private practice, Ganapathy Therapy, based in London.

Veena has a long-standing commitment to understanding the universal issues that affect us all, as reflected in her academic background (BSc Psychology, MSc Social Psychology) and previous role as a NHS mental health social worker (MA Dip SW).

She has a particular interest in exploring experiences of loss and issues relating to identity and belonging.

You are welcome to contact Veena at ganapathytherapy@gmail.com or to find out more about her private practice at ganapathy-therapy.co.uk

Jonathan Izard

Jonathan Izard studied at Cambridge University before training as an actor at Bristol Old Vic Theatre School. He worked in theatre, television and film for ten years and then moved into radio journalism, becoming a newsreader and presenter at the BBC, LBC and Melody FM.

He trained in person-centred therapy in the late 1990s and went on to study sex therapy and couples therapy. Jonathan has been in private practice for twenty years, working with heterosexual and LGBT clients, individuals, couples and groups.

For many years, he was a tutor at the City Literary Institute. He is a novelist and playwright; he also broadcasts for the BBC World Service.

Candice Johnson

Candice is a UKCP-registered psychotherapist with an MSc in Gestalt Psychotherapy, qualifying in 2008. She works in private practice in west and central London within three different locations.

Candice trained at The Metanoia Institute in West London, a highly respected organisation which has offered experiential and rigorous academic training in psychological therapies for over thirty years.

Since 2001, Candice has worked with a diverse group of people from differing ethnic backgrounds and facing a wide variety of challenges. Her expertise lies in building a solid therapeutic relationship based on trust, safety and non-judgement within which self-awareness, acceptance and change can come.

Visit Candice's website, candicejohnson.co.uk

Fiona Kennedy

Dr Fiona Kennedy is a consultant clinical psychologist, researcher, supervisor and trainer. Her website www.greenwoodmentors.com offers therapy and also mentoring for business.

She is interested in surviving trauma and in combining CBT and third-wave therapies. She is co-editor with Dr David Pearson of *Cognitive Behavioural Approaches to the Understanding and Treatment of Dissociation* and co-author of *Get Your Life Back: The Most Effective Therapies For A Better You*. Visit www.getyourlifeback.global for more info and free downloads.

She volunteers in India for www.dreamadream.org which helps Indian volunteers to mentor rescued children and young people.

Rachel Lewis

Dr Rachel Lewis is a counselling psychologist and family therapist. She has a private practice where she works with couples and families across all ages and stages of life. Rachel uses a team-building approach to support couples and families to stay emotionally connected in the face of life's toughest challenges.

In recent years, she has been privileged to work in the field of autism and has developed expertise in supporting couples where one or both partners have been identified on the autism spectrum.

Her website is freshpagetherapy.com

Tom Fortes Mayer

A Harley Street hypnotherapist and happiness author, Tom has built up a worldwide reputation for his powerful work. He believes passionately that hypnosis is the key to rapidly achieving real and lasting change.

In addition to his private practice, he is also the founder of the FreeMind Project charity, which aims to bring more happiness to the world. He also runs the FreeMind Hypnosis Training Academy, where his greatest passion lies in teaching other people to become ethical, highly effective hypnotherapists.

Please visit freemindproject.org/hypnotherapy-training and facebook.com/freemindproject for further details.

Elizabeth Wilde McCormick

Elizabeth Wilde McCormick has worked as a psychotherapist in both private and NHS settings for over fifty-five years. Her background is in transpersonal and humanistic psychology, social psychiatry, sensorimotor psychotherapy for trauma, MBSR and cognitive analytic therapy.

In the last fifteen years, she has maintained an interest in the interface between psychotherapy and contemplative practices. She is a founder member of the Association for Cognitive Analytic Therapy and the author of a number of bestselling self-help psychological books including *Change for the Better*, the CAT self-help book now in its fifth edition.

Liz McLure

Liz McLure has professional and academic qualifications in education, nursing, psychology and psychotherapy. She has specialised in the field of mental health for over thirty-five years, working with a wide variety of groups in different settings, including the NHS, HMP Grendon, drug and alcohol services, counselling and psychotherapy trainings and private practice. Liz is a training group analyst and supervisor with the IGA (Institute of Group Analysis) and has a small private practice in the West Highlands of Scotland. Contact details are on her website www.liz-mclure-psychotherapy.co.uk. For more information on group analysis or to find a therapist near you, visit www.groupanalysis.org.

Kate Moyle

Kate Moyle is an accredited psychosexual and relationship therapist in central London. She works with people to recognise their personal understanding of their sexuality and sexual health, with the view that issues have roots in psychology, emotion, the physical body, and a person's history and culture.

Alongside her work as a therapist she is also co-founder and partner at Pillow App for Couples (pillow.io) which helps busy couples to fit intimacy into their lives in a convenient and connecting way.

Kate is passionate about having open, honest and realistic conversations about sex that help people to feel educated and aware, in order that they can make informed decisions and feel comfortable in their sexuality.

Joe Oliver

Dr Joe Oliver is a consultant clinical psychologist and founder of Contextual Consulting, offering ACT training, coaching and therapy. He works at University College London as a course director for a psychology training programme.

Joe is a peer-review Association of Contextual Behavioural Science ACT trainer and regularly delivers workshops both nationally and internationally.

Co-author of the popular ACT self-help book, *ACTivate Your Life*, Joe loves to share ideas about ACT through writing, video or animation.

You can find him on Twitter at @contextconsult and his website is contextualconsulting.co.uk

Bob Pritchard

Bob Pritchard is a qualified social worker, and the team leader of Lambeth Early Intervention CAMHS. Bob is an IPT-A (Adolescents) supervisor, and practice teacher on the Children and Young People's Improving Access to Psychological Therapies programme. He is the communications lead for IPT-UK.

Before working in mental health, Bob worked in substance misuse services in the prison service, NHS and voluntary sector. He lives in south London, loves running and makes his colleagues groan with awful dad jokes.

Jo Ray

Jo Ray is an integrative arts psychotherapist and counsellor (UKCP and HCPC registered, registered member MBACP, full member of BAAT). She brings over twenty-five years' experience of working within creative environments, and spent over five years working psychotherapeutically using the creative process to facilitate change and help re-establish psychological growth. She has worked therapeutically with children and adolescents as part of the Kids Company schools programme; with adult survivors of childhood sexual abuse in an NHS clinical placement within the Oxleas Trust; with people living with cancer and their families and carers in an NHS clinical placement as part of the psych-oncology team at Guy's and St Thomas' Hospitals; with adolescents in a secondary school for boys; and in private practice with adults, young people and children, based in Dulwich, south London.

Visit Jo's website, www.artneurons.com

Graham Thomas

Graham Thomas is a private psychotherapist working in London. He also works online via therapyme.com. He trained at Regent's University London and has worked for the NHS and the charity sector.

David Veale

Professor David Veale is a consultant psychiatrist at the Maudsley Hospital and the Priory Hospital North London, and a visiting professor in Cognitive Behavioural Psychotherapies at King's College London.

He is also a past president of the British Association of Behavioural and Cognitive Psychotherapies, and a current trustee of the charities OCD Action and the BDD Foundation.

He has a special interest in treating obsessive compulsive disorder, body dysmorphic disorder and emetophobia, and in the rapid treatment of depression by triple chronotherapy. His website is veale. co.uk

He has co-authored three books in the Overcoming series on OCD, BDD and Health Anxiety and one on depression, *Manage Your Mood*.

Robert Weiss

Robert Weiss's first degree was in Photography. While he was on this course, which was divided equally between theory and practice, he became interested in psychoanalytic theory, and went on to take an MA in Psychoanalytic Studies at Brunel University.

He spent the next few years dividing his time between teaching, research and working as a photographer and printer, before starting his clinical training at the Site for Contemporary Psychoanalysis.

As well as his clinical practice, he serves on the governing body of the Site, teaches and designs courses, and is part of the editorial board of *Sitegeist*, a journal of psychoanalysis and philosophy. His website is www.robweiss.co.uk

Oliver Wright

Oliver Wright trained in Counselling and Psychotherapy at the University of East London after working in media and campaigning for many years. He is particularly interested in helping people who suffer with trauma and PTSD to process the disturbing thoughts and feelings that they experience and helping them to move on with their lives.

He works with a range of clients. Some have had one-off adult traumas, and others have lived with trauma for most of their lives.

He works in private practice in London and in a specialist trauma service within the NHS. For more information please see oliver-wright.net

Therapy Organisations

British Association for Counselling and Psychotherapy
itsgoodtotalk.org.uk
01455 883300
bacp@bacp.co.uk

UK Council for Psychotherapy
psychotherapy.org.uk
020 7014 9955
info@ukcp.org.uk

British Psychological Society
bps.org.uk
0116 254 9568
enquiries@bps.org.uk

Cognitive Behavioural Therapy
British Association for Behavioural & Cognitive Psychotherapies
babcp.com
0161 705 4304
babcp@babcp.com

Cognitive Analytic Therapy
The Association for Cognitive Analytic Therapy
acat.me.uk
01305 263511
admin@acat.me.uk

Acceptance and Commitment Therapy
Association for Contextual Behavioural Science
contextualscience.org
acbsstaff@contextualscience.org

Dialectical Behaviour Therapy
behavioraltech.org

Psychoanalysis/Psychodynamic Therapy
Institute of Psychoanalysis
psychoanalysis.org.uk
020 7563 5000
admin@iopa.org.uk

British Psychoanalytic Council
bpc.org.uk
020 7561 9240
mail@bpc.org.uk

Person-Centred Therapy
The British Association for the Person-Centred Approach
bapca.org.uk
01600 891508

Gestalt Therapy
gestaltcentre.org.uk
020 7383 5610

Psychosynthesis
Institute of Psychosynthesis
psychosynthesis.org
020 8202 4525
institute@psychosynthesis.org

Integrative Therapy
The United Kingdom Association for Psychotherapy Integration
ukapi.com

Existential Therapy
The Society for Existential Analysis
existentialanalysis.org.uk

Humanistic Therapies
UK Association for Humanistic Psychology Practitioners
ahpp.org.uk

Family/Systemic Therapy
Association for Family Therapy and Systemic Practice
aft.org.uk
01925 444414

Group Therapy
The Association for Group and Individual Psychotherapy
agip.org.uk
020 7272 7013

Relationship Therapy and EFT
relate.org.uk
0300 100 1234

Arts Therapies
British Association of Art Therapists
baat.org
020 7686 4216
info@baat.org

The British Association for Dramatherapy
badth.org.uk
01242 235515
enquiries@badth.org.uk

British Association for Music Therapy
bamt.org
020 7837 6100
info@bamt.org

Mindfulness-Based Cognitive Therapy
mbct.co.uk

Mindfulness-Based Stress Reduction
Mindfulness Works
mbsr.co.uk
01223 750430
michael@mindfulnessworks.com

Eye Movement Desensitisation and Reprocessing
EMDR Association UK & Ireland
emdrassociation.org.uk

Interpersonal Psychotherapy
Interpersonal Psychotherapy UK Network
iptuk.net
contact@iptuk.net

Hypnotherapy
National Council for Hypnotherapy
hypnotherapists.org.uk
0800 980 4419

The National Hypnotherapy Society
nationalhypnotherapysociety.org
01903 236857
admin@nationalhypnotherapysociety.org

Bibliotherapy
ReLit: The Foundation for Bibliotherapy
relit.org.uk

Reading Well Books on Prescription Scheme
reading-well.org.uk
020 7324 2529
readingwell@readingagency.org.uk

Mental Health Charities

Mind UK
mind.org.uk
0300 123 3393
info@mind.org.uk

Samaritans
samaritans.org
116 123
jo@samaritans.org

CALM
thecalmzone.net
0800 585858
info@thecalmzone.net

OCD Action
ocdaction.org.uk
0845 390 6232
support@ocdaction.org.uk

Bipolar UK
www.bipolaruk.org
0333 323 3880
info@bipolaruk.org

Acknowledgements

Thank you very much to my wonderful editor, Andrew McAleer at Robinson, for taking a chance on this book, and for being so calm, friendly and professional.

Thank you to my brilliant agent, Stephanie Thwaites at Curtis Brown, for being so encouraging and supportive – and to her assistant Isobel Gahan for being so helpful.

Thank you so much to all the contributors, both clients and therapists, who generously gave their time and honest insights on therapy. I'm truly grateful, and I hope you enjoy the book.

Thank you to all the celebrities who kindly read the book and gave me such lovely quotes.

Thank you to my colleagues in the editorial and content teams at VEON, including Kim De Ruiter, David Kane, Ed Lomas, Brad Finlay, Miles Chic, Nicholas Wodtke, Anastasia Nemchenok and Max Paradiso. I love working with you all.

Thank you to all my Patreon supporters, including Klaas Jan Runia, Chris Birkett, Mary Fowler, Mark White, Edd Edmondson, Matthew Sylvester, Brian Engler, Shane Jarvis, Dave Nattriss, Jack Scanlan, John Fleming, Emily Hill, Paul Gibson, Marcus P Knight, Max Harrison, Peter Weilgony and Tim Fowler, for being incredibly awesome and encouraging my creativity.

Thank you to Graham Nunn, who wrote, edited and proofed this book with me, and made me laugh throughout.

Thank you to my therapist for always being there for me, allowing me to be myself and making all my dreams seem possible.

Thank you to Nick Harrop, a great friend from whom I stole the original idea for funny Q&As.

Thank you to John Fleming for being Jon Bon Jovial and cheering me up when my marriage fell apart. Friendship like yours is rare and special.

And thank you most of all to the sweetest girl in the world, Lily, who makes me happier than I ever imagined. I love you impossibly much, and always will – so much, more than anything, all the numbers, till infinity.

Index